2/05

AN INSULAR ROCOCO

AN INSULAR ROCOCO

Architecture, Politics and Society in
Ireland and England, 1710–1770

Timothy Mowl and Brian Earnshaw

REAKTION BOOKS

For Geoffrey Beard and David Griffin

Published by Reaktion Books Ltd
79 Farringdon Road
London EC1M 3JU, UK
www.reaktionbooks.co.uk

First published 1999

Designed by Janette Revill
Printed and bound in Great Britain by
Biddles Limited, Guildford and King's Lynn

British Library Cataloguing in Publication Data
Mowl, Timothy
An insular rococo: architecture, politics and society in Ireland and England,
1710–1770
1. Architecture, Rococo – England – History – 18th century
2. Architecture, Rococo – Ireland – History – 18th century
3. Decorative arts, Rococo – England – History – 18th century 4. Decorative arts,
Rococo – Ireland – History – 18th century 5. Architecture, Rococo – Social
Aspects – England 6. Architecture, Rococo – Social aspects – Ireland
1. Title II. Earnshaw, Brian
724.1'9

ISBN 1 86189 044 3

CONTENTS

ACKNOWLEDGEMENTS

A book written by two authors on the architecture of two countries has inevitably to have two dedicatees: Geoffrey Beard for England and David Griffin for Ireland, but the authors wish to emphasize that neither of these are mere token choices. Geoffrey has been a pioneer in the study of English plasterwork and several years ago one of us stood in for him to lecture at a summer school on the subject. That was the start of an enduring fascination with stucco and stuccodores which Geoffrey has encouraged at every stage with his wide knowledge of English and European sources, and his considered judgements on many doubtful attributions. David Griffin is the Director of the Irish Architectural Archive. Its equivalent institution in England is housed in an enormous renovated train shed in Swindon, appropriate no doubt to a country which launched the Industrial Revolution; but David Griffin presides over exquisite, authentic Georgian premises in Merrion Square, South Dublin's most superior address. Simply to enter the reading room with its Michael Stapleton ceiling, horseshoe table and views out over the Dublin tree tops and Joycean back yards is a pleasure. With his relaxed welcome, hands-on management and scholarship, David has made every visit rewarding. This is how architectural studies should be conducted. We in England have lost the way, become impersonal and, as a direct result, less efficient. Now that we have shrugged off the last vestiges of Empire we need to make our institutions as human and friendly as their Irish counterparts.

Before thanking any other individuals we wish to express our gratitude to the staff of the Irish National Library. Over the past year we must have called up more than fifty books from their extensive collections and it was never longer than five minutes before one of the team of uniformed searchers laid the book on our desk. The computerized British Library never took less than an hour and sometimes took more than a day over an order. Research in Ireland is easy because one source can be followed up quickly by another. In London it is a labour that can require an overnight stay. The National Libraries of Wales and Scotland are as efficient and friendly in their service as the Irish Library. After the huge expense and long delays attendant on the new British Library it is a scandal that any book should take longer than minutes to deliver or that the service should be anything but cheerful and warm. We tend in this country to describe rigid and inflexible official attitudes as 'typically Germanic', but after our Irish experience we wonder if the Germans would not be perfectly justified in describing such frigid bureaucratic responses as 'typically English'.

The owners of Rococo houses in Ireland, Wales and England have all been equally kind to us. We have not been turned away from any door, however sudden and unexpected our descent may have been. One bank, or was it a building society, in Dublin insisted that we made an appointment to view their immaculately restored premises, otherwise to knock was to enter. Our particular thanks go to Sir Brooke Boothby at his enchantingly odd and little known Welsh castle, Fonmon, to Lady Rosemary Bellew who coped with one of us at Barmeath Castle at half past nine on a wet November morning, to Miss Pigeon and her brothers at quintessentially Irish Dowth Hall, to Hugo Merry in our favourite, though only just Rococo, Irish house, Kilshannig and to Patricia van Diest and Peter Mitchell who always exemplified Rococo hospitality at Beacon House, Painswick. Sister Theodore guided us around the Convent of the Holy Faith at Glasnevin and Ruth Ferguson around her remarkable twin premises at Newman House. Nigel Benford gave one of us an entirely unofficial and un-English welcome to those National Trust rooms at Claydon and Carol Love and Sue Baumbach to those at Saltram.

Where Irish scholarship was concerned we have leaned heavily upon Con Curran's writings which were polite as well as learned. Ireland owes him and the Irish Georgian Society a great debt for valuing the country's richest architectural treasures at a time when they were least in political fashion. Joseph McDonnell's book on Irish stuccowork has been an invaluable guide and a source of judgements to which we could take exception. We have never met him but feel we know him well. Without John Harris's writings we might never have noticed that there was such a concept as the 'Rococo Garden'. Roger White, Michael Liversidge, David Lambert, Michael Hall, Tim Knox, Lord and Lady Dickinson, Paul Moir, Richard Mullane, Paul Mitchell, Mark Bence Jones, Andrew Smith, Liam Daly, Simon Lincoln, Anne Henderson and Colum O'Riordan have all, in conversational exchange or heated argument, enriched our final text and so should shoulder some at least of both blame and praise for it. In their libraries, Anthony Beeson, Michael Richardson and Hannah Lowery were most helpful. Other scholars and friends we should like to mention are Martin Durrant, Julia Ionides, Peter Howell, Melanie Blake, Jaqueline Riding, Bruce A. Bailey, Jeffry Haworth, Lady Nutting and Alastair Laing.

Gordon Kelsey had to work much harder than usual with our photographs as white on white in a shadowy ceiling is a photographer's nightmare; in some desperation we turned to him to photograph personally many of our Bristol interiors and Fonmon Castle. For financial help with the illustrations one of us was the recipient of an Arts Faculty Research Fund grant from Bristol University, and we would like to thank Professor Charles Martindale and his committee members for their generosity.

Reg and Maureen Barton collated our typescript with their usual efficiency, and Harry Gilonis compiled an extensive index as well as organizing captions and tying up loose ends with fearsome meticulousness. We must thank Robert Williams for his recommendation of one of us to our publishers, Reaktion Books, who took a chance with us, and Timothy Mowl's wife, Sarah, and son Adam, who have put up cheerfully with this Rococo obsession for the last year.

Timothy Mowl and Brian Earnshaw
Bristol, Autumn 1998

INTRODUCTION –
RESERVATIONS AND
EXPLANATIONS

This book aims to trace the erratic but rewarding course of Rococo architecture and decoration in Ireland, England and Wales with an emphasis on the purer 'Insular Rococo' which developed in Ireland and the West of England, rather than on that Anglo-Italian compromise style which prevailed elsewhere in England and which still tends to be given undue prominence in architectural studies.

The Rococo as a style eludes easy definitions, as Gervase Jackson-Stops must have discovered when he described it as 'essentially abstract', which it is, only to find himself writing a line later that it was, 'ultimately based on the observation of natural forms', also perfectly true.[1] A contemporary description of it in the *Mercure de France* as 'des morceaux d'Architecture qui font des effets bizarres, singuliers et pittoresques'[2] might catch the impact of a really ripe Parisian interior of around 1730, but would be completely over the top as a description of a typical Dublin or Bristol interior of the 1750s and 1760s, where the feeling of the Rococo plasterwork is generally gracious, even soothing, while still keeping some elements of the perverse, the diverting and the unexpected.

It is more helpful to stop treating the Rococo as a distinct style in its own right and to approach it as a playful revolt against the architectural solemnities which preceded it, those of the Baroque. Louis XIV is personally supposed to have given the French Rococo the green flag in 1698 by telling his architect, Mansard, 'Il faut qu'il y ait de la jeunesse mêlée dans ce que l'on

1 The chimneypiece in the Great Hall of Castle Howard, Yorkshire (*c.* 1710) with the first hints of proto-Rococo decoration.

fera'. But here comes the English difficulty. Italy, Germany, Spain and France had all been exploring the Baroque for upwards of a century, France perhaps with its usual finicking mannerist reserve, so they all had ample theatrical heavinesses for their Rococo, their 'jeunesse', to rebel against. England had nothing. In 1699, when continental Europe was ripe for a change in mood, Sir John Vanbrugh was just beginning to build Castle Howard, the first great house in England that could reasonably be described as Baroque. To arrive at a party a whole hundred years late was insular indeed.

If one is unpatriotic but honest, England's seventeenth century had been a retardataire confusion, intensely interesting to an architectural historian but hardly impressive to an impartial outsider as any mark of national identity, purpose or prestige. That splendid flood of chivalric Elizabethan mock Gothic had run out in James I's reign into the sands of the Renaissance as interpreted at third hand by the Low Countries. Inigo Jones had returned from Italy infatuated with a Palladianism which was perfect for the small-time provincial nobility of the Veneto, and persuaded a cash-strapped Stuart monarchy to adopt it as its official style, fitting Whitehall's royal Banqueting Hall into the shell of a two-storey Vicenzan town house. Charles I had done his best to bring his country up to at least the stylistic standards of his father-in-law, Louis XIII, but his subjects, unimpressed by Franco-Venetian models, had executed him 'pour décourager les autres'.[3] The Commonwealth was a hiatus when a cost-cutting, stripped-down Classicism, ideal for developers making profits on the new London estates, took over as virtually a new national vernacular. One unfortunate result of this has been to set up an enduring English strain of aesthetics that equates drab simplicity with beauty. Only builders intent upon cost cutting have gained by this, but the mind set of 'Puritan Minimalism' has never been quite banished from English thinking about architectural style. In the eighteenth and twentieth centuries, though not in the nineteenth, it has usually been possible to suggest that a cheap design and gentlemanly understatement are one and the same.

The twenty-five year reign of Charles II was, for domestic architecture, a time of wasted opportunities which did much to prepare for the wrong turnings after 1714. By the accident of the Fire of London the country's leading architect, Christopher Wren, spent a disproportionate part of his design career working on a cathedral and a flock of City churches. King Charles himself set a confusing domestic lead. Sentiment for his mother's earlier stylistic patronage obliged him to focus the wing of Greenwich Palace that he managed to finance onto the existing Queen's House which was quite out of scale and out of style with what Webb was building for him. Then he had

Windsor Castle revamped in an ugly, unconvincing neo-Norman towered and battlemented style, its grim round-arched windows concealing vulgarly rich painted Italian interiors: another stylistic hedging of bets. The one palace at Winchester, where Wren was given his head, could have given the nation a route towards a reserved English Baroque, but it was never finished or occupied. Wren was given another chance at Hampton Court by Dutch William, but his Fountain Court there only proved that he could not turn corners gracefully when two of his multi-windowed and quite un-Baroque façades ran into each other. As for Kensington Palace, the London home of the House of Orange and the building which could have served as a national inspiration, the recent period of mourning for Diana, Princess of Wales, focused endlessly upon that dim, depressed garden elevation and demonstrated how completely royal patronage had failed to meet the challenge of a seat in the capital.

Lacking any authoritative guidance many English aristocrats were still, as the century ended, settling for the homely provincial charms of Carolean hangover houses like Hanbury Hall in Worcestershire: a demure brick box with all the air of having been modish in 1665 though it was only completed in 1701. Then there were the clumsy uncertainties of Kimbolton Castle, Huntingdonshire (1691–6), unrelated Francophile houses like Petworth, Sussex (1688–93) and Boughton, Northamptonshire (1683–1709) and the Genoese essay of Dyrham Park, Gloucestershire (1692–1703).[4] None of this amounted to an accepted and distinct national Baroque against which a light-hearted Rococo could skittishly rebel, until Lord Carlisle had the nerve to outpoint German princes and electors, go continental and build Castle Howard.

It was Castle Howard, together with the return of James Gibbs in 1709 from his Roman apprenticeship under Carlo Fontana, which let the Swiss-Italian stuccodores into English interior decoration. The invasion can hardly be described as a disaster for native English plasterwork as English plasterers had been stuck in a design rut for the last sixty years, turning out more or less skilful versions of those heavily compartmented ceilings, with fat swags of fruit and flowers, that Inigo Jones and John Webb had popularized under Charles I and the Commonwealth. These ceilings, versions of French designs of Louis XIII's reign, had never been appropriate interior forms for Jones's Palladian Revival buildings. Palladio himself would have employed fresco painters. But neither the Tudors nor the Stuarts had been public spirited enough to found a national academy to train artists. The money which the art-loving Charles I could have spent on such an institution he lavished either on his picture collection or on Van Dyck's enigmatically epicene men and exquisitely frail women. As a result Charles II's aristocracy had to rely on moderately talented artists from the Low Countries for portraits and expensive French and Italian painters, if they could afford them, for their walls and ceilings. James Thornhill was still only twenty-five at the turn of the century, so when it came to the interiors of Castle Howard it was natural for the Venetian artists, Antonio Pellegrini and Marco Ricci, together with the Swiss-Italian plasterers from Canton Ticino, Giovanni Bagutti and 'Mr Plura', to be employed.

Between them, as Gervase Jackson-Stops has noted, these artist craftsmen 'together produced a "proto-rococo" scheme of decoration which was to have immense consequences for the future'.[5] Not all these consequences, however, were healthy for English design. Bagutti and Plura were working at Castle Howard between 1709 and 1717. Anyone uncertain of the 'proto-rococo' nature of their designs needs only to look at the chimneypiece and over-mantel in the Hall where a double-winged shell supports massive C scrolls and twin mermaids, while the composition is topped with a whole battery of shell work (illus. 1). In 1710 the true French Rococo with that refined, obsessional quality of broken curvilinear strokes was not available as it was still evolving. In Italy, however, a half-hearted Rococo of asymmetrical cartouches and perverse auricular forms had been part of the stock-in-trade of Baroque designers since the 1650s. Even the French never denied their Rococo's design debt to Agostino Mitelli and Stefano della Bella,[6] two mid-seventeenth-century Italian artists. But this Italian 'proto-Rococo' was a heavy, indecisive compromise style. For the health of English plasterwork it would have been far better to have waited for a wave of French plasterers and designers in the 1720s and 1730s rather than to have fallen into the habit of employing the Swiss-Italians after 1710.

One result of the Swiss invasion has been the sterile debate in twentieth-century English Rococo studies as to how many Artari, Bagutti (illus. 21), Plura, Francini and Vassali can be balanced on the point of a pin, or more precisely which of these under-chronicled, wandering craftsmen was responsible for the plasterwork in any particular house. Far more seriously, their arrival coincided with the entirely unpredictable second revival, which will be considered in the next chapter, of Palladianism in England, a style intimately associated for the English with Inigo Jones's compartmented ceilings: heavy trabeation and fat swags of leaf, fruit and flower (illus. 2). With no easy supply of fresco painters to fall back on, indeed with fresco, the true Palladian interior form of decoration, seen by the English at that time as

2 Rigid, compartmented ceiling in the manner of Inigo Jones: the Saloon, Coleshill House, Berkshire (*c.* 1659).

old-fashioned and Baroque, there was nothing else to be done with these Palladian interiors but to give them the same old Jonesian ceilings, partly modified and enriched by the Baroque-Rococo compromises of the Swiss-Italians.

All of which may seem a very ungracious introduction to a group of highly talented craftsmen, but the Swiss did, inadvertently, cripple the full development of a true Insular Rococo based directly upon sophisticated French models. Ireland, as will be seen, was more fortunate. For economic and social reasons Ireland never became quite as engaged with doctrinaire Palladianism as the English. Its ruling class was, for a start, more Tory in sympathies than Whig, and Lord Burlington, the arch proselytizer for an antique Roman-Palladian, may have been hereditary Lord Treasurer of Ireland but, so far is known, he never crossed the Irish sea or set foot in the country. Also the Swiss-Italians, in this case the brothers Filippo and Paolo Francini, or Lafranchini as Irish scholars prefer to call them collectively, did not arrive in Ireland until about 1735, twenty-five years later than Bagutti and Plura reached England. This, together with a number of other enlightened Irish cultural initiatives, explains why it was the Irish who evolved from the French, with only a limited Swiss-Italian input, a true Insular Rococo which could then cross the seas to a receptive West Country (illus. 3).

As for these half-welcome Swiss not a great deal is recorded of them and virtually nothing of their personal judgements on the state of English plasterwork. Some authorities describe them as coming from 'barren valleys', like refugees from a rocky desert. In fact they came from a fertile Alp of mountain, pasture and vineyards a thousand feet up above Lake Lugano. Carlo Fontana came originally from the same area, which could explain some of the Gibbs connection with the stuccodores. In the large village of

3 The casual sophistication of West Country Rococo inspired by Dublin's example:
Stair-Hall, 15 Orchard Street, Bristol (1740s)

Rovio today Bagutti is still almost as common a family name as Jones in Merthyr Tydfyl, and the Casa Bagutti is a grand house with a blandly Classical front to the main street and four tiers of arcaded balconies to its gardens and lake views at the back.

Whether the fees which Giovanni Bagutti earned at Castle Howard paid for those wedding cake balconies is not known, but he and 'Mr Plura', no Christian name recorded, set Vanbrugh off with an interior style appropriate to his gloriously extrovert Baroque, one with sufficient hints of the Rococo to suggest the possibility of an easy evolution within a decade into the new continental Rococo. But Vanbrugh's architectural career was to prove a tragic instance of a direction and a genius denied. The style he projected was memorable with a masculine poetry of invention. If political events had gone another way, if one of Queen Anne's children had survived to succeed her or if the Tories had returned the Old Pretender to reign as James III, Vanbrugh, with the supporting cast of Nicholas Hawksmoor, John James and James Gibbs, could have produced a grand, though tardy, English Baroque. It was not to be. The fifteen years between the start of Castle Howard and the arrival of the Hanoverians in 1714 were not long enough to establish a Baroque tradition on which a Rococo could have developed naturally. It should have been taking hold in the country since at least 1660 to have stood any chance of outfacing Colen Campbell and Lord Burlington. While this book is not written to suggest that the second Palladian revival was an unmitigated disaster, neither does it assume that it was the best of all possible directions for the country to have taken. It was with this unrewardingly cold and, by European standards, desperately old-fashioned style that a lame and crippled English Rococo would have to co-exist.

While there are any number of Rococo interiors in English houses, that overmantel in Castle Howard (illus. 1) being arguably the first hint of the style, complete and perfect Rococo houses in Britain can be numbered on the fingers of one hand. Because the style only matured into a true native form of exterior austerity (illus. 4) and interior exuberance (illus. 5) in Ireland, passing to a fitful brilliance in the West of England, it would be fair to describe the following chapters as a study of Irish cultural colonialism, with England as the colony and Ireland as the benign invading power. Such a corrective balance to Anglo-centricity is overdue. Also, however, this book is undeniably a reconsideration of the Palladian Revival and a protest against it, a speculation on what might have been. To anyone interested in Georgian architecture, Ireland and Dublin are extraordinarily stimulating as an alternative England with country houses, towns and a great city that

4 Upper Merrion
Street, Dublin: the
tense refinement of
Rococo exteriors of the
late 1760s.

have followed a subtly different evolution of style and escaped much of the
destruction of industrialization and over-population.

In our Irish chapters we were always conscious of writing slightly against
the grain of modern Eire's self-image. After all the pioneering work of the
Irish Georgians over the last forty years and the rich accumulation of photographic records in the National Architectural Archive in Merrion Square,
the buildings of Ireland's eighteenth century have still not got the place in
Eire's esteem that its relics of Celtic monasticism hold. Historically this is
completely understandable, but it still makes no kind of aesthetic sense.
Between the two wars in the first years of the Irish Free State there was
an interlude of virtual state-inspired vandalism when the country allowed
its only real artistic treasure by European standards of greatness – its
eighteenth-century country and town houses – to be burnt or demolished
in a dismaying succession of isolated incidents. It was as if France had pulled down a third of its Gothic cathedrals because Catholicism had become
politically incorrect. But Georgian architecture was rightly seen as associated with a small Protestant elite and that small elite was also correctly
associated with political betrayal and famine.

Now in the last half of the twentieth century the official attitude has, theo-
retically, gone into reverse, but the Classical and chiefly Rococo excellencies
with which that despised Protestant Ascendancy had endowed a reluctant
majority has still to be genuinely liked, appreciated and guarded. It has been
since the 1939–45 war that Dublin's town houses have been ravaged, not
systematically, but by indifference: a row gone here where a major utility

needed prestige offices, new blocks of offices reared up elsewhere with the right height and an attempt at the right coloured brick but entirely wrong in every other detail. Six houses are demolished in another street when the tourist boom requires that another hotel should be built. Every time there are smiling faces and plausible words on TV to explain and excuse the destruction: that potent Irish charm of manners. Yet Dublin's beauty as a capital is singularly dependent upon its whole fabric of streets and not on a number of resounding buildings. There is one handsome confrontation between Trinity College and the old Parliament House, but everywhere else it is the quiet ease of architectural understatement which makes the city, and that cannot tolerate random rips and tears or slick patching.

It is easy to understand why the Irish are so disposed. If the Persians had conquered the Greeks at Salamis, raised the sublime temples on the hill at Athens and then, four hundred years later, had been thrown back across the Aegean, how would the Greeks have respected those Persian temples? Certainly not with reverence or affection. Instead they would have claimed that primitive Mycenae was the true relic of the Greek spirit and built 'The Greek Experience' for tourists to focus upon Agamemnon's gold mask and inlaid weapons. A few hotels would have been permitted on the slopes of the Acropolis to take advantage of the views. That is no more and no less than what Eire has done. 'The Dublin Experience', to which all the tourists flock in the undercroft of Trinity's Library, is brilliantly organized, but the Book of Kells which centres it is nothing when compared with the greatest of all surviving Georgian cities that surrounds it: Colonel Thomas Burgh's Library itself, Trinity's open grandeur, the first Parliament house in Europe, an inward facing Castle and all the elegant understatement of squares and residential streets.

Ireland did not come to a halt in the eighth century of the Christian era. Its 'Persian' invaders were an unlovable, selfish crew but at least they let the European Rococo flood into their reception rooms and made it their own distinctive style while England floundered in the grip of a stylistic anomaly (illus. 5). The authors have been visiting Ireland off and on, one of us since the 1950s and the other since the mid-1970s, but five times in this last uneasy year of 1997–8, up to and after the tragic bombing in Omagh. Reluctantly we have to admit that the Irish as a people are more at ease with life than we English: more likeable, warmer, more relaxed and welcoming, less hidden behind pretentious poses. Naturally we have encountered, in libraries, museums, country houses, lawyers' offices, the Gaelic League and the Archive, a shrewd, sophisticated intelligentsia which does care about the country's

5 The Stair-Hall, 20 Lower Dominick Street, Dublin (1756–8), illustrating the absolute contrast between a Dublin exterior and interior.

eighteenth-century riches. But the average Dubliner in the street is still genially indifferent and unaware.

We sat drinking one evening in a Malahide bar and saw all the television watchers in the place go wild with spontaneous joy as Manchester United scored against Turin's Juventus. It was precisely the opposite of what we expected. Manchester, after all, is a city of the 'Persians'. Would any one of those cheering have turned a hair if another set of Robert West's ceilings was removed to store and its parent house flattened for further hotels? On another occasion we were going around Russborough in a small party that included three graciously positive nuns. It was after bandits had made one of their periodic ritual raids on Sir Alfred Beit's art treasures, and as our guide related how all those great paintings had been stolen the nuns could only chuckle with admiration at the robbers' boldness, at a wealthy outsider being outpointed – what boys they must have been and them so bold! It was, we could not help thinking, a disturbing demonstration of national solidarity and, to us, a romantic irresponsibility. The Anglo–Irish relationship is a complex historical artefact and not one to take on trust with easy words and pleasant smiles. We, for our part, are grateful for the Royal Fort, Beacon House and Fonmon Castle: Irish interiors in England and Wales and evidence of cultural cross reference, and we hope that some chapters of this book will make correctional points. When Eire can accept the memory of the Protestant Ascendancy and its artistic legacy in the same way that the English accept the Norman Conquest and all that flowed from it: cathedrals like Durham, Ely and Peterborough, the carvings of Kilpeck, Barfreston and Malmesbury, our two countries will have reached a philosophical and neighbourly equilibrium. For the time being any appreciation of their Rococo by the Irish appears to lie somewhere between those cheers for Manchester United and the laughter of the nuns.

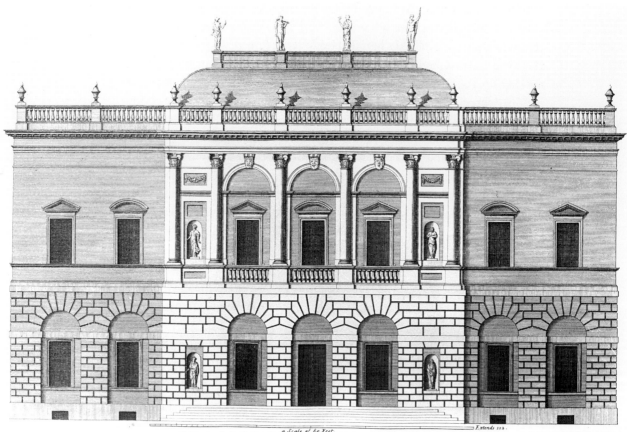

6 A Colen Campbell 'New Design' of 1715 intended to seduce the aristocracy to Palladian forms.

CHAPTER I

THE TROUBLE
WITH THE
PALLADIAN

The problem with any honest critical appreciation of the Rococo as it developed in the united kingdoms of England and Ireland is how to discuss, without seeming foolishly provocative or gratuitously unpatriotic, the neo-Palladian style with which it uneasily co-existed. The Rococo came in as a much needed decorative response to the inadequacies and the predictabilities of the average neo-Palladian interior. In the same way the Gothick was introduced as a relief from the neo-Palladian's unexciting exterior profile. Neo-Palladianism had from the start been more an imposition, almost a public relations effort, than a natural stylistic growth. As an icon or a house style for the aristocratic oligarchy of the Whigs, who ruled Britain for the better part of the eighteenth century, the neo-Palladian was distinctive. Its patrons would contrive to keep the balance of power in Europe, repress the conflicting nationalisms of their own three kingdoms and conjure up, not one, but two succeeding world-wide empires as emporiums for trade and an inventive industry. So for the image of such an imperial ruling caste the neo-Palladian, in villas, large country houses and public buildings, offered a refined architecture flatteringly appropriate to Roman Senators. It was also intellectually satisfying, cool and columned, the proper style for an Age of Reason.

The Classicism of Greece and Rome had already obsessed Europe for three hundred years, all that time putting a premium on scholarship and copying rather than on creative invention. Within that limited context the neo-Palladian was a badge of an erudite yet virile society. While the great nations of the Continent were allowing the dynamic of Baroque design to peter out in the effeminate scrolls and scribblings of the French-inspired Rococo, Britain, so the Palladian fanatics believed, could be seen as moving back to the Classical source springs, to Andrea Palladio's Veneto of the late sixteenth century. Palladianism had the additional advantage of being more than a mere style. It could easily become a cult, an aesthetic religion. There was a bible – Palladio's own *I Quattro Libri dell'Architettura* of 1570 – for exegesis and intense analysis by its devoted disciples. Any wealthy and personable peer could pose as its current apostle, and then there was a whole chain of delightful buildings still surviving in northern Italy to provide a pilgrim route for the faithful on their Grand Tours. There were villas of human scale and seductive, bucolic charm like the Foscari, the Badoer and the perfect Rotonda, town palaces like the Chiericati, the Barbarano and the Valmarana to suggest civic pomp, the Teatro Olimpico for a pasteboard illusion of the ideal and finally, though not hinted at in the pages of the *Quattro Libri*, in Venice there was S. Giorgio Maggiore, floating on the waters in an impossible perfection of the forbidden Catholic worship.

All this came with the advantage of an identity, an actual name – 'Palladian' – which no other rival Classicism possessed. The 'Baroque' would not be styled from the Portuguese word for a misshapen pearl until after 1765 when the style was already defunct. 'Rococo' was not coined as a term from the French 'rocaille' and 'coquille' (pebble and shell work) until the early nineteenth century. In their time the Baroque and the Rococo were simply seen as modern Classical architecture practised by various experts in their multiple, individual ways. Not one of the old masters – Raphael, Michelangelo, Guilio Romano or Bernini, certainly not Borromini – offered anything to equal Palladio's easily absorbed prototypes or the accessibility of his well-illustrated prose.

Even so, with all these advantages, the English return to Palladianism after the Hanoverian accession in 1714 remains perhaps the most unpredictable change of direction in the whole history of British architecture. For it was a return. It had all been tried out before and came now with what should have been the most unsuitable associations for the Whig party. From 1619, when Inigo Jones had devised the Whitehall Banqueting House for James I, the neo-Palladian had been the court style of the Stuart kings, while the Whigs were the direct descendants of the Parliamentary party which had executed Charles I and then, through their founder figure, the 1st Earl of Shaftesbury, given Charles II his most uneasy political moments.

The Glorious Revolution of 1688, which unseated James II and virtually turned Britain into an elected monarchy with William and Mary brought over from Holland, had been a Whig triumph. Now in 1714, while the Tories hesitated, it was the Whigs who had acted decisively and brought the Elector of Hanover, George I, over to reign when James II's son, James the Old Pretender, should have succeeded by right of birth. What then induced the Whigs to take up, in a second revival, this neo-neo-Palladianism of the discredited Catholic Stuarts when they were the true champions of the Protestant Hanoverians?

A number of theories have been offered. Sir Howard Colvin has written an impressive but not entirely convincing essay: 'A Scottish Origin for English Palladianism?' suggesting that the style had already been revived as much as twenty years earlier in the northern kingdom, and that it was brought down to London in the cultural train of a few opportunistic Scottish Whigs like the 2nd Duke of Argyll: men eager to prosper in the new Hanoverian environment.[1] Argyll's clan, the Campbells, were a byword for opportunism. Against Colvin's theory was the fact that Scotland in general had Stuart associations and was the natural base chosen in 1715 by the Old Pretender when he launched the first Jacobite Rebellion, an enterprise which failed, not so much from Scotland's lack of enthusiasm as from his own inept handling and dispirited image. In addition, the examples of this supposedly innovative Scottish Palladianism, which Colvin produced from old records and drawings, were unimpressive and provincial, as uncharismatic as the Old Pretender himself. In support of the Colvin theory there was, however, the undisputed fact that the first and most effective proselytizer for this second revival was a Scot, Colen Campbell, who had been trained as an architect back in Scotland by James Smith, himself the designer, on paper only, of some of Colvin's 'Palladian' prototypes. But in the aftermath of the '1715' any Scottish associations are more likely to have told against the Palladian rather than for it.

There is a more convincing, indeed obvious, theory on the source of the revival. The Hanoverian George came to the throne in 1714. In 1715 two splendidly produced and subsequently highly influential folio volumes were published: the first volume of Colen Campbell's *Vitruvius Britannicus* and Giacomo Leoni's first volume of his translation of Palladio's *Quattro Libri*, dedicated to King George. Both books praised Palladio's architecture in glowing terms and praised in almost equal measure Inigo Jones who had staged the initial Palladian revival. It seems highly probable that the new German dynasty favoured the style and that the Whigs adopted it as a mark of royal favour despite its earlier Stuart associations. George was, of course, James I's great-grandson and so in a sense a Stuart; the Palladian could with something of an effort be seen as a sign of his legitimacy.

Only the insular xenophobia and native arrogance of the English has obscured this plausible argument. It has been almost an article of faith among English historians that George I was a ridiculous figure who spoke no English, shut his wife up in a castle for adultery, had her lover murdered and took up with two notably ugly mistresses whom he absurdly elevated to the English peerage, Melusina von Schulenburg as Duchess of Kendal and Charlotte Sophia Kielmannsegge as Countess of Darlington. A reputable historian of the period like J. H. Plumb has described George as 'very stupid and lacking interest in the arts', even though, on the same page, 'His character was strong and powerful and complex'. But then 'George had a healthy animal appetite for women, he preferred them fat and complaisant', yet von Schulenburg, as Plumb records, was 'sixty, tall, thin, bony, more interested in money and power than the delights of the flesh.[2] The possibility that the King simply and sensibly enjoyed the company of an intelligent, cultured woman his own age and not fat at all is not considered. After all, he was German.

'We are ruined by trulls', Mist wrote in his journal of 27 May 1721, 'nay what is more vexatious, by old ugly trulls, such as could not find entertainment in the most hospitable hundreds of old Drury'.[3] Even Lord Chesterfield, an urbane and rational man, dismissed poor Schulenburg as 'little better than an idiot', claiming that the King's 'views and affections were singly confined to the narrow compass of his Electorate. England was too big for him'.[4] Yet George, a Protestant, had in his youth responded gallantly to the Catholic Emperor's appeal and fought to save Vienna from the Turk, but as Lady Mary Wortley Montagu noted dismissively, 'He could speak no English, and was past the age of learning'.[5] Horace Walpole, the homosexual authority for so much English historical writing on the eighteenth century, knew how to react to the other mistress, Kielmannsegge. She had 'an ocean of neck that overflowed and was not distinguished from the lower part of her body, and no part restrained by stays – no wonder that a child [Horace was referring to himself] dreaded such an ogress, and that the mob of London were highly diverted at the importation of so uncommon a seraglio'.[6]

No wonder too, that George spent as much time as possible in Hannover, away from his unpleasant and xenophobic English subjects. Recent research by German-speaking scholars in the more impartial airs of Canada's McGill University has revealed that, far from being the ruler of a 'beggarly Electorate'

7 Wilbury House,
Wiltshire as first built
(*c.* 1708): William
Benson's clumsy,
cut-down version of
John Webb's Amesbury.

The Elevation of Wilberry house in the County of Wilt the Seat of William Benson Esq. Invented and built by himself
in the Stile of Inigo Iones, to whom this Plate is most humbly Inscribed.
Elevation de la Maison de Wilberry dans la Comti de Wilt.

sunk in the culture of a provincial Baroque, George had, in 1709, long before his cold welcome in England, encouraged architectural projects of a Palladian character.[7] He was proud of the fact that his own family the Welfs (Guelphs as in the medieval Italian struggles between Guelphs and Ghibilines) originated, like Palladio, from the Veneto. One of his architects, Lambert Corfey, prepared a model of a Palladian villa with an octagonal central space and the characteristic centralized plan, like that which Lord Burlington was to build at Chiswick. When the King sacked Sir Christopher Wren as Surveyor General in 1718, he appointed the relatively obscure William Benson to the post and Benson, uneasily aware of his own amateur status, appointed the competent and confident Colen Campbell as his deputy. In 1716 Benson had created 'a curious waterwork' for the garden of George's palace of Herrenhausen;[8] much earlier, in about 1708, he had built for his own use in Wiltshire a deplorable bungalow in what Campbell in his *Vitruvius Britannicus* contemptibly describes as being 'the noblest Manner of Architecture . . . this beautiful and regular design'. Benson appears to have thought that by chopping off the roof and attic floor of Amesbury, a house by John Webb but attributed at that time to Inigo Jones, and simply applying a midget portico, a cupola and a few panels of relief, he could create an elegant Palladian lodge for a gentleman (illus. 7). Unaccountably Wilbury still features in some architectural histories as a significant early neo-Palladian house.

The King, however, had not visited Wilbury and thought he was putting an enthusiast for the Palladian into a position of great influence; though in reality Benson was a glove puppet for Colen Campbell's ambitions. Benson secured for Campbell the task of designing new state rooms at Kensington Palace between 1718 and 1720, but then the two men moved too quickly. They claimed that the House of Lords was dangerously unsafe and, before it collapsed in a holocaust of the entire peerage, proposed to build a new Palladian seat of government in its place. If they had succeeded, London in 1720 would have gained the prestigious complex which Dublin was to achieve in a dazzling feat of Irish one-upmanship in 1729 with Sir Edward Lovett Pearce's confident and virtually neo-Classical Parliament building. But London lacked the emulous spirit of Ireland's Protestant Ascendancy and the firm guiding hand of its Viceroy, Lord Carteret. Rival architects declared the House of Lords perfectly safe and both Benson and Campbell were sacked after a mere fifteen months in office.

What Campbell had, however, safely achieved was that 'our Trusty and Well-beloved' was given the royal licence and copyrights 'at Our Court of St James's, the Eighth Day of April, 1715, in the First Year of Our Reign' to publish the first of three volumes of his *Vitruvius Britannicus*, a work intended to prove, on pitifully slender evidence, that Britain had already a rich Palladian past and would soon have a far richer Palladian future. It was a literary confidence trick which worked exactly as Campbell determined.

Campbell's introduction was a head-on assault upon 'Baroque' design, though the term had yet to be invented:

How affected and licentious are the works of Bernini and Fontana? How wildly Extravagant are the Designs of Borromini, who has endeavoured to debauch Mankind with his odd and chimerical Beauties, where the Parts are without Proportion, solids without their true Bearing, Heaps of Material without Strength, excessive Ornaments without Grace, and the Whole without Symmetry?

In opposition to this supposedly contemptible Italian animation Campbell offered, yet without a single illustrated instance of his work:

the great Palladio, who has exceeded all that were gone before him, and surpass'd his Contemporaries, whose ingenious Labours will eclipse many, and rival most of the Ancients. And indeed this excellent Architect seems to have arrived to a Ne plus ultra of his Art.

All fine words, but with little substance. What carried this first volume of his *Vitruvius* was its weight and the sheer beauty of its plates. It is a huge and satisfying book to handle, so well presented and with such a determinedly optimistic text that the reader is soon persuaded to join Campbell in his reflection 'on the happiness of the British Nation, that at present abounds with so many learned and ingenious gentlemen', without realizing that none of the ingenious gentlemen in his list – Bruce, Vanbrugh, Archer, Wren, Wynne, Talman, Hawksmoor or James – could be described as Palladian designers by even the most generous definition.

The description of his *Vitruvius* as a literary confidence trick is not an overstatement. He had hijacked what, as recently as 1 June 1714, had only been intended by its backers as a proud reminder to the nation of all its recent architectural achievements, which were considerable, even by European standards. At least three of the names on Campbell's list – Wren, Vanbrugh and Hawksmoor – were great architects by any reckoning. England had been living through a golden age of design without any need for or inclination towards a second Palladian revival. Palladianism was dead, but Campbell, presumably with higher backing, was determined to disinter the stylistic corpse.

In her *British Architectural Books and Writers 1556–1785*, Eileen Harris attributes the hasty reshaping of the contents of *Vitruvius Britannicus*, which took place between 1714 and 1715, to its backers' panic-stricken reaction to the news that Leoni was about to publish his English translation of Palladio's *Quattro Libri*.[9] Campbell was brought in as a Palladian expert with a lively interest in Inigo Jones and a whole folio of house designs which could, charitably, be described as Palladio modernized or, more ruthlessly, as ostentatious piles of Palladian motifs heaped up to impress the vainglorious. Campbell was already engaged in building an enormous palace of a house, again vaguely Palladian, at Wanstead in Essex for Sir Richard Child, so he had a reputation to offer, not just drawings. His name was given on the title page, and he was allowed to write the introduction and explanatory notes. A number of house illustrations which were to have been included were cut out and Campbell's 'inventions' were slipped into their place. The first volume of *Vitruvius Britannicus* came out before Leoni's Palladio (Rudolph Wittkower believed that Leoni, mortified, put a false date, 1715, on his book which did not actually appear until 1716).[10] Campbell's second volume would come out in 1717 with the promised illustrations of the 'Inigo Jones' designs for a palace at Whitehall. The third volume came out in 1725 when Campbell's architectural practice was riding high and was, therefore, a celebration of an established career.

His three volumes, spanning ten years, record an extraordinary reversal of architectural fashions. The first volume only included one realized modern 'Palladian' house, Wanstead, and even that would never have been recognized by Palladio himself as designed in his spirit. Yet with no fewer than fifteen plates devoted to Campbell's sumptuous Palladian inventions (illus. 6) the book spearheaded a second Palladian revival. In addition to his inventions, all dedicated impressively to individual aristocrats like the Duke of Argyll and the Earl of Halifax, Campbell had squeezed in ten plates of four buildings either by, or attributed to, Inigo Jones. Wisely he illustrated none of Palladio's buildings as these would have shown up the tawdry pomp of his own designs.

The visual impact of the first volume depended initially on St Paul's cathedral, St Peter's, Rome and a rival to St Peter's which Campbell was hoping to 'invent' on Lincoln's Inn Fields. After that ecclesiastical parade the volume was dominated, and impressively dominated, by Vanbrugh. No one would have dreamt that Sir John's career had peaked, would now decline, and that his last designs for Grimsthorpe in Lincolnshire, which would feature in the third, 1725, volume, would represent an ignominious capitulation to the Palladian. Yet Vanbrugh was the architect who had so imaginatively reflected English triumphalism in Marlborough's wars and directed the English Baroque into a distinct national form worthy to be set against the best in Italy and Germany. In the 1715 volume there were six tremendous views of Blenheim, six of Castle Howard and two of Kings Weston, near Bristol.

In his notes Campbell was all unctuous praise of the master. At Blenheim, 'The Manner is Grand, the Parts Noble, and the Air Majestick of this Palace, adapted to the Martial Genius of the Patron'. While in acknowledgements he wrote:

> I am at a loss, how to express my Obligations to this worthy Gentleman for promoting my Labours, in most generously assisting me with his Original Drawings, and most carefully correcting all the Plates as they advanced.[11]

So in 1715 Campbell had everything to play for, but was playing hard. The native lines of English and Scottish architecture were still idiosyncratically glorious and inventive. Scotland's Drumlanrig Castle was allowed to flaunt its outrageous towers, turrets and ducal coronet-cap without a word of shame. There was nothing to represent the cowed and nervous kingdom of Ireland. Her builders were for the most part raising barracks for the fifteen regiments of the great garrison which kept the Protestant Ascendancy secure.

Only one plate in the first volume hinted at the Achilles heel of the future neo-Palladian: its interiors. This was a cross-section through the centre of Campbell's second (and built) design for Wanstead. Here alone in all these

The Section of Wansted house.   *Le profil de la Maison de Wansted*

impressive views there was just a hint of an inside decorative treatment (illus. 8). Campbell showed one large wall of the Saloon covered with a huge mural on the Race of Atalanta, a favourite theme of Sir James Thornhill. Painted frescoes were strictly correct as treatment for true Palladian interiors and at this date, 1715, there were still signs that England might produce its own school of painters in the Thornhill tradition. In reality Sir James was the end of the line. The future for painted interiors, in so far as there was any future, would lie with the French and the Italians; English Palladians would rely upon plasterers for their interiors and the true Palladian vocabulary for plasterwork work was very limited (illus. 22). Tedium and predictability were only a little way ahead and they would be the opening for the Rococo. If they would not or could not paint, the islanders would have to resort to plaster, and against all expectations at this time it would be the Irish who would deploy their plasterwork with the more open invention and an acceptance of Rococo themes and styles.

Campbell's second, 1717, volume of *Vitruvius Britannicus* recorded a nation's architecture in suspension. Eastbury Park, a manic new Vanbrugh house, was threatened for Dorset, but the plates were dominated by fourteen for Inigo Jones and eleven for Campbell, Inigo's self-proposed successor. A few of Campbell's designs were actually built though they were excessively modest, mere merchants' town houses, the rest were inventions 'in the

Theatrical Style'. He had still to find his balance, there was as yet no authentic contemporary English Palladianism. Jones's supposed Whitehall Palace designs and his Wilton House, Wiltshire had the positions of authority which Vanbrugh's palaces had held with more confidence in the first volume. And with the Wilton plates there was a second pointer to the basic weakness of Campbell's campaign for the Palladian. One plate was devoted to two of Wilton's celebrated interiors, the Double Cube Room and the Dining Room. Campbell made no attempt to indicate the paintings by the de Critz brothers on its ceilings, but he did convey the main outlines of the John Webb–Inigo Jones decorations – heavily pedimented doorcases, panelled walls, long drops of heavy plasterwork to punctuate those panels, an acanthus cornice and a compartmented ceiling. This was the Louis XIII treatment offered for copying in 1717. If it was good enough for Inigo it was good enough for Campbell. In the third volume of *Vitruvius Britannicus* Campbell would follow up this implicit direction with illustrations of three of his own interiors, for Houghton Hall, Norfolk, Mereworth Castle, Kent, and a garden house at Hall Barn in Buckinghamshire, all in very much the same style. Shades of a decorative prison house were already closing in.

It is in the third, 1725, volume that the Palladian tide has turned and the native Baroque is in retreat. The book is dedicated to George, Prince of Wales, by Colen Campbell, not just his 'obedient servant', but his 'architect' [on what grounds the volume is silent]. It was not possible for the author to close the door entirely on the rich and stimulating Baroque past, as a number of plates that had been removed from the first volume to make way for Campbell's inventions had to be used somewhere: a view each, for instance, of Greenwich and Castle Howard. Sir John Vanbrugh, obviously the greatest living British architect, could still not be completely excised. His riotous Eastbury for Bubb Dodington was well illustrated and there were two plates of Seaton Delaval, Northumberland. But now Campbell's time had come. Since 1717 he had enjoyed eight highly successful years and he impressed his commissions, even a few of his manifestly unremarkable town houses, into the contents.

There remained much of which to be proud: Ebberston Lodge, a light-hearted nest for a mistress in Yorkshire, made the desperately important point that the Palladian style could play, had in fact been originally designed in part for holiday retreats on the farm. Stourhead, Wiltshire, Baldersby, Yorkshire, and Pembroke House in Whitehall firmly established what was already becoming the standard neo-Palladian villa pattern in England, the one Andrea Palladio would have recognized: the frontal elevations with

9 Houghton Hall, Norfolk as Colen Campbell intended it in 1725 and before James Gibbs devised a Baroque roofline.

the 1–3–1 pattern of windows, the central three bays slightly advanced on the flanking single bays. Rather like a class of the old steam locomotives, the 4–6–2s and the 2–4–2s, they were a design concept which could be easily grasped. Modest, economical and civilized, they tended to make Vanbrugh's Eastbury look slightly ridiculous, too assertive, too inventive, 'not quite English', the phrase could be breathed. And in addition to three proto-types for gentlemanly understatement Campbell could reasonably boast his English Villa Rotonda, Mereworth Castle with its central dome, handsomely supported by expensive hexastyle porticoes, Italy translated to Kent with none of Lord Burlington's pedantic nonsense about recreating the villas of the ancients. Houghton Hall, designed for Sir Robert Walpole the power broker and First Lord of the Treasury, gave Campbell his final imprimatur of arrival and yet, ironically, Walpole at the same time undercut him, nudged him sharply in the ribs with a reminder of more relaxed architectural manners and the presence of James Gibbs.

In his plate of Houghton's entrance front Campbell showed the house as he had intended it should be built with austere end towers on the Wilton pattern (illus. 9). Walpole, not a man much inclined to the austerities of life, brought in Gibbs to give the towers comfortable rounded tea-cosy tops and an old-fashioned Baroque profile. Houghton makes the point that Palladio's villas simply do not adapt easily to the scale of a great English country house. Campbell tried gallantly with a Venetian window in each tower, but he was up against the basic dysfunctionalism of all accurate Palladian architecture in England's cloud-confounded climate. In a true Palladian façade the windows should be small, in order to ration the generous Italian sun, and there should be very few of them in relation to the wall surface. The larger the house the more meagre and forbidding its allowance of window openings will appear. Another consequence is that a big house will tend to look smaller than it really is because of that economy in fenestration. That is an issue which will need to be aired in a later chapter when the vast neo-Palladian country houses were going up and the *aficionados* were attempting to intellectualize their failings.

At this point it is enough to leave Colen Campbell riding high on the wave of his own brilliant self-publicizing, with his 1–3–1s streaming out over the parklands of England and Lord Burlington in the background preparing to launch a much tighter but less attractive version of a style which had already moved dangerously far from the exquisite casualness of its Italian origins.

CHAPTER II

THREE VILLAS
TO THE
ROCOCO

Campbell, and after him Lord Burlington, chose their time to wage style wars in England with strategic good sense. Now the long French war was ended, the native Baroque of Vanbrugh seemed an embarrassment, over-stated and vainglorious, a soldier's triumphalist style. If past precedent was any guide the natural stylistic course for the country would have been to follow its great continental neighbour after the usual twenty-year time lag. There were, however, serious technical obstacles to the adoption of the brilliant new Rococo of France, and Campbell was probably aware of them when he made his shrewd stand for Classical simplicity and economy.

Since Britain is an island it is not helpful to complain that its arts are, and always have been, insular. Artistically, though not strategically, France has always had one enormous advantage over England. She has frontiers with Italy, Germany and the Low Countries and has always been able to draw from them not just inspiration and novel fashions, but an inexhaustible supply of skilled craftsmen and brilliant artists in stone, wood, metal and paint. Poor England and even poorer Ireland tended to get the skilled foreign workers who had failed to find patrons in France. So there is no excuse for ignorance about the stylistic activities and technical strength of France. In the eighteenth century there was never any possibility of the English adopting the true French style of the Rococo because that was an intensely sophisticated decorative process. A French Rococo interior depended upon an integrated team of joiners, wood carvers, wood painters,

painters on canvas and upholsterers, all highly skilled and consequently highly paid, working together with one mind under an experienced director. Plaster and stucco work came into such a team practice but it was not even secondary in importance, it came fourth or fifth down the scale. Plaster was a cheap material, easily handled and not, therefore, highly regarded, it would be used as a substitute for wooden wall panels in middle class interiors.

A number of supremely finished and exquisitely mannered Régence (1715–23) interiors were being created in great Parisian town houses throughout the second decade of the century. It was a style feeling its way from the grotesqueries of Jean Bérain, Louis XIV's *Dessinateur de la Chambre et du Cabinet du Roi* from 1674 to his death in 1711, through Claude Audran and Charles Antoine Coypel's more nimble-footed pastoral and fairground fantasies – monkeys, fairies, tightrope walkers and chimeras – to the true Rococo, the 'Genre Pittoresque'. That, as shaped by designers like Gilles-Marie Oppenord (1672–1742) and Nicolas Pineau (1684–1754), would be a natural but distinctive variant of the Louis XIV style, lighter, more elegant, more allusive, but still technically overwhelmingly rich and using the same teams of decorators who merely updated their designs.[1]

In 1719 William Kent spent several months in Paris, waiting for Lord Burlington to return from his strangely planned tour of the Veneto. After ten years in Italy, studying painting, architecture and antiques, Kent would have had no trouble in recognizing the high level of the French decorators' skills and the impossibility of equalling and copying them in Britain. A natural pasticheur himself, he would have sketched and absorbed this French fashion and was able, ten years later, to insert a few French Rococo details, primarily into the overdoors, of Lord Burlington's otherwise obsessively 'Ancient Roman' villa at Chiswick. But even in a minor decorative detail like an overdoor Kent must have realized that France had artists like Guillaume Martin, Hyacinthe Rigaud, François Le Moyne and Jean Restout who, though only middle ranking in French esteem, totally outclassed any British painters in their ability to provide such decorative trifles with stunning technical competence.

A real Palladian villa in the Veneto tends to cheer and enliven its chaste proportions by confident Mannerist frescoes. There are the loves of Antony and Cleopatra in warm autumnal colour on the walls of the Villa Caldogno, not great art but wonderful wallpaper. Battista Franco's giants tumble head-over-heels in the rooms of the Villa Foscari (La Malcontenta) and Giambattista Zelotti's sensual histories of Venus give the Villa Emo the airs of an elegant country bordello. But none of this was available in early

10 *Thetis visiting Vulcan's Forge*, illusionist decoration by James Thornhill at Hanbury Hall, Worcestershire (*c.* 1710, oil on plaster).

eighteenth-century England. There were always a few expensive, competent foreign fresco painters around for those who could afford them: men like Antonio Verrio, Giovanni Pellegrini and Francesco Sleter. They were the equivalents in talent of those sixteenth-century hack-painters like Franco and Zelotti, but they did not come at hack-painter prices, and in provincial England they passed as great artists not as the kind of jobbing painter who would come down for a week, enliven a room to a patron's theme then go away modestly remunerated.

For a number of complex, debatable reasons England simply did not produce even mildly talented artists to make fresco popular. It may have been the Black Death, the philistine nature of successive monarchs, or the repressive quality of England's Protestantism, but whatever the cause, artistic poverty was a fact. The twenty-odd years it had taken James Thornhill (illus. 10) to paint one, admittedly large, ceiling at Greenwich and the dismal grisaille work with which he covered the dome of St Paul's cathedral were not calculated to inspire enthusiasm for much further experiment in fresco. At plasterwork, however, the English had a more encouraging record, not perhaps in design, but certainly in technique. No one who studies the intricate wreaths of flowers, fruit and leaves on the great ceilings of a Carolean house like Sudbury Hall in Derbyshire, or the cherubs and lions playing in the Vitruvian scrolls of plasterwork in a minor country house like Eye Manor, Herefordshire, can doubt that good plasterers were common in the shires.

11 A ceiling painting by William Kent of *Mercury Watching Herse and her Sisters before the Temple of Minerva* (installed *c.* 1724, oil on canvas) in the Hall at Chicheley Hall, Buckinghamshire.

Something which needs to be borne in mind when approaching the Rococo is that plasterwork is a very forgiving art form. The materials come cheaply – lime, sand, hair and water – even the more refined stucco only needs the addition of a little marble dust. Mistakes can be corrected and gross errors thrown away without too much pain. Skills can be acquired very quickly as Sir Roger Pratt found when he taught himself to hang the Inigo Jones-designed ceilings for Coleshill, Berkshire, in a few weeks. With a good stock of moulds and dextrous fingers for improvisations a master plasterer was soon established in his trade and even able to style himself as a 'stuccodore', which was only an impressive sounding title for a plasterer with a portfolio of foreign designs and aspirations to serve the gentry.

A painter takes longer to train. The young William Kent set out in 1709 for a ten-year apprenticeship under Guiseppe Chiari in Rome, but talent as well as application is required to make an artist and Kent, paradoxically, seems on his return to have done more than anyone at this period to make English patrons despair of fresco painting and turn to plaster. If there is an element of the subjective in that judgement then it can be tested at Kensington Palace. A viewer should pause long enough on the stairs to take in the peculiar perspectives, clumsy compositions and lifeless faces of Kent's illusionist frescoes on the walls. He was a man of considerable designing talent but as an artist not even third-rate, only fourth, and he was the painter

whom Lord Burlington brought back from Rome to be his paid friend and to paint interiors for a new architecture (illus. 11).

All this explains why, when the Rococo finally worked its way through the stylistic block of the Palladian, and the even more artificial Palladian–Ancient Roman compromise imposed by Lord Burlington, it was not a French Rococo of sculpted wooden panels, inset mirrors, painted overdoors and silken upholstery. It was an Italo-British Rococo of fine inventive plaster-work, chiefly concentrated upon ceilings and isolated wall events – overmantels and drops (illus. 12). Because it owed so little to French design and crafts-manship directly, the characteristic C and S scrolls of the original French Rococo tended to become mere adjuncts to the livelier figurative work of the native, or Italian invention. The Earl of Chesterfield's town house, designed by Isaac Ware and built as late as 1749, is often quoted as an example of real Rococo styling, but the French nobility would have sneered at it as an example of English insularity, a cheap copy of the tightly stylized and perfectly crafted French prototypes in great Parisian town houses like the Hôtel de Soubise, or de Matignon or de Richelieu. No English joiners would have been capable of work that required the three skilled stages of panelling, sculpting and painting soft, almost unknotted French oak. In the other main reception rooms Ware retreated thankfully to a thin washed-out Palladian. When the English Rococo was finally allowed off the leash of Palladian convention it would produce rich figurative invention and concentrations of dramatic detail with less constraint from panels, beams or any patterned confinement. The artistic tragedy was that it had to wait so long to demonstrate its range, adaptability and potential. Quite how it had been put on hold for almost twenty years is a complex story.

The building history of three villas, all more or less inspired by Palladio's Villa Rotonda, illustrates not simply the internal vulnerability of English Palladianism to Baroque and Rococo decorators, but a failure of fresco to become the legitimate medium for interiors in that style.

Mereworth Castle was the first of these villas, built between 1720 and 1725 by Colen Campbell for Colonel John Fane, later 7th Earl of Westmorland. It is a house of the most satisfying mathematical beauty, not simply a copy of Palladio's Villa Rotonda but an improvement on it. Inexplicably it has failed to capture the English imagination in the way that, for example, Leeds Castle or Stourhead have done. This is probably because it has only very rarely been open to the public and is not even easy to see from a road or right-of-way. It lies low under the lee of a wooded western hill in orchard country, the property now of a rich Arab who has restored it admirably and bedizened its interior gloriously with art works and modern constructs. Only a short drive down from London, a visit to it could save a deal of complex travel and uncertain knocking on doors in the Veneto. In an ideal state all students on fine arts courses should spend a morning there to experience those celebrated Palladian 'harmonic proportions' as realized by an ambitious Scot. England has its own great Palladian villa but it is a well kept secret (illus. 23).

The house is a domed circle set in a square with towering hexastyle porticoes on all four sides. As originally built it was even more poetic than its hilltop Palladian prototype, for Mereworth rested magically on the waters of a broad moat which it bridged, from north and south, by grand flights of steps arching up over the water. The other two porticoes, east and west, served as belvederes or alternatively as platforms for anglers. Even in its interior Campbell improved on Palladio. The Rotonda's central hall has no windows. Its dramatic frescoes of gods and goddesses in illusionist architecture – seventeenth-century work by Ludovico Dorigny – exist in permanent twilight, only lit from the distant portico doors. Palladio's inept lighting of this villa is a puzzle. In the second book of his *Quattro Libri* he stated: 'The hall in the middle is round and receives its light from above', but there are no windows shown on the cross-section. Campbell gave Mereworth a much steeper dome (so steep in fact that Christopher Hussey

placed this most Palladian of houses in the Baroque section of his *English Country Houses: Early Georgian*)[2] and this pitch allowed for four round windows which give ample direct light to the circular central hall within, but not to light frescoes, for its walls are bare.

While the other principal rooms of the house, the long South Gallery and the east and west bedroom suites have ceilings richly frescoed in a compromise between contemporary Baroque and the style of Inigo Jones's Double Cube Room at Wilton, the central Hall was the first of those severe 'staccato' rooms which were to become the orthodox English neo-Palladian interior. So a golden opportunity for a dramatic display of fresco was lost. Instead of giant animated figures Campbell gave the walls a calm punctuation of Palladian architectural features: white doorcases with well-dressed nymphs seated on their pediments, busts and square blind window openings with long plaster drops in between, but no painter's work (illus. 13).

The other state rooms are quite different in their colour and visual attack. Francesco Sleter and another, possibly Kent, painted bright pictorial panels for the compartments of heavily trabeated ceilings, some with deep covings frescoed in blowzy gilded work: armorial achievements and heavy grotesques. Below friezes of swags, masks, cherubs and scrolls the walls are enriched by white marble doorcases, pedimented and topped by frolicking children. These interiors, more than that steep dome, go some way to justify Hussey in describing Mereworth as Baroque. What Campbell and Sleter were doing here was close to what Thornhill, Sleter and Amigoni were doing, also in the 1720s, at Moor Park, Hertfordshire: the same pedimented doorcases with seated figures, the same rather coarse Baroque scroll work around panels of brightly painted allegorical canvases in compartmented panels (illus. 21) . As his *Vitruvius Britannicus* reveals, Campbell had devised no original scheme for decorating a Palladian interior. At Mereworth, with one exception, he simply phased an English Baroque interior with Jonesian undertones into the Palladian shell.

That significant exception was the domed Hall. There Campbell, perhaps still hopeful of another commission from Burlington, deliberately imposed a cold Ancient Roman restraint. The dome of Palladio's original Rotonda was wild with Mannerist stucco work. There are figures poised upon its cornice and the panels have frescoes by Alessandro Maganza; but Mereworth's dome has only austere Roman coffering by Bagutti: it was the under-use of a skilled stuccodore but it was Burlington's preferred style.

Campbell had been reading the signals coming from Burlington House, though not soon enough to please. His designs for Mereworth had been offered first, with the optimistic embellishment of an earl's coronet, to Burlington, not Colonel Vane. It had been rejected despite, or even perhaps because of, its Palladian credentials and Burlington had settled down to design himself, the confident amateur in the Vitruvian tradition, a pavilion-villa to stand next to his old Jacobean house at Chiswick, a structure which he intended should be more Ancient Roman than Palladian.

Meanwhile Colonel Fane, eminently satisfied with his Baroque-Palladian compromise, went on to add, probably to designs by Roger Morris, hand-some pedimented twin pavilions to flank the main approach to Mereworth from the north. It was entirely in keeping with this house's relaxed and natural decorative tradition that the east of these two pavilions was given, around 1740, the most 'coquille', as opposed to 'rocaille', Rococo interior in Britain. This is a superb fantasy chamber of birds, dolphins, floral wreaths and scrolls, all created entirely from iridescent sea-shells which frame mirrors and shelves for the display of china and cover all the walls and ceiling in textured patterning. Horace Walpole described this room as 'extremely pretty',[3] which is an understatement. It could be used as a barometer of taste. After experiencing the Roman gravity of the dome and the Baroque decor of the main villa, a visitor should come into this exotic garden room to absorb the spirit of the Rococo: uninhibited, naturalistic and dedicated to charm.

Before making any harsh criticisms of Richard Boyle, the 3rd Earl of Burlington, two things need to be stressed. He was a genius at persuasion, the successful advocate of an inappropriate architectural style whose antecedents and implications he had never bothered to master. But by pressing the merits of his Ancient Roman under the cloak of a neo-Palladian revival he set back the course of an English Rococo by twenty years and permanently crippled its development. He is, therefore, comparable with such stylistic manipulators as Le Corbusier and Warhol in his ability to convert a society to the improbable, to change art history. The second point to be made about him is that, however much of a disaster his villa at Chiswick, constructed between 1723 and 1729, may appear in retrospect, it was and remains a brilliant though not necessarily likeable or beautiful building.

One reason why such an influential figure has attracted so few biographies is that Burlington had the instinct to keep himself to himself. The general outlines of his life are well known, but he committed singularly little to paper or to print about his personal feelings, relationships and judgements. This may be why he tends to be accepted as a much deeper scholar than he actually was. He had a whim, it seems to be nothing more – the revival of Ancient Roman architecture as a contemporary form – and he had the willpower and the worldly influence to impose it to some extent upon an English school of Baroque design. His cleverness was to use the political ascendancy of the Whig lords and the fashion which Colen Campbell had created for a compromise English Palladian as the vehicles for his more revolutionary obsession with a Roman rather than a Palladian revival. With his wealth and his political connections he hijacked Campbell's pet scheme.

What makes Burlington's one-man neo-Classicism so unsatisfactory as a movement was its timing. He came roughly forty years too soon to be a scholarly or convincing neo-Classical architect, and he was personally far too impatient and superficial a scholar to do much to extend the existing knowledge base. On his first conventional Grand Tour of 1715 he was four months in Rome but spent three of them ill in bed, so his knowledge of the monuments on which he was to base so much was limited to what he observed in one winter month of convalescence when, in any case, his architectural ambitions were probably still quiescent. Even more telling was the itinerary of his second, brief sortie down to Italy between August and November of 1719. It was an illogically planned, even mysterious visit. He met William Kent, as if by pre-arrangement at Genoa, but if Burlington intended to launch an English neo-Classicism, an Ancient Roman revival, why did he not travel on down to Rome to sketch and study its remains with Kent as his artist guide?

Instead he sent Kent on to Paris and then, in Kent's words, 'was agoing to Vicenza and Venice to get architects to draw all the fine buildings of Palladio'.[4] Burlington did, it is true, go to Venice, where he bought from the Barbaro-Trevisan family a collection of Palladio drawings of Roman antiquities. These he would carry home as a great treasure and ultimately publish in a limited edition for connoisseurs as *Fabbriche Antiche disegnate da Andrea Palladio*: elevations and details of Roman baths; much later Robert Adam found them conjectural and inaccurate. Burlington, though obsessive about correct detail, was not a hands-on scholar himself, he was too impatient.

As for Vicenza and 'all the fine buildings of Palladio' he spent two days in the city unable to see more than two villas because the countryside was flooded. Then he made his way home, picking up Kent to begin a life-long partnership in design. He was an arrogant aristocrat in a hurry. For him Palladio was a short cut to the Roman past, someone who shared his Roman obsession but who had been obliged to earn his living churning out villas for a small-time Veneto aristocracy when he really had his eye on the half-ruined grandeurs of Rome. It was not Palladio's Second Book with all its delightful villa variations which interested Burlington, it was his First Book on the 'correct' orders, and his Fourth Book of reconstructions of large Roman public buildings. The flaw at the heart of Burlington's architectural work was that he was content to recreate ancient Roman interiors by cannibalizing parts of the exteriors of Roman public buildings. This accounts for the inescapably 'municipal' air which clings to his domestic work and the work of architects constrained to follow him too closely: William Kent at Ditchley House, Oxfordshire, Campbell at Houghton, Henry Flitcroft at Wentworth Woodhouse, Yorkshire and, most chillingly of all, the team of amateurs and professionals who devised Holkham Hall in Norfolk for the Earl of Leicester.

Vincenzo Scamozzi's oddly proportioned Villa Rocca Pisani could only have attracted Burlington as a model by the oddity of its over-sized and awkwardly supported dome – a domestic Pantheon perhaps rather than a conventional Renaissance villa. It was his misfortune that Herculaneum and Pompeii still lay unexcavated at the time when he could have learnt from them. Some two hundred years earlier the remains of Nero's Golden House had been explored and quite extensive wall paintings discovered. Raphael had made these into a decorative cliché with his grotesque work at the Vatican so they could be used as a plausible Roman decorative treatment, but there was little other guidance for an impatient man. Those Palladio drawings which Burlington had bought explain the impression which his

Chiswick villa gives of being impersonal, a miniature and lavishly gilded version of Roman public baths, all Caracalline coffering, washable surfaces and municipal statuary rather than a gentleman's polite country retreat.

It must, however, have been Chiswick Villa rather than any of his other buildings that was Burlington's prime instrument in converting a number of his peers to the Ancient Roman manner. It was sited near London on the most fashionable reaches of the Thames where everyone could inspect it while enjoying the remarkable gardens and its impressive concentration of features. Basically what the Villa offered for easy imitation was a staccato method of decorating a room, in striking contrast to the rival Baroque method whereby every decorative feature is connected and works as a perceived unity. Chiswick's rooms are rich, even overwhelmingly so, but they still depend upon areas of completely plain walling on which events – a pedimented doorcase or chimneypiece, a bust on a bracket, a statue in a niche or a carved plaque – are isolated almost as carefully placed museum pieces, that municipal element again. Because most Roman ceilings had collapsed and Burlington had no really satisfactory models to follow, he either used the coffering (illus. 14) which survived in the Pantheon and in the ruins of many major public buildings, or else he fell back on Inigo Jones-type ceilings, heavily trabeated and compartmented, concealing the anachronism with a heavy show of painted grotesque work and Kent's inimitably embarrassing paintings.

Ditchley House illustrates how quickly this staccato treatment caught on for the more formal rooms of a house, the Hall in Ditchley's case. It also illustrates the competition which the Ancient Roman was up against, because the Saloon was being decorated at exactly the same time (1724–5) in a connected Baroque style already edging so close to the seductive forms of the Rococo that it is not easy to say whether the stuccodores – the Italian-Swiss team of Vassali, Artari and Serena – were not consciously trying out a compromise between the two styles. William Kent handled the Hall in a loyal version, though on a much grander scale, of the rooms he was helping Burlington to decorate at Chiswick. He even contrived to isolate the ceiling by a wide, bare cove surrounding his heavily trabeated roundel within a square; the roundel occupied by one of his most amusing paintings: a vast Assembly of the Gods. Everything on the walls is equally isolated, the perfect staccato treatment: pedimented doorcases, niches and chimneypieces, rectangular plaques, roundels and busts. Because Kent designed it, the effect is impressive, harmonious and balanced as well as icily formal (illus. 15). A few steps away in the Saloon there is a different, more sensual world of linked forms. Fluted Corinthian pilasters tie cornice and dado firmly together; rich swirls of almost Rococo scrollery top the niches which again link cornice and dado; on the ceiling in shallow relief within shallow compartments crammed with overlapping, overspilling scrolls and anthemions, a goddess floats, supported by cherubs among soft clouds. Classical busts occupy the corner roundels, a Baroque rather than a Rococo device, but the animation of forms about the roundels cancels out any severity (illus. 16).

Both rooms are beautiful and succeed by opposing visual methods, afterwards it is fascinating to visit Chiswick to see what was Kent's inspiration for that formidably confident Hall at Ditchley. At this point it is only fair to add that the Villa has always been, as Burlington intended, more of an icon than a house, a challenge rather than a residence, attracting potential house builders and architectural historians in the way the Great Pyramid of Cheops attracts a certain kind of mathematician, or the books of Nostradamus attract self-appointed visionaries. It is a structure that seems to invite interpretations. John Harris once described it as a house that has had too much written about it, but then went on to undercut himself by writing the definitive analysis to accompany his catalogue for the 1994–5 Burlington exhibition. In this he called the Villa 'the most pedantically composed house ever built in Europe' and proved his point by relating virtually every feature to some

15 The Hall, Ditchley House, Oxfordshire (1724–5): sumptuous but staccato.

detail in Palladio's works or writings, except those motifs inspired by Kent, an important exception.[5] Richard Hewlings, in a long essay on Chiswick, carried out a similar exhaustive exegesis relating those same features to precise parts of ancient Roman buildings, which amounted to much the same thing. The Hewlings essay also finds some remarkable parallels with world architecture. He even suggests that the Link Building, which Burlington built in 1732 to connect his Villa with the old house next door, could have been influenced by links between buildings in the Moscow Kremlin. The rats and mice painted among acanthus fronds in the cornice of the Blue Velvet Room are, Hewlings believes, the rats and mice which 'ate the body of Hiram Abif, architect of Solomon's Temple, and that information would be intelligible to a Mason'.[6] Chiswick has this effect upon its admirers.

A first sighting of it is liable to come as a disappointment to anyone expecting conventional Palladian harmony as at Mereworth. Unkind similes come cheap but the dome is singularly graceless, too large and rests without apparent convincing support on a sloping slate roof. It hangs there like an ugly toadstool or a Montgolfier balloon preparing for take off. Immediately

Burlington's arrogant indifference to expectations can be sensed; it is a stimulating experience and the size of the dome is an early indication of his priorities. This was no pretty garden building but a suite of rooms for entertainment and refined retreat, a demonstration of principles. The interiors came first and the grandeur of the Tribunal, the first reception room, demanded the height of that unhappy dome.

It is an overwhelming, even a bewildering experience to walk around the eight, quite small but densely compacted and aggressively rich, rooms of the Villa. Nothing quite prepares a visitor for the absence of corridors, spaces to connect spaces, the visually in-your-face way that the spatial variety of octagons, rectangles, squares, a circle and an apsed rectangle crowd in, one room upon another, and interconnect in a maze of cross vistas, red, blue and white interiors and all of them golden at every gildable point. The verdict of 'nouveau riche vulgarity' hovers at the back of every new response, but is never quite justified because as well as being so rich the detail is also brazenly 'correct', so derivative of the best models and authorities, and therefore lacking in imagination or individual invention. Chiswick is stylistic bullying. It is easy to sense how it made converts by cowing them. It was not the staccato impact of Burlington's style which was wrong; Kent showed how well that could be handled; it was the way it killed invention by its insistence on scholarly forms. It was a pedant's architectural manner and it has made pedants, nervous conformists, of its patrons and admirers then and ever since.

A style which combines purity with richness of detail, and yet verges by its excess upon attractive bad taste, can work on this scale, like an expensive toy. It is when it has to be expanded to cope with much larger rooms that the endearing joke becomes lost in an impersonal predictability, a recipe for rooms, not an inspiration. The Sculpture Gallery at Holkham is only Chiswick's tiny Gallery writ tediously large to emphasize its institutional potential; the Great Hall at Wentworth Woodhouse, all sixty square feet of it, proves the aridity of a convention deployed over a wide space without visual invention. And Chiswick was the show house responsible for that fatal reliance upon correct detail. It rolled back in England the advancing European tide of the Rococo invention and charm, replacing it with scholarship of a kind and a derivative grand manner. The rooms in Chiswick impress by 'book architecture', the full enrichments of the Corinthian order leave no place for any individual artistic statements. At every possible point the proper mouldings from Palladio or an illustration in Désgodetz's *Les Edifices antiques de Rome* or Fréart's *Parallèle de l'architecture antique et de la moderne* have been layered one above the other. There are at least fourteen of them in the Tribunal before its coffered and guilloched vault can take off; bead-and-reel (three times repeated), palmette, guilloche, Greek key fret, egg-and-dart, dentil and waterleaf. The same mechanical treatment has been laid out on the double apsed room of the Gallery where a light touch and artistic invention were needed to complement its delightful spatial qualities. A heavily gilded 'Roman Bath' cornice dramatizes that shaming moment when Burlington, or whoever he found to blame among his assistants, discovered that this main cornice was running several feet higher than the cornice of the Venetian window which it was supposed to meet. Harris charitably describes the effect as 'mischievous'; 'amateur bungling' would be more accurate.

Since the English and particularly the Irish Rococo are at their best with ceilings, the ceilings of this alternative Ancient Roman style at Chiswick are of prime interest. Burlington abandoned his Roman templar detail except in the Tribunal and retreated to the heavily beamed compartments of Inigo Jones, that early French Baroque devised to make Queen Henrietta Maria feel that she had not left civilization entirely behind when she crossed the Channel. But with the ceilings Kent could be restrained no longer.

He had managed to make his occasional marks on the walls. Those saucy girls with their S-curled locks and upward cast eyes in the Circular Closet have been traced back by Cinzia Sicca to the concave niche in the loggia of Rome's Villa Madama.[7] Kent must have remembered them from that source, sketched them and given them that naughty air of blasé patience as they carry the Corinthian order on their golden heads (illus. 17). As handled here they are a peculiarly Rococo conceit, a refreshing snatch of the figurative in all these abstract orders. That overdoor too in the Bedchamber has two mer-boys flanking a cavalier portrait, their tails are boldly chubby S scrolls that spout C scrolls, and the acanthus and corn stalls below them bend in a C scroll Rococo wind.

It was on the ceilings, however, that Kent's slight talents as a painter were given full play. The beams themselves are so smothered in wreaths of fruit, Greek key frets and guilloche, all gilded, that Kent's poor sense of colour in the recessed panels, his weak handling of perspective and the boring predictability of the grotesque work are decently lost in the standard Chiswick overkill. It was perverse in a space as small as the Blue Velvet Room to giganticize the brackets supporting the ceiling. The device may have precedents in the Ducal Palace at Mantua, but at Chiswick it gives the effect of being trapped in a biscuit tin with nothing to look up at except Kent's awful

17 William Kent adds
saucy maidens to
otherwise Palladian
detail in the Circular
Closet at Chiswick
Villa, Middlesex
(*c.* 1725–9).

allegory of architecture, tilting drunkenly against a background of golden
stars. When Lord Burlington's debt to Kent is being obsequiously rehearsed
this particularly terrible painting and grossly overscaled room should not be
forgotten. The ceilings at Chiswick are a disaster, ill-suited to the rooms
which they cover and a complete anachronism for anyone attempting to
suggest an antique manner. From this time onwards ceilings would be the
weak link in the stylistic continuity of the neo-Palladian, and the area where
contemporary decorative work, first the Baroque, but very soon after in
houses like Rousham, Oxfordshire, and Stanmer Park, Sussex, the Rococo,
would break through.

It was an irony, which Lord Burlington would not have appreciated, that
the next English house to be modelled on the Villa Rocca Pisani should have

had its interior decorated, not in any antique Roman manner, but in the most uninhibited and superlatively fine Rococo work ever to be created in Britain. This was in the central octagonal hall of the Nuthall Temple, a house built between 1754 and 1757, though the Hall was not transformed by its stucco work until 1769. Only ten miles to the north-east of the Temple is Southwell Minster with the 'Leaves of Southwell' in its Chapter House, the most perfect naturalistic Gothic carving in the country. It is not pressing comparisons too far to suggest that Thomas Roberts's stucco work in the Temple was as fine and as artistically important as the stone-carved leaves in the Minster. They were twin pinnacles of two schools of decorative design, the Gothic celebrating forms of nature, the Rococo celebrating, with equal joy, the artefacts of man.

Only one art critic has ever given the Nuthall Temple its due, probably because only one ever got inside it. Christopher Hussey, clearly overwhelmed by his visit to the house, wrote a delighted description of the Octagon in a *Country Life* article in September 1923. Six years later, in an act of casual vandalism unequalled even in the destructive 1950s and 1960s, the house was demolished and all that lyrical, carefully crafted work returned to dust. If it had been even hinted in 1929 that the Leaves of Southwell should be ground down to make road aggregate there would have been a national outcry. The stuccoed trophies of the Nuthall Temple went with hardly a protest; such is the imbalance of esteem in which Rococo work has been rated in Britain. Yet the Chapter House and the Temple's Octagon were both thoughtful and observant work of native craftsmen and should have been equally valued.

The inspiration behind the Octagon seems not to have come from the architect of the house, Thomas Wright of Durham (1711–86), but from its genial bachelor owner, Sir Charles Sedley, of whom very little is known other than that he bet successfully on horses, was awarded a doctorate of laws by Oxford University and was 'a gentleman highly esteemed in the county and will long be remembered for his amiable disposition'. Thomas Wright, whom Sedley chose to design his new house, was a moody and temperamental man, an eccentric scientist and astronomer with a facility for impressing princes of the blood and influential aristocrats; the Duke of Portland probably recommended him to Sir Charles. Better known today for his savage grottoes and rough hermitages than for complete country houses, Wright favoured, rather surprisingly, the Rococo for interior decoration at Shugborough, Staffordshire, and the Horton Menagerie, Northamptonshire.

Once Wright had completed the Temple, a massive overscaled block of a house with a recessed hexastyle portico and a shallow dome set much lower than that on its Scamozzian model, Sir Charles sacked him before the Octagon had been fitted up. A scheme which Wright proposed for that formidable space, 36 feet across (5.49 m), has survived but it was quite inadequate. There were to be small decorative plaques on each of its eight sides at the gallery level, and if Wright's work at the Horton Menagerie is any guide these would have represented astronomical symbols (illus. 24). Whatever the reason his patron was not satisfied. Wright retired to his own house at Byers Green near Durham where he was constructing an observatory. For twelve years the cavernous spaces of the Octagon remained bare apart from the sixteen decorative round arches on brackets, eight at ground floor level, eight at gallery level, and the eight columns with capitals of Wright's own quirky design that supported the gallery. It was a formidable decorative challenge. Then in 1769, well into the period dominated by Robert Adam and with the Rococo already becoming unfashionable, Sir Charles, after a particularly successful coup on the racecourse, brought in one of the very few great native English plasterers, Thomas Roberts of Oxford. Roberts did not so much decorate, the word is too tame, as exhilarate the Octagon with his last and finest Rococo achievement.

Roberts's favourite motifs and his increasing mastery of the art can be traced in his surviving commissions: splendid wall panels in the Library of Christ Church College, some of the ceiling panels in Queen's College Library, plasterwork at Kirtlington Park and at Rousham House a little further north in the same county. At Kirtlington he appears to have worked with the Danish stuccodore Charles Stanley and got from him the designs for his first set of roundels on the theme of Aesop's fables. In the Dining Room his first birds, eagles apparently, hang the drops from their claws. Roberts's picture frames in the Old Library at Rousham pick up the line of Rococo design which William Kent had begun in the Parlour in 1738 with crouching eagles and scalloped guilloche. At Heythrop Roberts executed a second set of Aesop roundels, so when he came to Nuthall he had been thirty years in his profession and must have seen time was running out for the rich three-dimensional figurative work in which he was skilled.

From the old photographs which illustrated Hussey's account, the Octagon must have been a space where Wright's shallow, repetitive arches were almost lost in Roberts's enchanting excess of detail (illus. 18). As Hussey, bowled over by that torrent of invention and morally disturbed by his own response, wrote: 'where can such another haunt of rococo be found? – that airy, insouciant extravagant spirit whose sole function was to delight,

18 The Hall, Nuthall Temple, Nottinghamshire (1769), demolished in 1929.

whose only justification is irresponsibility'.[8] There is an intriguing under-current to Hussey's choice of words. Does 'delight' have to be associated with 'irresponsibility'? Or is there something very Protestant working away there? Are 'airy', 'insouciant' and 'extravagant' exactly the right words to praise an artistic composition which celebrates human arts and sciences? Are representations of moral fables, violins, weather glasses and terrestrial globes in any sense 'irresponsible', or was Hussey, for all the obvious pleasure he took in that great room, reacting nervously to that sad Puritan concept that has underlain whole centuries of English critical thinking – that true Beauty is somehow inextricably tied up with Simplicity? Whatever the truth, the Rococo has never had an easy ride in Britain.

Underlying the profane decoration of the Octagon were several worthy themes. On the cove of the wall which supported the gallery the theme was earth, air, fire and water; on the walls above the gallery were expressed exuberantly the four pursuits of civilized man, a very eighteenth-century selection: war, the hunt, music and divine philosophy. Around each arch hung swags and drops of delicately figurative plasterwork. The drops dangled from lions' mouths and the swags hung over flamboyant cartouches above which an angry dragon bird – wyvern or gryphon – spread its wings and flaunted its horrid tail. Those birds of Kirtlington and Rousham had grown now to mythic dimensions, but such monsters rampage everywhere in Irish plasterwork, in St Stephen's Green, Malahide Castle and Newbridge House, but nowhere else in England on this scale and with identical barbed-tail modelling. From these dragon-birds and from the brilliance of the detail there has to be a strong probability either that Roberts was employing some Irish craftsmen, or that he had himself worked in Dublin, had copied Irish motifs as his Aesop's roundels, the Bear and the Bees, the Fox and the Crane, copied Stanley's designs at Kirtlington.

Those roundels were mere applied plaster pictures, the very best of the modelling was in the drops, the sixteen trophies hanging around the gallery walk: tambourines, trombones, violins, drums, quivers, muskets, swords, pikes, globes and weather glasses, all shaped with illusionist accuracy but all grouped with stylized artifice, that elegant rightness which is the prevailing mark of the Rococo and could make the juxtaposition of a cutlass and a battle-axe a thing of abstract beauty. Slung above the drops were the swags with nets wreathed in flowers, bulging with fruit and beset with scientific instruments. In the shadows of the columned ground floor the pattern of swags, dragon-birds and drops was more modestly scaled. The vault of the dome had been completed to Wright's proposed scheme and probably in Wright's time. That shameless display of S and C scrolled acanthus writhing in the soffits of the eight round-arched windows was easily the most French element in the whole interior, those 'raffle leaves' which Isaac Ware viewed with such suspicion. Those windows and the shallow arches gave a discipline which the omnipresent gaiety of the drops denied, creating a necessary tension. It was one of the great rooms of the eighteenth century, rich even by South German standards, with the Rococo flourishing at last, as it should have done over the past three decades, within Palladian shells, a craftsman's art and technique redeeming an architect's inadequacy.

In his defensive nervous way Isaac Ware had described the new style as 'only pleasing to the light eye of the French, who rarely carry their observation further than a casual glance',[9] which was a justifiable observation if he was thinking of the predictable, abstract flourishes of S and C scrolls on the more run of the mill French work, the kind of decoration which he himself delivered for Lord Chesterfield's London town house. But that was an unfortunate exception, England got its Rococo not from its French neighbour where the style originated, but from Italian-Swiss stuccodores practised in the Baroque but perfectly able and ready to go with fashion and deliver a rich figurative Rococo when required. Hussey, that last witness to Thomas Roberts's achievement, analysed the style accurately:

> to the true rococotte every object of nature or man's creation was a legitimate object for inclusion in purely decorative designs, where every rule of science was subservient to the one law – pleasure: on one condition – that it was deliberately and perfectly portrayed.[10]

It was Classicism's last and most successful attempt to contain the real world within its boundaries.

The destruction of the Octagon in 1929 was a tragic limitation of our experience, but in its time it was virtually inevitable. We preserve only an acceptable selection of our past and at that time the Rococo was associated with cinema interiors. The style has never really won the hearts of many architectural historians, conditioned as they tend to be, to admire 'correct' forms, as at Chiswick, and of course the beauties of noble simplicity. Giles Worsley's *Classical Architecture in Britain: The Heroic Age* is a definitive study of Classicism's evolution in this country, a distillation of the best articles produced in his time as architectural editor of *Country Life*; but Worsley seems not to rate the Rococo as 'Heroic'. He gives Gothick architecture a whole chapter to itself but in a book of over three hundred pages the Rococo only gets six. 'Generally', Worsley wrote, 'Rococo can be seen as fitting into the concept of propriety [a puzzling phrase as 'impropriety' might seem more appropriate] which overlays English Palladianism. It was certainly no threat to Palladian architecture'.[11] Worsley is dismissive but Gervase Jackson-Stops, whom he quotes, was more generous, as well he might be having rescued and restored the Rococo interiors of the Horton Menagerie from the very brink of ruin and lived in it himself. He wrote:

To a large extent rococo in fact became the official style of interior decoration, particularly for smaller and more intimate rooms, among this new generation of Palladians in the 1740s and '50s, but posed no threat to established conventions of exterior architecture.[12]

Here again we have that phrase 'no threat', this sense almost of something insidious, lurking to weaken something noble and right.

It could reasonably be proposed that houses by Robert Taylor, like Harleyford Manor, Buckinghamshire, and Henry Keene's entrance front to Bowood House in Wiltshire, did offer a very real, functional as well as aesthetic, challenge to Palladian exterior forms (illus. 19). The Rococo was also most at home in large spaces, as at the Nuthall Temple, and in stair-halls, as at Bristol's Royal Fort, where its flexible forms were peculiarly suited to decorative movement within complex geometry. But both comments, by Worsley and Jackson-Stops, are typical of the general disparaging tone which the Rococo has seemed to excite. Is it seen as feminine because it was so eager to explore the figurative? Is it too attractive, even seductive to the senses? Do the critics feel that it was not quite English? Perhaps, like Isaac Ware, they still mistrust all things which they believe to be of French derivation.

CHAPTER III

THE GARDEN AS AN EXPRESSION OF ROCOCO REVOLT

Although Desmond FitzGerald wrote a very comprehensive account of Irish gardens in the Rococo period for *Apollo* as early as 1968, suggesting that they were a distinct type and tracing their English sources,[1] the concept of an English Rococo garden was effectively launched by John Harris in a stimulating and perceptive *Country Life* article of 7 September 1972, entitled 'Painter of Rococo Gardens: Thomas Robins the Elder'. It was established firmly in the vocabulary of garden historians by an exhibition of Robins's water-colours held at the Royal Institute of British Architects' Heinz Gallery between 1975 and 1976, with John Harris as curator. His wife, Eileen Harris, had written a three-part article on Thomas Wright in *Country Life* in 1971[2] and the very different work of the two contemporaries, Robins and Wright – Robins's airy, delicate temples and bridges, Wright's rough, boulder-strewn grottoes and gnarled bark houses – have come to be associated together as typical features of a recognized garden type.

What was most valuable about the Harris article was that he swept away the legend that the 'Jardin Anglais', so popular on the Continent in the later eighteenth century, owed anything to 'Capability' Brown and those green deserts which Brown and his imitators inflicted on so many great English parks and gardens. A catchy nickname can work wonders on a reputation. Over the years so many accounts of landscape gardening have rehearsed that trite anecdote of Lancelot Brown visiting an estate and announcing that it 'had capabilities'. In effect this meant that the owner could cut costs on his previous, labour intensive, formal garden, invest profitably in forestry by art-fully clumping his plantations and secure a lake for fishing and bathing by damming up a small brook. Brown, earning in a good year £15,000, was only the most successful of several such estate advisors – William Eames, Richard Woods, Thomas Leggett and John Davenport were others – who travelled the country with a group of skilled labourers. The process was a capitalist response to parkland carried through under cover of the new aesthetic vision of Nature. Stephen Switzer had initiated the movement in his *Ichnographia Rustica* of 1718, urging gardeners to make their designs 'more rural, natural, more easy and less expensive'.[3]

But what impressed French and German park designers and persuaded them to follow the English was not Lancelot Brown's elegant economy, but the trick of turning an estate into a polite eighteenth-century anticipation of the Disneyland concept: a place for pleasure, leisure and surprises. This the English had achieved by a clever scatter of exotic garden buildings in a medley of styles: Gothick, Turkish, Egyptian, Tartar, Hindu, Tahitian and, of course, Classical; and because the Classical garden buildings were only one among several other styles, these gardens escaped the tyranny of several centuries of Roman and Greek influence. In exactly the same way, a Rococo room decorated with capering monkeys, a singerie, such as featured at Kensington Palace and Kirtlington Park in Oxfordshire, represented eman-cipation from, or even revolt against, omnipresent Classical themes and motifs. To that extent these gardens of eclectic pleasures were expressions of a Rococo mood, a natural interlude in a century otherwise obsessed with the Classical ideal.

Before John Harris drew attention to the Robins paintings, the gardens of the 1740–70 period had been inadequately recorded when compared with the pre-1720 formal gardens of the Kip and Kynff era, but the new enthusiasm for Robins's work has had one unfortunate effect. Essentially a miniaturist, Robins has given some garden historians the impression not only that Rococo gardens were toy-like in scale, but that they were a middle-class phenom-enon of a very limited period, that of Robins's span as a painter – 1748–65.

This incorrect impression was strengthened soon after John Harris had popularized the Rococo idea when it emerged, by a stroke of luck, that one of the gardens which Robins had illustrated, or even perhaps designed, still survived, though only just, as it had been overplanted with conifers. This was at Painswick House, Lord Dickinson's seat in the high Cotswolds. Now that there was an image at which to aim and all Robins's precisely drawn details to aid the restoration, work began. The conifers were uprooted before

they had permanently wrecked the grounds; the Red House, a charmingly asymmetrical Gothick pavilion (illus. 25), was repaired and a programme for rebuilding all or most of Robins's features was set in train under the guidance of a scholarly committee. The garden was opened under the 'Rococo' label and, when it produced great drifts of snowdrops at an otherwise vacant slot in the stately homes and gardens visiting calendar, its future was assured.

Yet when the Robins view of the garden is studied critically it only has one serpentine feature, a path connecting the Red House and the Exedra. All the main axes of the garden are ruthlessly straight and a hard geometrical diamond of paths criss-crosses its central area (illus. 20). If anything makes it 'Rococo' it is not a prevalence of S and C scroll curves but its eclectic mix of styles, its amusing surprises and its deliberate invocation of a fantasy: that this was a garden sacred to the great god Pan whose statue presided sinisterly over a large cold bath, where naked frolics could take place. It was an earthy English equivalent to Jean Antoine Watteau's Arcadian painting of an 'Embarkation for Cythera', the island of love. At Painswick a Gloucestershire gentleman had prepared an actual garden of love. In that sense it was Rococo, but it was only a small-scale, crowded version of other gardens and parks scattered all over Britain in a style that had been popular for the last twenty-eight years. The English and Irish Rococo garden is a valid concept and one worth exploring because it had a wide influence over western Europe, but its time span, scale and social context have to be reconsidered on the lines which Harris originally suggested, but which subsequent garden historians, with the usual English relish for class distinctions, have unhelpfully narrowed.

In a recent study, *The English Rococo Garden* (1991), Michael Symes actually dismissed the most royal and obviously Rococo of all English gardens, that created for Princess Augusta at Kew, because Sir William Chambers's Pagoda there 'was too large and dominant. When we think of rococo chinoiserie', Symes concluded 'it is much more on the scale of the small temple in Robins's water-colour of Woodside, Old Windsor, Berkshire'.[4] Yet in its prime Kew had the richest show of eclectic park buildings in Britain. In addition to the Pagoda there was a House of Confucius, a Gothic Cathedral, a Roman Ruin, nine Classical temples, a Mosque and an Alhambra. Apart from the unimpressive flatness of its terrain it was the perfect Rococo layout.

Influenced by this restricted, Robins-related definition of the style (illus. 26), Symes was uncertain whether the first of all English Rococo gardens, that designed by Pope at Twickenham, qualified as authentic. He wrote:

> So much was crammed into the limited space – amphitheatre, bowling green, wilderness, hothouse, vineyard, kitchen garden, grotto, obelisk, urns, cypress walk, shell temple – that one has to ask whether this garden, which dates from 1719 to 1744, can be described as rococo.[5]

Symes's conclusion, however, was that it could not, because the ultimate point of the design was reverential: the climax was the cypress walk that led up to the obelisk which commemorated his much loved mother. But one of the aims of a Rococo garden was to play with the creation of mood, reverent melancholy for Pope, cheerful lust for Benjamin Hyett at Painswick; and in any case Pope's bowling green could hardly have been intended to create a mood of reverence. This was not only England's Rococo trend setter but the direct inspiration for Ireland's first Rococo garden, that created at Delville, just outside Dublin, in the late 1720s by Pope's close friend Dr Patrick Delany. It was Delany and his grotto-decorating, letter-scribbling wife, Mary, who spread the Rococo garden aesthetic among their friends all over the Pale in the next two decades, a sign of how closely the Protestant Ascendancy was linked to English fashions.

The problem with a correct but broad definition of the term 'Rococo garden' is that it can appear to cover almost any garden. Italian Renaissance gardens of the sixteenth century were often places with sudden surprises, grottoes of the gods, trick fountains, rocky cascades and alcoves of privacy. Elizabethan gardens followed the same formula. That essential Rococo garden feature, a pavilion on an island in an artificial lake, had been anticipated at Hatfield by the Cecils in James I's reign and by John Evelyn at Sayes Court, Deptford very early in the Commonwealth. The truth is that the seventeenth century with its formal Franco-Dutch gardens was the Dark Age of garden design, a time when autocratic princes and enterprising nursery gardeners joined hands from mutual interest to impose an expensive reign of order. It was the exception and an aberration from good garden sense. Informality is the natural rule. The whole point of a garden is that it offers a contrast to the rigidity of a house. As the diplomat Sir Henry Wotton observed in 1624, 'as Fabriques should bee *regular*, so Gardens should bee *irregular*, or at least cast into a very wilde *Regularitie*'.[6] Sir William Temple, a timid gardener but a sensitive observer, wrote in his 1685 book *Upon the Gardens of Epicurus*, that he had experienced a delightful irregularity in an old, mature garden at Moor Park, Surrey, laid out in Wotton's time by the Countess of Bedford. He was well aware, partly from his reading of Fernão Mendes Pinto's *Travels in the Kingdoms of Ethiopia, China, Tartaria* of 1653 and Jan Nieuhof's *An Embassy . . . to the Grand Tartar Cham Emperor of China* of 1669, but even more so from the daily use of his own 'Purcellan' plates from China, that the Chinese had a great contempt for regularity in a garden. They claimed that a 'Boy that can tell an Hundred, may plant Walks of Trees in straight Lines'. Instead, 'their greatest Reach of Imagination is employed in contriving Figures, where the beauty shall be great, and strike the Eye, but without any Order or Disposition of Parts, that shall be commonly or easily observ'd'. But despite this uneasy awareness of the charm of asymmetry, Temple shrank back from attempting to achieve it himself: 'I should hardly advise any of these Attempts in the Figure of gardens among us; they are Adventures of too hard Achievement for any common Hands'.[7]

Temple was an aesthetic coward writing in the heyday of the Franco-Dutch formal garden, but he did pass one valuable word down to the next generation: '*sharawadgi*', from the Chinese 'Saro Kwaichi' meaning 'impressive by careless grace', which the Chinese used to praise this quality of deliberate informality in a garden. Once people have absorbed a word, even one as artificial as '*sharawadgi*' or 'Rococo', to express a quality, then that quality tends to become fixed as a concept. Horace Walpole was still impressed by '*sharawadgi*' and using the word when he wrote his *History of the Modern Taste in Gardening*, just prior to 1770. The writer who made this irregularity acceptable to a particularly formal-minded generation of Whig lords after the Hanoverian succession was Anthony Ashley Cooper, 3rd Earl of Shaftesbury. He was the theorist behind the contradictory stylistic directions of Lord Burlington.

Shaftesbury was the Whigs' home-brewed philosopher, the master of a persuasive poetic prose style and prestigious as a grandson of the great 1st Earl, the party's founding father. Recent commentators have claimed that Shaftesbury's raptures on the subject of 'Nature' in his *The Moralists* of 1709 have been misread, that he really favoured a sublime order. If that is true then Shaftesbury is to blame for the misreading by putting into the mouth of Philocles, in a dialogue, speeches like the following:

> I shall no longer resist the Passion growing in me for Things of a *natural* kind; where neither *Art*, nor the *Conceit* or *Caprice* of Man has spoil'd their *genuine* Order, by breaking in upon that *primitive State*. Even the rude *Rocks*, the mossy *Caverns*, the irregular unwrought *Grottos*, and the broken *Falls* of Waters, with all the horrid Graces of the *Wilderness* itself, as representing NATURE more, will be the more engaging, and appear with a Magnificence beyond the formal Mockery of princely Gardens.[8]

While in an earlier exchange Theocles declaimed a new TE DEUM:

> O Glorious *Nature*! Supremely Fair, and sovereignly Good! All-loving and All-lovely, All-divine! Whose every single Work affords an ampler Scene, and is a nobler Spectacle than all which ever Art presented! O mighty *Nature*! Wise Substitute of *Providence*! Impower'd *Creatress*! O Thou impowering Deity, supreme Creator! Thee I invoke, and Thee alone adore.[9]

All this was potent writing and easy to interpret as virtually a religious justification for abandoning formalism in gardens and adopting 'all the horrid graces of the *Wilderness* itself'; which was exactly what Vanbrugh at Castle Howard and Lord Burlington at Chiswick proceeded to do. But while the 'horrid Graces of the Wilderness' came easily to the already theatrically inclined and castle-charmed Vanbrugh, the winning over of Lord Burlington, a desperately formal classicist, was a real conversion on the road to Damascus. A more unlikely father of the 'Rococo' garden could hardly be imagined.

The origins of Ireland and Britain's deviant strain of the Rococo, as a decorative house style and a garden style, lie in that strange about-face of stylistic direction which the United Kingdoms were persuaded to take in the years immediately after the Hanoverians came to the throne. While a notably formal house style was being adopted, one with dysfunctional small windows, tomb-like monumental façades and a stony reserve, garden design was swinging around in an entirely different direction, towards relaxed and entertaining wildernesses threaded with winding paths that led to sudden vistas of columned temples, exedrae, obelisks and amphitheatres, with serpentine lakes and geometrical basins of water: the Classical world achieved in a game of virtual reality. Vanbrugh had made a move in that direction with his Wray Wood at Castle Howard, but that was far away in Yorkshire. It was Lord Burlington's garden at Chiswick which focused the minds of fashionable London society upon the creation of Arcadian woodlands strewn, as in some painting by Claude Lorrain or Nicholas Poussin, with Roman remains.

No one has yet written a convincing biography of Burlington to explain his self-image, his hold upon his contemporaries, or exactly what his relationship was with William Kent, that fat, jolly, clown-like, inventive genius, whom he released onto the English cultural scene. One aim behind Burlington's garden plan was certainly the recreation of the Younger Pliny's garden in his villa at Tuscum (sometimes referred to as 'Tusculum'). He paid Robert Castell to research Pliny's letters for him and to publish the *Villas of the Ancients Illustrated* in 1728, with detailed, hypothetical maps of the original complex grounds. In his analysis Castell claimed to find two garden types in Pliny's letters and then, by an almost imperceptible deviation from his Latin sources, he slipped in a third type from China and attributed that also to Pliny. This is so illogical and so unscholarly that there has to be a suspicion that Castell was finding in his sources what his patron wanted him to find.

His first two garden types were total opposites: Nature left to itself, 'well-water'd Spots of Ground, irregularly producing all sorts of Plants and Trees', was one and the other was 'Gardens by the Rule and Line', all straight walls and avenues laid in geometrical patterns. The third garden type, 'By the Accounts we have of the present Manner of Designing in China', came some way between the other two. It was 'a close Imitation of Nature; where, tho' the Parts are disposed with the greatest Art, the Irregularity is still preserved . . . an artful Confusion . . . Rocks, Cascades, and Trees, bearing their natural Forms'.[10]

If the plan which Castell devised, a conjectural reconstruction of the grounds around the Tuscum villa, dated 1728 (illus. 29), is compared with Rocque's 1736 plan of Chiswick (illus. 30), the similarities are striking. Both villas have hippodrome enclosures terminated by exedrae to the front and rear. Tuscum has the three garden types set out in three distinct areas. To the bottom left is a 'Rule and Line' garden; top left is a 'Natural' garden with two irregular belts of trees and clumps of trees set over wide grassland

21 Decorative Baroque detail in the Hall of Moor Park, Hertfordshire (*c.* 1728).

22 Baroque detail in a proto-Palladian house: a chimneypiece in the Hall at Barnsley Park, Gloucestershire (*c.* 1731).

23 Palladio improved: Mereworth Castle, Kent (*c.* 1720–5), Colen Campbell's masterpiece.

24 A detail of Rococo plasterwork in the Horton Menagerie Saloon, Northamptonshire (*c.* 1760).

25 The Red House, Painswick Rococo Garden, Gloucestershire (*c.* 1748) squints down two paths in a Rococo-Gothick compromise.

26 Thomas Robins's painting of a Chinese seat in the gardens of Honington, Warwickshire (1750s, gouache and watercolour on vellum).

27 A view of Sanderson Miller's Sham Castle, Hagley Park, Worcestershire (1747–8).

28 James Gibbs's Temple of Liberty, Stowe (1741–4).

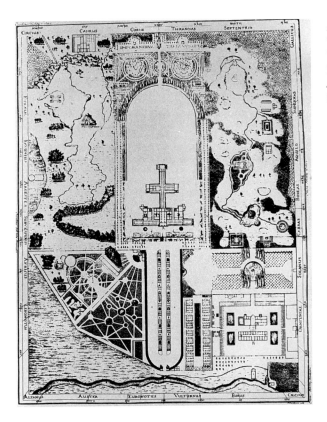

29 Robert Castell's 'Plan of Tuscum, the Villa of Pliny' from his *The Villas of the Ancients Illustrated . . .* (1728).

through which a stream wanders to a lake. The only man-made intrusion is a temple built on a peninsula jutting into the lake. To the top right of the plan is a garden 'after the present Manner of Designing in China' and this is a prototype for a Rococo garden. Every line in it is still casual: a continuous but irregularly planted woodland encloses a long oval of open land. A lake at the top is linked to another lake by a second wandering river which divides at one point to create a large island. A few trees are scattered across the plain and the island is thickly wooded. What is so striking and Robins-like is the number of small buildings and features set artfully into this landscape. There are two miniature formal gardens, one hidden within that island wood, a three-sided court with a little pavilion, a round pool set about with columns, a circular temple on a hill, a rectangular moated pavilion and three other indeterminate structures.[11]

Lord Burlington had, apparently, no faith in the ability of rural Middlesex to stand unaltered as a garden in its own right, but Rocque's plan of Chiswick (illus. 30) has all the features of the second and third Tuscum garden types. His villa has its exedra-hippodromes fore and aft with a trio of formal

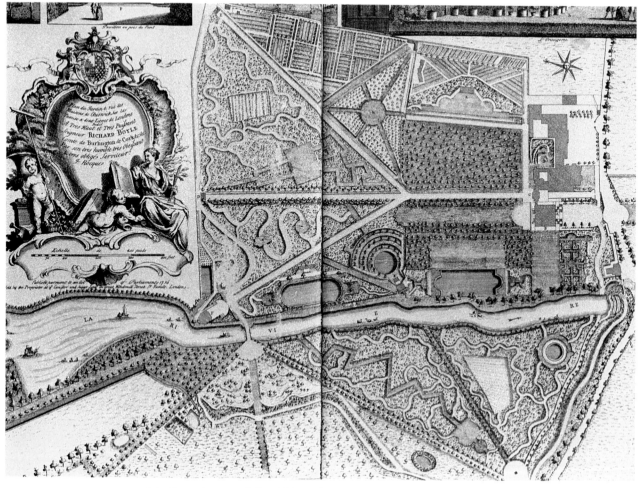

30 John Rocque's engraved plan of Chiswick Villa and Gardens, Middlesex (1736).

avenues leading away from the end of the larger exedra. Scattered about the ground are garden buildings and features – temples, a bagnio, a deer house, a triple-caverned cascade, an orangery, an arch and a serpentine lake with islands. What Chiswick has but Tuscum lacks is a highly complex, winding, twisting pattern of paths overlying the main features of the grounds; these are, however, mentioned in Castell's text. Referring to 'the Manner of Designing in China' he wrote 'through its winding Paths One, as it were, accidentally fell upon those pieces of a rougher Taste, that seemed to have been made with a Design to surprize those that arrived at them'.[12]

So Tuscum and Chiswick were similar in design, but the important question is which had precedence? Did Burlington lay his grounds out first, starting in 1722, and did Castell then conveniently find that he had copied Pliny perfectly? Or did Castell's scholarship persuade Burlington to follow an ancient Roman precedent? The most likely answer is that the grounds were laid out over the years when Burlington and Castell were discussing Pliny's letters and deciding together, possibly with William Kent as a third in a committee of taste, how to interpret the Latin texts.

What mattered was that the new gardens were strikingly innovative, enjoyable and rewarding to visit. In pursuit of Roman authenticity Burlington had hit accidentally, while pursuing his antique vision, upon the formula for an ideal modern pleasure garden. Chiswick was quickly copied in that tight cluster of gardens of the rich and famous laid out along those sylvan reaches of the Thames. If Burlington, with his own obsessions, Castell's scholarship, Shaftesbury's precepts and Kent's practical advice, had not quite devised the perfect Rococo garden, he had come very near to it. All that Chiswick required to make it entirely Rococo was the eclectic element of the Gothick, which in 1720 was not fashionable, but very soon would be. The Chinese element was apparently already present, not in an actual building but in the 'artful confusion'; Chiswick's grounds were *sharawadgi* realized.

As a gardener, William Kent tends now to be associated with Horace Walpole's neat aphorism that he 'leaped the fence and saw that all Nature was a garden', but Burlington allowed no leaping of fences at Chiswick. It was, and even now remains, an enclosed, even slightly claustrophobic Arcadia, a group of wildernesses such as Shaftesbury had urged, tightly packed with references to Pliny, Shaftesbury and the exotic Chinese notion of *sharawadgi*, a fertile fusion of disparate influences.

The only problem in accepting this interpretation is Lord Burlington himself. Where architecture was concerned he was so desperately formal and precise, so bloodless and tied to precedent, that it appears improbably paradoxical that he should have created a garden of *sharawadgi*. Could he really have believed that Pliny designed in a relaxed Chinese spirit? He certainly owned a copy of the celebrated thirty-six prints of the imperial Chinese palace and gardens at Jehol which Father Matteo Ripa had brought back from his mission to China. Ripa had personally presented another copy to King George I so those novel oriental visuals would have been much discussed in polite circles. Then again William Kent was Burlington's arbiter of taste, always urging him on to take risks, and Kent's illustrations to Spenser's *Faerie Queene* prove his fondness for random rocks and sudden craggy islands.

The winding paths were not the important feature at Chiswick. There was nothing inherently Rococo in such a curvaceous entanglement of wilderness ways. Even in the worst days of the seventeenth century there had always been a place for a wilderness set a little aside from the geometric formalism. Inigo Jones had laid one out in about 1636 for the 1st Earl of Bedford's London garden overlooking Jones's new urban development in Covent Garden, and the 1st Earl of Shaftesbury had a wilderness at Wimborne St Giles. Even Versailles, the black heart of formalism, had a celebrated 'Labirinthe' with a maze of largely geometrical paths penetrating a square bosquet. Le Nôtre, the gardener, and Bishop Bossuet, the Dauphin's tutor, had co-operated to set up thirty-nine allegorical groups which, followed through these paths, would reveal a moral mystery to a wise visitor, though the 'Labirinthe' was actually a favoured resort for courtesans. At Chiswick Burlington offered something more impressive than a mere curvilinear wilderness. His entire garden was laid out as if by an artist, someone confident in handling asymmetry with deliberately random architectural and visual delights. Someone had managed to persuade Burlington that there had been in the great Roman gardens a third way, and that third way had been identical with this mysterious but alluring Chinese way.

In France it had been the impact of Chinese forms on Classical practice which had inspired the first Rococo experiments in interior decoration, so it would not have been remarkable for the new 'Rococo' fashion in English gardens to have been similarly fired by the interpretation of Latin texts in the light of prints of Chinese gardens. Chinoiserie was at the heart of the Rococo movement; not so much in actual Chinese forms, though these did play an active role, as by the sheer stimulating awareness that there was, far away across the Continental land mass, another and alternative civilization, just as ancient, just as imperial, as the Roman. That was the release, the culture shock, which set Rococo designers free to vary, to invent and to observe with open eyes.

In 1728 an ambitious nurseryman, who was to have almost as much influence on taste and style in eighteenth-century England as Lord Burlington, published a large, lavishly illustrated book. The nurseryman was Batty Langley of Twickenham and his book, *New Principles of Gardening or The laying out and planting of Parterres, Groves, Wildernesses, Labyrinths, Avenues, Pools & etc After a more Grand and Rural Manner than has been done before.* The book represented a considerable capital expenditure and was a very clever piece of salesmanship. What the book basically sold, being both 'Grand and Rural', was eclecticism on a massive scale and the idea of the garden as a 'fun' place, a return to the Italian sixteenth-century concept of the garden as a grove of surprises and marvels, something again remarkably like what Lord Burlington and Kent were creating down the river. Fun would have been the last consideration in Burlington's mind, but in Kent's it could easily have been the foremost.

The plans in Langley's book open into three folds of elaborately complex grounds. A first reaction is that no landowner would ever construct such extensive mazes of paths and hedges as Langley was proposing, but a glance back at Rocque's 1736 'Engraved survey of Chiswick' will reveal a similar entanglement threading its way through the groves, sometimes in loops and twirls, sometimes in fierce zig-zags. Each fold-out in Langley's *New Principles* offers four separate gardens (illus. 31). There was never any intention of selling the lot any more than a modern mail-order shopper is expected to buy everything in a catalogue, which is what the *New Principles* was. At this stage in his career Langley's importance was only as an eager and plausible purveyor of the latest garden novelties, he had not begun to invent the novelties himself.

The sales technique is surprisingly aggressive. While the book gives an old-fashioned patron all the expensive gear: statues, urns, fountains and topiary work 'greens' for a Franco-Dutch formal layout, at the same time it sets out to make such a customer feel thoroughly inferior. The introduction opens accusingly:

> Our Gardens are much the worst in the world . . . the Pleasure of a Garden depends on the variety of its Parts . . . a continued series of Harmonious Objects, that will present new and delightful Scenes to our View at every Step we take, which regular gardens are incapable of doing. Nor is there any Thing more *shocking* than a *stiff regular Garden*; where after we have seen one quarter thereof, the very same is repeated in all the remaining Parts.[13]

This reads like a definition and a defence of a Robins garden of the 1740s and 1750s yet it was written in 1728, and is such a significant generalization

on garden design that a question arises. Was this nurseryman, with his
memorably familiar Christian name, making a genuinely innovative,
ground-breaking statement about the way ahead for English gardens, or
had his alert mind merely picked up from his fashionable Twickenham
customers a trend already accepted? His nursery garden was sited strategically among the Thames-side parishes most popular with Londoners
seeking a rural retreat. Aristocrats, gentry and rich widows were thick on
the ground. The King hunted regularly in Richmond Park where Sir
Robert Walpole was the acting Chief Ranger. The Duke of Newcastle and
his brother Henry Pelham, both eventual Prime Ministers, lived across the
river at Claremont and Esher. At Petersham the Duke of Argyll had
Sudbrook House which had been designed for him by James Gibbs between
1715 and 1719. Alexander Pope, the poet and garden expert, lived in
Twickenham as did the King's official mistress, the Duchess of Suffolk.
Soon Horace Walpole would be drawn irresistibly into this sylvan suburbia
of the rich and influential. Langley claimed to be an innovator: 'this Method
of laying out Gardens, after the manner exhibited in the following plates,
being *entirely New*', but a man who needed to make fast profits in a labour-

A VIEW OF TWICKENHAM

intensive business would be more alert to follow fashions than to make
them.

William Kent was not only active at Burlington's Chiswick villa, where
he was helping out around 1726–9, in 1730 he was designing garden buildings and ornaments for Pope at his Thames-side villa. With Alexander
Pope and William Kent among his likely customers, Batty Langley had
picked up rather more than one idea of the garden as an area where 'we are
continually entertained with new unexpected Objects at every step'. Those
winding reaches of the Thames must have been an experimental ground
where idle wealthy Londoners (illus. 32), with little else to do apart from
entertaining each other and showing off their gardens, tried out new
concepts of landscape and, naturally, consulted their nurserymen on the best
way to realize them. Surrey and Middlesex were, to eighteenth-century
England, what the Loire valley had been to sixteenth-century France, a
favoured riverside where new architecture and new garden design could be
explored. In Batty Langley's prophetic, or perhaps simply very well informed,
book he offered, in addition to recipes for a charming 'Rococo' confusion,
plans for *ferme ornée* gardens, years in advance of the celebrated farm
garden which Philip Southcote created in the 1730s at Woburn in Chertsey,

five miles up the Thames from Twickenham. Then, following Switzer, he delivered the formula on which Capability Brown's landscapes were to be shaped from 1751. Attacking the formalism of earlier gardens he wrote:

> Those great *Beauties of Nature*, HILLS and VALLEYS, were always levelled at very great Expenses, to complete their Regularity, or *the total ruin of the Gardens*. Their GROVES (whenever they planted any) were always regular, *like unto Orchards*, which is entirely wrong; for when we come to *copy* or *imitate Nature*, we should trace her steps with the greatest Accuracy that can be . . . no three Trees together range in a straight line . . . *Parterres* are most beautiful when entirely irregular.[14]

Being a nurseryman with a business to run Langley realized that such 'natural' gardens could spell ruin to his trade, so the profitable parterres of the old formal garden had to be retained in 'regular Irregularities' and 'pleasant Meanders', while each tree was to be surrounded by 'cut Circles about fourteen or sixteen Inches in Breadth sown with Dwarf Stock, Candy Turf, Pinks, Sweet Williams, Catch-fly & etc'.[15] It is easy to see where Horace Walpole would get his idea of sweet scented woodland glades when he came to plan out the grounds of Strawberry Hill.

All that was lacking to make Batty Langley the perfect purveyor of Robins-type gardens were the eclectic elements, Chinese and Gothick, which differentiate those Robins gardens from a Palladian garden like Chiswick. Langley had not long to wait for the Gothick. In 1733 the ever-inventive William Kent revived the medieval style resoundingly by adding large Gothick wings, with the canted bays which are generally described as the exterior mark of a Rococo building, to an existing fifteenth-century tower at Esher, just up the Thames from Twickenham (illus. 38). This was done to create a country villa for an eventually mildly popular Prime Minister, Henry Pelham. The Gothick could hardly have had a more prestigious launch. Quick as ever to cash in upon a trend Langley did some hasty research into what he called the 'Saxon' architecture of his country, feminized it acceptably with ogee curves, lent it a spurious air of scholarship with Gothick orders and published in 1741–2 (re-issued in 1747) his handsome and influential *Ancient Architecture Restored and Improved by a Great Variety of Grand and Useful Designs, entirely New in the Gothick Mode for the Ornamenting of Buildings and Gardens*. So from the very first the Gothick was aimed at garden buildings and, from the price and quality of the book, at rich clients, not tradesmen as is so often assumed.

Chinese architecture was not so well served by precedent and publication; but that it took the public fancy as readily as the Gothick indicates the

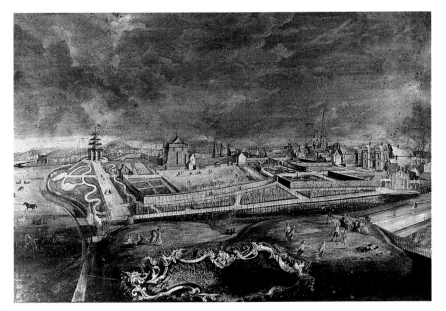

33 The Chinese pagoda in the garden of Marybone House, Gloucester: a view in gouache and watercolour on vellum by Thomas Robins (1750s).

temper of the times. There was an eagerness for novelty, a lively curiosity about other historical periods and other places; both history and geography were in the ascendant after the long reign of the Classics. Early in the 1730s William Kent designed three perfect Chinese garden houses, no ramshackle wooden structures but substantial octagons with two tiers of tiled roofs, bell hung, saucy and inventive. They were probably never built but his designs survive.[16] A two-storey Chinese gazebo built to overlook the Watling Street at Orleton in Shropshire still preserves the charm of these inauthentic and, therefore, uninhibited experimental buildings. Unfortunately Benjamin Hyett's four-storey pagoda raised in his Gloucester back garden at Marybone House only survived a few winter storms (illus. 33). A Chinese house took its place among the Classical temples at Stowe, Buckinghamshire, in 1738, but then, after a subterranean and unrecorded progress, the style erupted. In 1749 the Prince of Wales became aware of Chinoiserie and commissioned a thoroughly convincing, even scholarly Chinese temple, the House of Confucius for Kew, from either William Chambers or Joseph Goupy. By 1751 there were extrovert and cheerfully incorrect Chinese pavilions at both the big London pleasure gardens, Vauxhall and Ranelagh. In his *Analysis of Beauty* of 1753, Hogarth allowed that 'buildings . . . might be much more varied than they are' but gave no warm welcome to the Chinese with his 'There is at present such a thirst after variety that even paltry imitations of Chinese buildings have a kind of vogue, chiefly on account of their novelty'.[17] In 1756

John Shebbeare in his *Letters on the English Nation* admitted that 'The simple and the sublime have lost all influence [by which he must have meant classicism] almost everywhere all is Chinese or Gothic'.[18] In a more positive and fashionable spirit Horace Walpole had told his friend Sir Horace Mann in 1750, 'I am almost as fond of the *Sharawaggi*, or Chinese want of symmetry, in buildings, as in grounds or gardens', promising that if Mann returned to England 'you will be pleased with the liberty of taste into which we are struck, and of which you can have no idea'.[19] Lord Kames in his *Elements of Criticism* of 1762, felt that the eclectic tide was still running strongly, 'Judged by numbers, the Gothic taste of architecture must be preferred before that of Greece, and the Chinese probably before either'.[20]

It is evident from such comments that these gardens of eclectic confusion and charm were by no means confined to a few middle-class landowners who happened to patronize Thomas Robins. They had become the general fashion throughout the country. What has tended to conceal this truth has been the frailty of these Gothick and Chinese garden buildings. It is almost by a miracle that the Chinese House at Stowe has survived three subsequent moves. Lastly there was the tendency of park owners in the neo-Classical decades after 1770 to prune away the eclectic buildings from their parks and gardens in order to achieve a more pure Claudeian image.

CHAPTER IV

A
WANDERING
BISHOP

Reputations in the garden world depend upon the accident of survival. Unless a garden has been pickled at some stage in its growth, or was unusually well recorded and illustrated, it is forgotten and garden histories get written by a subjective process of selection. The safest way to test whether those Robins gardens were typical or highly unusual is to find a contemporary who visited a broad selection of gardens in England, Wales, Ireland and Scotland, recorded his or her impressions and was, if not an impartial judge, at least an informed and sophisticated one. Fortunately there was just such a prodigy of travel and painstaking recording: Richard Pococke (1704–65), a Hampshire-born Englishman who eventually became Lord Bishop of Ossory, an Irish diocese with its cathedral of St Canice in Kilkenny.

Pococke was himself a wonderfully Rococo figure. He had a unique familiarity with those exotic styles of architecture from which a garden designer could draw inspiration. His travels between 1736 and 1742 had taken him, not only over the usual western European areas of the Grand Tour, but up the Nile as far as Luxor where he measured Egyptian temples and drew the head of Ozymandias, King of Kings, lying forlornly on the desert sands. Then he toured the Holy Land, Syria and the Lebanon, found the temple at Baalbeck, 'a most exquisite piece of workmanship',[1] visited the Great Mosque at Damascus, sketched Greek reliefs along the coasts of Turkey, paused in Constantinople and returned home via Athens, Naples and Chamonix in the Alps to be rewarded for his discoveries by being made a fellow of the Royal Society.

34 Jean-Etienne Liotard, *Portrait of Richard Pococke*, oil on canvas, showing Pococke posed in Turkish costume at Constantinople in 1741.

There is a portrait of him 'à la Turque', painted in Constantinople by Jean-Etienne Liotard, which catches the essence of a mischievous poseur (illus. 34). A huge black turban crowns his head like a candle-snuffer, but cannot extinguish his amused gaze, the wide intelligent eyes or the air of self-conscious nobility.[2] He exudes that disastrous over-confidence which in a few months would lead him to suggest that the Doric order on the Parthenon was a mistake, that it should have been Corinthian (a very Rococo judgement) and that the sculptures in the pediments, while 'doubtless the finest adorned of any in the world', were probably put there by the Emperor Hadrian in the third century of the Christian era.[3]

Born into a clergy family he had been made Precentor of Lismore and Vicar General of Waterford even before he set out on his eastern travels. In 1745 he tactfully dedicated the second heavy volume of his *Description of the East and some other Countries* to a thoroughly committed Rococo enthusiast and Francophile in the ruling Whig junta, Philip Dormer Stanhope, 4th Earl of Chesterfield. This was well timed as in 1745 Chesterfield was appointed Lord Lieutenant of Ireland. Pococke became Chesterfield's chaplain for that brief but brilliant tenancy of Dublin Castle when, by mild measures and bawdy wit, the Earl kept Ireland tranquil through the testing months of Prince Charles Edward's seizure of Scotland and invasion of England. Pococke and Chesterfield not only shared the same aesthetic tastes, but an equal enthusiasm for the technical education of the children of the poor and for raising the prosperity of their adopted island by trade and manufacture.

These two interests are not as oddly matched as might appear. The Rococo style has acquired an image of frivolity and boudoir feminism in this century, but in its time it was a decorative fashion associated with innovation, technical advances and foreign skills in design, metalwork, printing and the whole range of the arts. If Pococke had a favourite word in his diaries after 'serpentine' it was 'improvement' and in each town he visited he faithfully recorded the manufactures and the educational establishments. In Ireland Lord Chesterfield gave active encouragement to the Schools of the Dublin Society; rather less happily, Pococke founded and assiduously inspected the schools of the Incorporated Society for English Protestant Schools in Ireland. One of the Society's aims was to convert Catholic boys to the Church of Ireland, which explains why Bishop Pococke is not celebrated in twentieth-century Eire.

Before he left the capital Chesterfield made Pococke Archdeacon of Dublin in which office he carried out an unprecedented inspection of the clergy. With their shared interest in Rococo gardens and especially in shell grottoes, it might have been expected that Pococke and Mrs Delany would have become friends, but she found him a bore at the dinner table. It is possible that his inspection had offended her husband, Patrick, who was Dean of Down and Chancellor of St Patrick's cathedral in the city. Regrettably Pococke left no account of the innovative Delany garden at Delville.

The omission must have been deliberate as Pococke's appetite for recording improved gardens was as strong as ever. He covered the south-western counties of Ireland in 1749. In 1750 and 1751 he was travelling England. Then in 1752 he made an arduous circuit of all those parts of Ireland which he had missed in 1749, writing a fascinating and at times shocking account of the conditions of the poorest peasantry in Connaught with, in sharp contrast, a description of the idyllic Rococo parks of the Anglo-Irish aristocracy in Leinster and Munster.[4] He was touring England again in 1754, 1756 and 1757, winding up with a final six-month investigation of Scotland and the Isles. Not one of his diaries was published in his lifetime. An apoplectic fit carried him off in 1765 when he was on the road again, conducting a visitation of his new diocese, Meath.

In his lumbering prose style he strained more often to express pleasure over the parks and gardens of his native country than he had ever done over the wonders of Egypt, Syria and Greece. He was a sincere connoisseur of the picturesque with a precise and limited range of appreciation where landscape was concerned, but in that he was exactly typical of the decades in which he was writing. Mountains as such had little appeal for him. The excursion at Chamonix up to the Mer de Glace was taken for reasons of geological curiosity, not to enjoy the Alpine skyline. To please him, hills had to be modest and very sharply defined in outline, as in a Chinese landscape where abrupt and shapely rocks rise straight out of a level plain. He described Poulton in Lancashire as 'exceedingly fine country with small hills finely improved'.[5] The lumpish and unsatisfactory hillocks around Bridport in Dorset delighted him: 'the beauty of this place is greatly increased by the fine improved single hills, which form a semicircle, and by other pointed hills rising up behind them'.[6] Predictably when he came to those most Chinese of British hills, the Breiddens in Montgomeryshire, which are modest in height but shoot up almost vertically from the alluvial plain of the Severn, he was in raptures and struggling for words:

> All this country is most beautiful in hills, which are divided by lawn and wood, and where the river turns and locks in the land there is the most finest group of hills I ever beheld.[7]

What immediately delighted his eye was the discovery of a weathered rock face from which gnarled and grotesquely shaped trees and bushes grew. These suggested the stylized linear landscapes of Chinese lacquer and porcelain, English glimpses of the world of the willow pattern plate. At Gowlorn Head, again in Lancashire, was: 'a very fine rocky cliff, out of which many trees grow in a most beautiful and extraordinary manner, and particularly the yews, which are so shorn with the wind that they turn up against the rock and grow like a hedge'.[8] In Tunbridge Wells he found 'there are rocks on some of the hills which have a beautiful effect' and,

> a pleasant valley, beautifyed with rocks and wood on each side, this leads to what they call 'the rocks' on the south side, which are towards the top of the hill, and are perpendicular, and about twenty feet high, with large cracks in them through which one may pass, there is a walk on them, and seats under the wood, some of which grows out of the rocks.[9]

To us these may read like the minor pleasure of some municipal park, but to Pococke they were aesthetic treasures with a Far-Eastern exactness of outline. Such precise hills and rocks needed water to reflect them and to be perfect the water had to twist. Pococke found 'serpentines' almost everywhere. East Malling, Kent, had 'a most beautiful park in which two rivulets meet and are made into serpentine rivers . . . and a high island is forming below the meeting of the rivers'.[10] At Lewes, Sussex, was 'the river running through the fields in the most beautiful meanders and the hills forming a most romantic amphitheatre'.[11] Where these artful waters could be combined with an eclectic scatter of garden buildings the Bishop was most warm in his praise. At the Earl of Shaftesbury's seat, Wimborne St Giles, Dorset, he discovered that,

> The gardens are very beautifully laid out in a serpentine river. One first comes to an island in which there is a castle, then near the water is a gateway, with a tower on each side, and passing between two waters there is a fine cascade from one to the other, a thatch'd house, a round pavilion on a mount, Shake Spear's house, in which is a small statue of him, and his works in a glass case. There is a pavilion between the waters and both a Chinese and stone bridge over them. I saw here a duck which lays in rabbits' burrows.[12]

Lord Shaftesbury was no middle-class upstart merchant trying his hand out at garden design nor was Wimborne a small park, but the effects described here feel miniature, just as Robins gives a delicate miniature air to the landscapes which he painted. It was a 'small is beautiful' time, and if Wimborne faintly recalls a willow pattern plate then Richard Bateman's garden at Old Windsor, Berkshire evokes the linear landscapes of Chinese porcelain with more deliberate precision:

> at the former garden is a sort of grotesque shell work with a summer house over it, and beyond that a Chinese alcove seat, near which is a Chinese covered bridge to an island, and another, uncovered, beyond it to another island. This and the swans on the river make it a most delightful piece of scenery.[13]

Bateman was a friend of Horace Walpole and at this stage of his life he was a fanatic for things Chinese, but Thomas Robins's two paintings of these grounds underplay their Chinese elements. One of Pococke's two bridges can be glimpsed at the bottom of a picture otherwise dominated by straight rows of trees, the antithesis of sharawadgi. For all the charm of his detail, Robins was only a fan painter by trade; hills and a difficult perspective gave him problems. But it is possible to identify on one painting several other features of the Bateman estate which Pococke had noted: a *ferme ornée* 'with a walk round it of about half a mile, part of which is close, in the Wilderness way', also a farmhouse with a garden and a greenhouse 'in the Chinese taste; in the room below this they commonly breakfast in Summer'.[14]

Most revealing of all Robins's landscapes are the trio which he painted of

Davenport in Shropshire, the last of which is a tacit admission of failure in the other two.[15] First comes a study of the whole park taken from an imagined aerial viewpoint somewhere to the south. Much of the park, the large area north of the plain brick box, Smith of Warwick house, is not Rococo at all, but an old-fashioned seventeenth-century *patte d'oie* of three straight clearings sentinelled by columns and sliced through woodland. Curiously, the three choice Rococo features: a hermit's grotto, a cascade and a Gothick octagon, all laid out on a path following the contour of a steep, sandy hill, must have been invisible from the house yet wide open to inspection from travellers on the main Bridgnorth–Wolverhampton road. As if to make up for this Robins has drawn a Classical ruin and seat on the south side of the road from which the Rococo trail could have been enjoyed if the seat had really existed. Another feature, a towering Gothick pigeon house to the east, could only have been visible from a few side windows of the main house.

The second painting (illus. 35) illustrates the modest improvement which has been carried out in a little valley west of the house, but again invisible from its windows. To command the new lake created by damming up the river Worfe a ludicrously out-of-scale Gothick oriel-apse has been clamped onto the side of an otherwise unaltered black-and-white timbered cottage. In such a narrow valley a serpentine was not possible, but one side-vista has been cut up through woods to the left towards a Gothick seat and another to

36 Thomas Robins, *Capriccio*, gouache and watercolour, showing a landscape idealized in Rococo terms at Davenport House, Shropshire (1755).

a Classical urn. To enliven this oddly focused view Robins has set a group of anglers fishing from the dam while a dairy maid milks cows upon the green: it is all charmingly bucolic but rather tame.

In the third painting Robins has expressed his dissatisfaction in a capriccio (illus. 36): a wishful elaboration of the second painting and a Romantic dream landscape. Now a huge gnarled oak occupies the foreground and the placid Worfe rages in a ravine under a frail Chinese bridge. An overloaded punt braves its rapids which are all of four feet wide and two feet deep; rough fishermen, or possibly children paddling, stand knee-deep in the shallows. Finally Robins has stolen the Bristol High Cross, or something like it, from Stourhead and dropped it down to dominate the savage idyll. Two prim ladies sit with their backs to the old oak enjoying the animation and a whole picnic party, a *déjeuner sur l'herbe* straight out of Watteau, clusters beneath another tree. The Shropshire out of doors has suddenly become both elegant and faintly dangerous.

The practical social utility of the eclectic garden buildings of these landscapes is a constant in Pococke's diaries. They have taken over the function of privacy provision which Elizabethan houses supplied through roof pavilions, as at Longleat, Wiltshire, or terrace wall banquet houses as at Montacute,

Somerset. A faint air of sexual impropriety has always hovered over garden buildings. In Shakespeare's *Measure for Measure* Angelo's mistaken tryst with Mariana takes place in 'a garden house'. Paul Stamper has come across the papers for a divorce case of 1775 where the witness relates how, hidden in the branches of a pine tree, he saw Edward Corbet of Petton Hall, Shropshire, retiring with Anne the dairy maid into his summer house. There the couple disappeared from his sight below the level of the sash window for four minutes. Hannah Corbet won her divorce.[16]

Most of the pleasures associated with garden houses were, however, strictly respectable and domestic. At Bramham in Yorkshire, 'late Lord Burghley's', in the midst of a concentration of Robinesque eclecticism was 'a thatched house to which the family sometimes go for variety, and take some refreshments'.[17] The same alfresco delights were popular at Wentworth Woodhouse, near Sheffield. There the very rich Marquis of Rockingham and his wife took their bucolic picnic meals seriously, building a number of garden dining rooms for shelter from the uncertain Pennine weather. They escaped from their immense palace to a wilderness, an open Ionic temple, a greenhouse, a dairy and 'a poultry' with rooms 'where they used to dine and drink tea'. The Marquis had built a pyramid topped with a viewing platform and 'a rustick Dorick octagon temple', but as if that were not eclectic confusion enough the Marchioness had added a new pleasure area:

> an house with a large room, two smaller offices under, and here the family dine often in the summer. There is a walk on the south and west with a little serpentine river and a bridge, several winding walks through the wood, and a view made by a moss hermitage. There is a skittle ground for the youth to divert themselves, not to omit a beautiful temple to Cloacina with a portico round it, supported by columns made of the natural trunks of trees.

Pococke added coyly, 'and my lady engaged me to dine that day in the wood. She is the great Earl of Nottingham's daughter',[18] so even bishops might live briefly in Arcady. There could be no clearer demonstration of the social disfunctionalism of such a vast Palladian house. By their monotony, their insistent grandeur and their vast rooms, they drove normal inhabitants out into Rococo gardens, the one required the other. Obviously Robins could have painted there for weeks. It was a large park but divided, like Chiswick, into smaller units and, as the creation of a Marquis who was twice Prime Minister, it was anything but middle class.

In Ireland, at Caledon, Co. Tyrone, Lord Orrery, who was Jonathan Swift's biographer and a friend of Pope, was developing his park at the same time as the Rockinghams and to almost exactly the same social pattern. In addition to 'an ivory palace' made entirely from bones bought from local butchers, he had built, he claimed,

> at the expense of five pounds, a root house, or hermitage, to which on Sunday the country people resort, as the Londoners to Westminster Abbey. For gayer scenes, I have a lodge near a mile distant from the hermitage, and large enough to contain a good number of friends at dinner or supper, or to entertain eight couples with a country dance. Behind this room are three little rooms, besides a cellar. These buildings are in the form of Buckingham House. And the courtyard is filled with various fowls, and admits the most lively and innocent scene imaginable. All the buildings command a view of the river, of groves and of various agreeable objects.[19]

In all the favoured parts of Ireland the social and eclectic scene was the same. Lord Limerick at Tullamure (Tollymore) Park had 'over the rivulet' built 'a thatch'd open place to dine in, which is very Romantick, with a stove near to prepare the Entertainment: above on the North side of this He has begun to build a pretty lodge, two rooms of which are finished, designing to spend the Summer months here'.[20] The same peer had another eclectic park at Dundalk in Co. Louth with 'an artifical serpentine river, a Chinese bridge and a thatch'd open house supported by the bodies of fir trees'.[21] A few counties further north Lord Antrim defied the rains of Ulster to bring the shepherd pleasures of Arcadia to his park at Glenarme: 'The most beautiful and romantick ground I ever beheld', Pococke declared, 'a beautiful mount which commands a fine prospect, where My Lord often dines . . . the perpendicular rock at least a hundred yards in height, out of which shrubs and trees grow in the most beautiful manner, just at the entrance of this wood on an eminence is a banqueting house in a very romantick situation'.[22]

Even Connaught had, around Westport, 'fine low hills which are planted and improved',[23] but, despite its 'improvements', Powerscourt House among the Wicklow hills with its 400-foot waterfall was altogether too much for the Bishop with his 'Rococo' sense of appropriate scale. He dismissed it with 'the slopes are rather too steep and unnatural',[24] which was a perfect mid-century judgement. Dangan, Lord Mornington's house on the more modest slopes of Co. Meath, was the Bishop's favourite Irish garden with toys, temples and just the right kind of hill. There was a redoubt,

> it is a regular fortification, there is a ship, a sloop and boats on the water . . . the hill beyond it is improved into a beautiful wilderness: on a round hill near the house is a Temple, and the hills round are adorned with Obelisks, Pillars and some buildings, altogether the most beautiful thing I ever saw.[25]

Hills, serpentines and aesthetic judgements are all, in this mild Rococo mid-century, safe and moderate. At Altadora, cut into a tablet of white marble under a bust of the laughing philosopher, Pococke found a poem which encapsulated his own outlook, and liked it so much that he recorded its selfish self-satisfaction:

> O Sacred Solitude! Divine retreat!
> Choice of the Prudent! Envy of the Great!
> Here from the wayes of man, laid safe ashore,
> We smile to hear the distant billows roar.
> Here, blest with health, with business unperplext
> This Life we relish and insure the next.[26]

In Pococke's endless peregrinations what comes over most consistently is the universality of what he calls 'improvements' but which seem to be nothing less than a reshaping of whole tracts of countryside into areas of fantasy where the real world has been tamed and cosmeticized. New wealth was pouring in from Empire and conquest, and this remarkable creation of private play-grounds was very high in the ruling classes' priorities of expenditure. It was as if the ordinary world was so dull and unaesthetic that most families with money and property felt socially constrained to create areas of illusion. Even now, after two hundred years, so many survive that we tend to take them for granted, but in the middle of a so-called Age of Reason they are an extraordinary phenomenon: so many cantos of Spenser's *Faerie Queene* realized with hermit's cells, Phaedria's island on the Idle Lake, Bowers of Bliss and Enchanter's Castles for wicked Archimago to inhabit. William Kent loved the *Faerie Queene* and prepared fantastical illustrations for an eventual 1751 edition; it is easy to see why he was so enthusiastic. It was a Romantick age before Romanticism, which offers yet another definition for that elusive term 'Rococo'.

Every so often Pococke's laboured entries break out into a prolonged rapture and the Bishop reveals his top ratings for Rococo 'landskip'. When he entered the Duke of Cumberland's royal improvements in and around Virginia Water near Windsor he found that strange park the epitome of the eclectic Rococo.[27] First, inevitably, there was a pond with an island – the Sino-Rococo motif – with a room 'in the figure of a Greek cross', a couch for dalliance in each of its arms. 'The Duke often comes here and spends an hour or two and sometimes dines', for a kitchen was concealed in the trees. Then on an eminence was more ducal geometry, 'a triangular tower which is a hexagon within, with a hexagon at each corner, which are round within', a pure Spenserian creation, echoes of that 'House of Temperance': 'The frame thereof was partly circular/And part triangular – O work divine'. Did Cumberland, gross, red-faced and apoplectic, the military hero Britain loved to hate, see himself as some allegorical figure out of Spenser, partying there in a delicately feminine Rococo interior absurdly inappropriate to someone of his fearsome reputation?

> The hexagon is most beautiful, the sides are adorned with festoons of flowers and fruit hanging down from them on each side of the doors and windows in stucco, and painted in their natural colours; over each door is a bas relief, in white marble . . . in the centre is a branch adorned with Chelsea china.

Obviously 'Butcher' Cumberland was more of a Rococo addict than his brother the Prince of Wales who is often described, on little solid evidence, as the Rococo Prince.

From the leads of the hexagon tower there were views of a 'Serpentine River' with cascades and caves around its shores. A wooden Chinese bridge spanned the serpentine in one swoop of 110 feet and under it sailed 'a small yacht, which has sailed on the sea, a Chinese ship, the middle of which is high, covered and glazed, a Venetian gondola, and five or six other different kinds of boats': a fleet of eclectic fantasy. 'Twenty men are employed all the summer', Pococke noted approvingly, 'in mowing the grass in different parts. The Duke has wild beasts here, and I saw an ostrich walking in the lawn near the house'. So yet another essence of Rococo devices was public entertainment, royalty, as always, providing it.

'It is incredible', Pococke concluded, 'how fine a place this is made, from being the most disagreeable and uncultivated, and the whole country round it is in a state of great improvement. In the harvest time the Duke carries on no improvements, but in the winter he has commonly a great number of men at work'. So here a new equation had been added to all the others: the Rococo garden equalled prosperity and high employment.

It is easy, and in a scholarly sense satisfying, to emphasize some relatively obscure Classical allegory and interpret a whole complex garden in its terms when the reality is as complex and happy-go-lucky as Cumberland's Virginia Water. Stourhead garden in Wiltshire for example is often explained by careful analysis of Aeneas's journey in Virgil's epic poem. But Aeneas never visited a Jacobean structure like St Peter's Pump up in its side valley, or a Convent in the Woods. There was a Chinese house on the hill slope below the house but Aeneas never went so far afield as Peking. Pococke noted on his visit to the garden in 1754 that the lake was to have islands with buildings on them 'one of which is to be a Mosque with a Minaret'[28] – Aeneas in Baghdad? So Stourhead originally was Rococo, a Robins-type garden, like

Kew which, under Princess Augusta after the Prince of Wales's death in 1751, acquired a galaxy of such exotic structures and yet more Classical temples. There was nothing essentially small about a Rococo garden but, unlike one of Lancelot Brown's carefully composed pastoral landscapes with its beautiful (and economical) vacant spaces, a Rococo layout gave an impression of the miniature, a Robins-like air, by the multiplicity of its ornaments, often delicately detailed.

Like Castell, Pococke also divided his improvements into three categories, though two seem often to be enclosed together within the same confines. His three were 'the wilderness way' (the most common), 'the farm way' and 'in the park style'. All the wilderness gardens are groves with serpentine winding ways that lead, usually between hedges, to surprise features. The farm way is a large open area bordered by a path which slips back occasionally into the surrounding belt of trees. The most famous of these *ferme ornée* layouts was Philip Southcote's Woburn Farm at Chertsey, laid out in the late 1730s which, in Pococke's description, 'is the first improvement in the farm kind, and is esteem'd the most elegant, in England . . . It consists of walks to the left, first round two meadows on rather high ground and then round another two on low ground . . . there is a bridge that leads to several small fields mostly of corn and some meadows with walks and plantations round them'.[29] At Thomas Shenstone's The Leasowes near Halesowen the circuit path took in a grove dedicated to Virgil, but also skirted farm fields with barns and hayricks. These open 'farm' fields appear to have functioned rather like a modern County Show, an area to display one's agricultural refinements to the neighbours.

Batty Langley's *New Principles* has a list of the appropriate items which could be included in such a farm field to interest a visitor:

Paddocks of Sheep, Deer, Cows & Hop Grounds, Nurseries of Fruit and Forest Trees, Vineyards, Inclosures of Corn, Grass, Clover & etc, Cones of Fruit Trees, Warrens of Hares and Rabbits, Hay Stacks and Wood Piles, as in a farmer's yard in the Country.[30]

So the County Show parallel is not far-fetched; the bucolic simplicities of eighteenth-century life should never be underplayed; haystacks and wood piles had their place in the Rococo garden. Buckland House in Berkshire retains its Richard Woods-designed 1760s park encircled by such a route and until as late as 1905 it was still the custom every Sunday for the family and weekend guests to make the entire circuit of stewardship, ending at the Arts and Crafts dairy for a sampling of the home-made cheeses. That was

37 One of several
gouache and
watercolour views
painted by Thomas
Robins in the 1750s of
the gardens at
Dorchester House,
Surrey.

how the farm way garden was intended to function.[31] The park style, on the other hand, appears from Pococke's vague references to have been no more than an anticipation of what Capability Brown would soon impose: a gracious open land with clumps of trees which neither surprises nor meanders, probably no more than an elegant pasture land or paddock for horses.

Whether the three Pococke garden types were ever very distinct is doubtful. That Buckland farm way circuit, for instance, passes several interesting temples and cold baths. There was often a strongly competitive element in what went into a garden. On one southward bend of the Thames at Weybridge, Pococke noted three celebrated gardens literally bordering each other and vying for a polite visitor's attention. There was Lord Lincoln's Oatlands with its 'serpentine river', shrubberies, parterres and 'all sorts of exotic plants . . . In the lawns sheep are grazing; and at the end of the terrace is one of Inigo Jones's gates',[32] Lord Portmore's Dorchester House which Robins painted three times with its triumphal arch gateway, 'beautiful round Temple' and enchanting Gothick garden house 'a little spire to make it appear like a Church' (illus. 37),[33] and Southcote's Woburn Farm; the three forming a weekend circuit for Londoners with a horticultural bent.

It is not easy to fit Mr St John's park at Dogmersfield in Hampshire into any of Pococke's three types. A visitor would find, beyond the first predictable serpentine river and Gothick arch, 'an imitation of a British or

Druid avenue . . . of large stones set up on end for half a mile'. Had Mr St John visited the prehistoric avenues at Carnac in Brittany or was it Avebury he had in mind? Then came in Pococke's progress 'a colonnade . . . call'd the Temple . . . an octagon turret' and, at Sir Maurice Cope's, in the middle of a thirty acre lake, 'a small low turret on four Gothick arches, called the Chinese building, but is rather defective in the execution, and near the water is a cottage built to resemble a Gothick chapel'.[34] Neither wilderness, farm nor park, this must have been fantasy land, but precisely which fantasy?

Hagley Hall in Worcestershire had to be left to the last, for there Bishop Pococke was already arrived in Heaven, a Rococo Heaven with a new picturesque vista to be relished at every few paces.[35] Much of the garden and its buildings survives, if a little over-threaded by busy roads, and some of its buildings are consequently isolated. But the small shapely hills – Pococke-sized – and their improved woodlands are still recognizable while the house itself is appropriately alive in most of its principal rooms with inventive, figurative Rococo plasterwork. The place with its set walks so excited the Bishop that his prose style, never exactly winged and vaulting, becomes at times rapturously incoherent. Hagley had so many 'seats', so many prospects, lawns, woods and features that the Bishop hardly knew which way to turn:

> Ascending up the valley there is a walk on each side, one winds up to the prospect and also along the side of the hanging ground. Going into the other to the left we come to a head, which is a bay to the water above, and on this is a rustick seat of bricks opening to the water above it in form of a Venetian window; a large piece of water comes up to this seat and a beautiful cascade falls down the rocks into it, by which it is divided into two parts, all finely adorned with wood.

Leaving this oddly suspended 'water' Pococke came to a 'half octagon open building and a tent at the further end to the east; from this half octagon there is a view of the castle as in a woody vale between the hills, which rise over it, also the Prince's pillar'. The Prince was Frederick Lewis, the pillar his gift to the Lytteltons, and the castle was that Sanderson Miller creation which so pleased Horace Walpole with 'the true rust of the barons' wars'. It survives intact, four towers about a court, but engagingly perverse in its lopsided profile (illus. 27). Pococke described it 'with a turret at each corner, that to the southeast is entire, the others as well as the walls of the castle are made as ruinous, and the Gothick windows rising above the ruins have a beautiful effect'. Here, as much as anywhere in England, the Gothick and the Rococo have fused together, the former supplying the asymmetry of the latter in an acceptably historicist and patriotic union.

Statues of Apollo and a vale of Venus were not seen in any sense as inappropriate to this presiding Gothick castle, and the Bishop found nothing incongruous in Classical gods being neighboured by 'an alcove seat, covered with pebbles curiously figured, in which are represented a cross, beads, and ornaments of pots of flowers'. His path led him on by more waters and seats,

> and going up at the end of the vale, it passes by the hermit's fountain, cover'd with an old trunk of a tree, and so leads to the Hermitage at the south-east corner made with roots of trees, with a seat round it cover'd with matting, a rail and gate before it made of rude stakes.

When hermits are mentioned in any contemporary account there is always this curious fascination with the details of holy squalor, an interest perhaps in the possibility of retirement and preparation for death in a setting of natural beauty and horrid simplicity. Pococke never questions the bizarre contradictions of the aesthetic trail which he is following: 'Venus of Medici as coming up out of a fountain'; 'a little dip adorned with a variety of flowers in a constant succession'; 'a rock work of rough materials of the glass-houses and quarries'; Pope's urn 'on a pedestal and crowned with a double mask, as I suppose of Satyr and Philosophy'.

In the end, exhausted by the many ascents and descents, delighted by all the indigestible variety of visuals he declared:

> I could not but give you this account, tho' very imperfect, of one of the finest and best improved spots I ever saw, and the finest ground, in which nature is only helped by art, with the greatest taste and in the most elegant manner.

The Bishop could hardly have found a fairer description of the Rococo garden than that: nature 'helped by art, with the greatest taste and in the most elegant manner'.

38 Esher Place, Surrey (*c.* 1733): the country seat of a popular Prime Minister.

CHAPTER V

GOTHICK AND ROCOCO – THE EARLY DAYS OF A SUBVERSIVE DUO

The first important Gothick building of the English eighteenth century was planned between 1729 and 1731 and built by 1733 at Esher, Surrey, as the country seat of Henry Pelham, brother of the Duke of Newcastle. At that time the Pelham brothers were powerful members of Sir Robert Walpole's cabinet. Esher Place (illus. 38), a strikingly innovative house, entirely Gothick in appearance and featuring four large new canted bays, had been designed by William Kent, one of the country's best known, and certainly most original, architects. Henry Pelham was to live at Esher for the next twenty-one years, until his death in 1754, and for the last ten of those years he would be Prime Minister and First Lord of the Treasury (illus. 39), leading the country through the trials of the War of the Austrian Succession and then through six years of peace and increasing prosperity with falling taxation and a reduction of the national debt. He died in office, popular and respected, to be succeeded as Prime Minister by his brother the Duke. In all those twenty-one years, when the Palladian is generally supposed to have been the Whig party's house style, Esher Place was Pelham's family home and centre of hospitality, a large Gothick country house surrounded by a Rococo garden of great beauty, laid out by Kent. As such it was visited regularly by the great and the influential, and being only a few miles from the capital, its imposing new style was, inevitably, widely noted.

In this first half of the eighteenth century, when a polite style war was being conducted and four styles were competing for the attention of would-be builders, terms need to be clearly defined. The Gothick and the Rococo were the two unofficial or pirate styles which had moved to occupy the stylistic confusion and decorative vacancies created by the artificial imposition of the Palladian onto a native Baroque. Sometimes the two styles, Gothick and Rococo, interacted so closely with each other as to become one; usually however they co-existed, side by side, but still distinct in the same house. The Gothick is, therefore, an essential chapter in any account of the English, though not the Irish, Rococo. In Ireland the Gothick never took such a firm hold as in England. Some architectural analysts tend to patronize the Gothick (with a 'k') as a puppy stage to the mature dog – the Gothic Revival. It was not; it was a style in its own right, a deliberate development of original Gothic medieval motifs within the conventions of Classicism, hence Esher's symmetry, it was more a richly rewarding protest movement than a whole-sale revolt. It could lead eventually, as it did in Horace Walpole's Strawberry Hill, to Gothic Revival forms, to the conscious scholarly replication of accurately observed medieval details. But at that point the cheerful improvi-sations of the Gothick have been lost, creativity is in decline and copying is at a premium. It was because the Gothick and the Rococo both accepted some Classical conventions, while striving to enliven them, that they could often work unselfconsciously together. The characteristic S and C scroll forms of the Rococo accorded naturally with ogee Gothic arches and cinquefoil tracery. Consequently while ogee arches were relatively rare in medieval Gothic work they became almost standard in the Gothick.

There were two important interchanges between the two styles. The Gothick gave the Rococo its most distinctive outward form, that of the canted bay, so prominent at Esher, while the Rococo, by its example, persuaded the Gothick into a pleasant decorative excess which at the outset, and this is a feature not always noted, the style tended to avoid. The Gothick began as a surprisingly austere style while the Rococo was initially restricted to interior decorative design; so they both had much to gain from each other. There will be no attempt in this single chapter at a complete history of the Gothick taste, only a study of the interdependence between it and the Rococo before the dead hand of scholarship brought in the application of correct Gothic forms and the revival began its not always satisfying course into nineteenth-century eclecticism.

No Gothick narrative would be complete without a devious plot. The Gothic novels of the Minerva Press which deluged British lending libraries at the turn of the century with tales of sinister titled villains, haunted castles and the threat of rape in gloomy cellars, had their origin and inspiration in

Horace Walpole's *The Castle of Otranto* of 1764. So it is only appropriate that Horace Walpole's own personal vendetta against the house of Pelham should be central to this real-life plot. It concerns high politics, frustrated love and, if not a haunted castle, at least two Gothick houses. One was Esher Place, castle-like in style and social consequence, and the other was Strawberry Hill, smaller and more frail, but eventually towered, a house which has unexpectedly outlasted its grander rival. What needs to be emphasized from the start is the time scale of the two buildings. Walpole did not begin to make Gothick additions to his small modern house until 1748, by which time Gothick Esher had been flourishing for fifteen years. Esher Place was Walpole's inspiration: 'Esher I have seen again twice', he wrote in 1748, 'and I prefer it to all villas, even Southcote's; Kent is Kentissime there'.[1] By his writings he may have contrived to obscure Henry Pelham's political reputation and virtually ignore his architectural initiative, but bricks, mortar and that date of 1733 give Esher a primacy which should never have been forgotten by architectural historians. When Giles Worsley in his *Classical Architecture in Britain: The Heroic Age*, described Strawberry Hill as 'the first important Gothic house within easy reach of London'[2] he had fallen victim to Horace Walpole's persuasive rewriting of architectural sequences. Equally when, earlier in the same book, he dismissed Henry Pelham as 'an intimate of Sir Robert Walpole'[3] though in fact Pelham was a rather more successful Prime Minister, Worsley was again accepting, unconsciously, Horace Walpole's sustained campaigns of denigration against the Pelhams. He is not alone in this. Terence Davis in *The Gothick Taste* describes Pelham as 'the financier',[4] as if he were a mere London banker, while Michael McCarthy in his *The Origins of the Gothic Revival* contrives not to mention Pelham at all except in a quotation from a contemporary poem by William Mason:

> There was a time 'in Esher's peaceful grove,
> Where Kent and Nature vied for Pelham's love'[5]

Yet all three historians, aware that the house must, by its date, be significant, illustrate Esher Place in their books while underplaying its owner.

In these open and politically correct times it is possible to relate the source of the Walpole vendetta against the Pelhams without making moral judgements. The Duke of Newcastle had no children, but his brother Henry had two sons and three daughters. In November 1739 Henry's two little boys died within a day of each other. This left the Pelhams' nephew, the 9th Earl of Lincoln, Henry Fiennes Clinton, a young man of nineteen, an orphan,

39 Henry Pelham, First
Lord of the Treasury
and builder of Esher
Place, Surrey.

Newcastle's ward, and the male heir to the Pelham fortunes. In the practical, family-centred way of the times the brothers decided that Lincoln
should marry Pelham's eldest daughter, his cousin, Catherine. It was arranged that the King, obedient to the Pelham interests, should recreate the ducal
title of Newcastle with reversion to Lord Lincoln: a satisfactory solution to a
dynastic difficulty.

At that time Lincoln, an amiable, handsome sportsman, impressionable
and impetuous, was in an adolescent stage of bisexual attachments. He and
Horace Walpole, who was three years his senior but very much his junior in
sexual experience, began a passionate physical love affair while they were
both on their respective Grand Tours in Italy. A virtual honeymoon followed
on the Riviera and for the next three years in England, while Lincoln kept a
mistress, fathered a bastard and generally behaved like a roistering young
man about town, he and Walpole continued in a physical relationship. This
appears to have been shallow but enthusiastic on Lincoln's part, while for
Walpole, who was a fastidious and non-promiscuous homosexual, it was the
great emotional affair of his life. Its course can be followed in the twenty-five
letters of volume thirty of the Yale edition of Walpole's correspondence.

In October 1744 the Pelhams decided that it was time for Lord Lincoln to
settle down. He was married off, probably quite willingly, to his cousin
Catherine and soon became an affectionate, though still occasionally riotous,
family man. Walpole had hoped to continue the relationship, but the uncles
had laid down, or so Walpole assumed, a stern censure. From that month

onwards there was to be no further contact of any significance between the two old lovers, however hard Walpole might try to engineer responses with little gifts of books and brief pathetic letters.

While never losing his affection for Lincoln, Walpole blamed their separation entirely on his uncles, Newcastle and Henry Pelham, and took his revenge most effectively over the next thirty years. Walpole is well known, from his delightful gossipy letters, as an admirer, and if his own account is to be believed, the source of the Gothic Revival in England. But by his two serious, posthumously published, works of political record, *Memoirs of the Reign of George II* and *Memoirs of the Reign of George III*, he made himself the prime source on parliamentary intrigues in the mid-century for all subsequent historians, however much they might claim to mistrust him as a partial authority. Macaulay seems actively to have disliked him, but he still took his Whig theory of constitutional history straight from Walpole's seductively persuasive directions. Walpole had, after all, been an MP for twenty-five years, known everyone, plotted industriously and been the son of the most efficiently corrupt and long serving British Prime Minister, Sir Robert. So who could be better informed?

Admitting, with disarming honesty, that he had 'a strong aversion'[6] to Pelham but only because the Prime Minister had once refused him a request on pension rights, Walpole proceeded in his texts to blacken the Pelham names, ridicule their motives and ensure that posterity would see Henry as a weak, drifting compromiser and Newcastle as a buffoon. At every point in the *Memoirs* when a Pelham can be made to seem mean, foolish, corrupt and contemptible, Walpole seized that opportunity and trickled out mingled humour and bile.

Sometimes, because Walpole was, behind his spite, a shrewd and fair observer, he had to struggle hard to conceal Henry Pelham's decency and good judgement, as when, writing of the conclusion of the 1739–48 war he noted that Pelham, 'concluded an ignominious peace; but the circumstances of the times made it be thought, and perhaps it was, desirable'.[7] Or when he was summing up Pelham's life he allowed reluctantly, 'Let it be remembered, that though he first taught or experienced universal servility in Englishmen, yet he lived without abusing his power and died poor'.[8]

But these were only rare flashes of truth; more typical of the blizzard of denigration were:

Mr Pelham was timorous, reserved, fickle, apt to despair. He would often not attempt when he was convinced it would be right.
All men thought Mr Pelham honest till he was in power.

He supplied the deficiency of genius by affected virtue; he had removed superiors by treachery, and those of whom he was jealous by pretexting or administering to the jealousies of his brother . . . He enjoyed the plenitude of his ministry but a short time; and that short period was a scene of fretfulness.[9]

After which a reader has to be reminded that in 1715 Henry Pelham volunteered to fight against the forces of the first Jacobite rebellion and acquitted himself bravely at the battle of Prestonpans. He refused to join in the general panic when Prince Charles's army reached Derby in the second Jacobite Rebellion and, as a result of his handling of the Rebellion's aftermath with a wise blending of firmness and justice, England and Scotland remained a united and world dominating power for the next 250 years. Even Walpole had to allow that Pelham was a popular Prime Minister, who not only won a war but established a prosperous peace and died in office. Nevertheless,

nothing tended so much to unravel the mystery of devotion which the nation had conceived for Mr Pelham, as it appearing that it had not been the genius of the man, but the servility of the times which had established his authority.[10]

Even Pelham's death did not end the hate campaign: 'his brother, who whimpered for him like a child for the first hours, like a child forgot him to run after his rattle as soon as he formed the plan of inheriting his power'.[11]

Whether Walpole consigned Pelham to lie among the ranks of forgotten Prime Ministers purely for being the father-in-law of Lord Lincoln, or whether that frustration was mixed with a resentful awareness that Pelham had easily outpointed him in the Gothick stakes, it is impossible to say. But Pelham's building programme in the early 1730s was far more single-minded and confidently Gothick than Walpole's building efforts in the late 1740s. Having bought the Esher estate in 1729 he first rejected an attractive but conventional 1–3–1 neo-Palladian villa design which Kent had offered to build on a hillside, overlooking Bishop Waynflete's old brick Tudor gatehouse in the valley below,[12] then commissioned Kent to build an entirely symmetrical yet wholly Gothick nine-bay house of three storeys with Waynflete's gatehouse retained as its centrepiece. This established Classical symmetry and Gothick fenestration as the future norm of the style. Kent refenestrated the gatehouse and then, as if a battery of large, ogee-arched, bifora windows with quatrefoils as variants was not innovative enough, he echoed the small canted bays on the fifteenth-century gatehouse with two large three-storey canted bays on the entrance front and two more single-storey canted bays on the river front, built out as extensions to overlook the gardens. This gave Pelham four large octagonal rooms on the principal floor, each one commanding the sunlight from three angles and marking a dramatic escape from the Classical box. Visitors would have approached between Kent's twin Gothick lodges, driven down a long straight avenue and arrived in a theatrical Gothick courtyard, three-sided with a battlemented roofline, two four-storey, ogee-domed towers and two tower-like canted bays. It was a proto-Otranto, and achieved thirty years before Walpole would write his novel of that name.

Inside Esher Place Kent kept his nerve and did not retreat, as he so easily could have done, to Classical decoration. Instead he devised his own version of a Gothick star vault for the ceilings, with pendant features. His doorways and chimneypieces were deliberately schizoid – Tudor arches below, broken Classical pediments above. He was engaged at the same time, 1732, in building a pastiche Tudor tower in the Clock Court of Hampton Court Palace, a medievalism which had been urged on him by the Prime Minister, Sir Robert Walpole.[13] Pure ogee arches are not common Tudor forms, but Pelham's Esher should be seen as a deliberate linking of an eighteenth-century version of Tudor motifs with those varied spatial effects, octagons included, of the interiors recently completed by Burlington at Chiswick. It was Esher that established the ogee and the quatrefoil as a standard cliché of the Gothick to be used when other inspiration failed. Not perhaps a very beautiful house, it was certainly a very memorable one and its interiors offered an attractive spatial freedom which the conventional Classical rectangular ground plan denied. An innovative example had been set, but no established architect was in any hurry to follow it up.

Between the completion of Esher in 1733 and the publication in 1741–2 of Batty Langley's celebrated *Ancient Architecture Restored and Improved* not one significant Gothick building went up anywhere in Britain. James Gibbs's brilliant Temple of Liberty at Stowe (illus. 28), begun in 1741, was exactly contemporary with Langley's book. It is not possible, therefore, to describe *Ancient Architecture* as a book published in response to a new public enthusiasm for the medieval. This leaves a question: what gave a nursery gardener, with a reasonable track record of publishing helpful architectural pattern books of an exclusively Classical nature, the confidence to publish a large, expensive book on a new style in which no one, up to 1741, except Henry Pelham, seems to have been interested? The Rococo was beginning to infiltrate English interiors through the influence of Continental craftsmen, but why now the Gothick? Who was behind it?

Dr Eileen Harris earned the gratitude of architectural historians in her *British Architectural Books and Writers* of 1990 by stating the obvious, which earlier historians had hesitated to state for fear of ridicule, that Batty Langley was heart and soul an enthusiastic and committed Freemason and that Masonry lay behind all, or most, of his publishing activities. Dr Harris did not quite press her evidence to suggest that the entire projection of Gothick design in the 1740s was an unconcealed Masonic project ('conspiracy' would be the wrong word as there was no concealment) but that was her implication and one which it is hard to avoid.

Langley had drawn favourable attention to himself by a series of articles published in the *Grub Street Journal* between July 1734 and March 1735. These constituted a fierce defence of native English architecture, in particular of Westminster Abbey, 'that Venerable and August Pile, being the most Magnificent in this Kingdom'; he praised his hero, Nicholas Hawksmoor's faithful restoration work on the west front remarking: 'how he puts in new stone where the old is found to be infirm and sculpts down the sound so that when 'tis completed 'twill appear with equal beauty, as the first day it was erected'.[14] Langley's favourite Gothic was slim, plain thirteenth-century work: the nave of the Abbey and the Temple Church off Fleet Street. The 'Filagree Work' of Henry VII's chapel, 'though admired by some', he considered, 'not worthy of imitation by any'.[15] So he is not likely to have been in favour of the rich decorative effects of the Rococo (illus. 40).

Then in 1736 Langley had published *Ancient Masonry both in Theory and Practice*. This was a two-volume work and only those who have seen library staff staggering under the weight of its enormous twin volumes will appreciate what an enterprise and an investment it must have represented for a self-taught nursery gardener to publish. But it was dedicated to past Grand Masters of the Order, starting with the Holy Roman Emperor and listing seven dukes (one of whom was Newcastle, Pelham's brother) and sixteen earls (more Scots than English, but including Pembroke and Chesterfield). It is obvious that Langley was only able to publish such an expensive and ambitious work because he had the security of a resounding subscription list and Masonic backing. *Ancient Masonry* was intended as the last word on Classical design and the construction of Classical details, it brims over with exuberant self-taught scholarship. The Ionic capital for instance is listed and illustrated in twenty different versions from twenty different authorities. Langley noted piously that 'it is the duty of every man to communicate such knowledge as he is blessed with that will be of Service to the Publick'.[16] Freemasonry was flourishing in the 1720s and 1730s, not only as a society for associating groups of the great and the good in various lodges or for the mutual insurance of trades-people, but it had also the genuinely benevolent purpose of improving

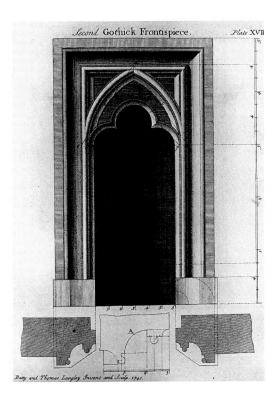

Second Gothick Frontispiece.   Plate XVII

Batty and Thomas Langley Invent and Sculp. 1741.

40 Batty Langley in austere mood: Plate 18 from his *Ancient Architecture* (1741–2).

technical skills and industry to bring about national prosperity. Somehow Langley had convinced his Masonic superiors that he could further this last aim; hence his *Ancient Masonry*. With the same powerful backing, six years later, he published his *Ancient Architecture*, proposing to do for the Gothic, with illustrations by his brother, what he had just done for the Classical. In a preliminary essay to this next book he wrote with engaging confidence:

> And as this Specimen of my Endeavours to restore and illustrate the beauties of *the Saxon Architecture*, for the Good of Posterity, is *honoured* with the Encouragement of the preceding *Nobility* and *Gentry*, I make no Doubt but that by their good Examples, all other *Lovers* and *Encouragers* of Art and Industry will further encourage it . . . the Works of the Ancients, whose magnificence and Beauty greatly exceed all that have been done by both *Greeks* and *Romans*.[17]

It was a confidence justified by a subscription list which included, this time, fifteen dukes (virtually the entire ducal register), twenty-six earls, three viscounts, twenty barons and seven justices, ensuring that the book was bound to make some aesthetic impact.

Here, however, it needs to be stressed, to counter the general view of 'Batty Langley Gothick' as something light and frivolous, that the greater

41 Batty Langley in a
tentative compromise
with the Rococo: Plate
38 from his *Ancient
Architecture* (1741–2).

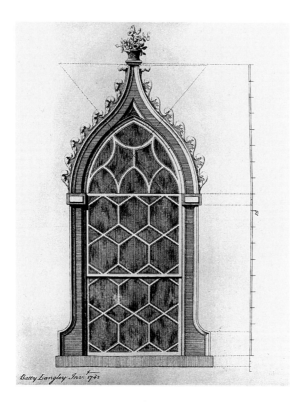

number of its 63 illustrative plates are serious, austere and thoroughly practical suggestions for carrying medieval forms into a Classical world. Only
one of his plates (36) a cinquefoil ogee bifora window can be accurately
described as linking Gothick and Rococo detail. The window has garlands of
flowers with gryphons' heads following the curves of its arch and each ogee
top sprouts either acanthus leaves or a flower basket. Five other plates (38, 42,
43, 47 and 48; illus. 41) have some Rococo flourishes; plates 9 and 12 are
Jacobean in feeling. That leaves 55 plates which, while often geometrically
inventive and inclined to curvaceous ogees, cinquefoils and trefoils, suggest
practical, sensible models for adding Gothick doors, windows, chimneypieces and orders to existing houses. The book ends with fourteen delightful
designs for garden buildings. It seems increasingly probable, on the evidence
of this book, his previous *Ancient Masonry* and the combined subscription
lists, that Langley, with his abounding self-confidence and his undoubted
scholarship, had persuaded the superior lodges of London Masonry to
support him in a patriotic revival of the arts of medieval masons. The Gothick
or as he called it the 'Saxon' style might, therefore, be legitimately described
as part of a Freemasonic projection with political undertones.

At the time of its publication Lord Cobham and his group of dissident Whig politicians were exercised over the constitutional liberties supposedly enjoyed in the early Saxon kingdoms of England, claiming them as precedents for their own political programme. Cobham had erected a 'Saxon' temple in his park at Stowe. If, therefore, Gothic architecture could be seen as 'Saxon' in origin it could be projected as the true architecture for liberty loving Britains. Langley was too well informed on English architectural history to have believed that any surviving Gothic buildings dated back to Saxon times. His dating, for example, of the various parts of Westminster Abbey is impressively accurate. But if some of his Masonic sponsors wanted to describe the most attractive medieval work as 'Saxon' then he was ready to oblige, thereby exposing himself to the ridicule of later historians.

This explains why his first edition of 1741–2 has as its title, *Ancient Architecture Restored and Improved*, and a grovelling dedication to 'The Encouragers to the Restoring of Saxon Architecture' and to the Dean of Westminster Abbey, a 'Structure . . . of the Saxon Mode (tho' vulgarly called Gothic)'. This is followed by his notoriously foolish essay describing all medieval Gothic work as a mere memory of superior Saxon buildings which had been destroyed by the Danes. When he published his second edition in 1747 political pressures had lessened, the style he urged had begun to take off, allowing him to scrap the ridiculous introductory essay and give the book a more realistic title: *Gothic Architecture*. Now it was the illustrations which made the impact.

Langley never risked designing an entire Gothick house but, in 1743, a year after his first edition came out, William Halfpenny, a fellow author of pattern books but also an active provincial architect, took up Langley's implicit challenge and completely reconstructed Stouts Hill, a house at Uley in the Gloucestershire Cotswolds, using Langley's plates. Stouts Hill together with its brilliant follow-up, Halfpenny's garden pavilion, the Orangery, at nearby Frampton Court, marks the coming of age of the Gothick in buildings where its native clumsiness has been caught up within a Rococo grace and curvilinear charm. The two buildings also mark the beginning of a West Country and Bristol bias to the way the styles developed.

By copying Esher's canted bay towers at Stouts Hill, Halfpenny escaped that two-dimensional cut-out effect to which the simple applied forms of the Gothick were subject. It is unfair to compare Stouts Hill with Esher now that only Bishop Waynflete's original gatehouse survives on that site, but some cross reference is unavoidable. Esher was approached formally between Kent's neat twin box lodges, two mantlepiece ornaments enlarged.

The drive marker to Stouts Hill is bucolic and dramatic: an ingenious Halfpenny improvisation, a Cotswold farmhouse masked on two sides by high Gothick façades of Y-tracery and quatrefoils (illus. 55). These give it the air of a Nonconformist conventicle and the whole pasteboard composition seems to be holding its breath until the gentry's carriages have rolled past and normal life can return to pigs and hens. The drive then ambles on up the valley to a house where Esher's canted bays have been much reduced in height, spaced out and softened. Halfpenny designed a two-storey, three-bay centrepiece with a canted bay swinging out boldly in apparent symmetry on either side (illus. 56). Topped by token battlements his elevation is dominated not only by its seventeen windows, cinquefoil-headed ogees below (Langley's plate 39), flattened ogees (plate 18) above, but also by the insistent hexagonal patterning (plate 38) of the glazing bars. Away to the right the domestic range of the earlier core retreats and advances with quiet echoes of the main façade. The porch is a jewel of Gothick invention with more plagiaristic hints of Langley's plate 49: 'An Umbrello'. Frail, curvaceous yet also angular, it demands attention where a Classical portico would be taken for granted. Inside the hall the chimneypiece subdues every other element, even the delicate cluster of columns to the double doors devised from one of Langley's often scorned but actually beautiful Gothick orders (perhaps plates 12 and 13). The chimneypiece with its overmantel rises like a church monument only cheered by its hunting trophies (illus. 57). Plates 24, 41 and 44 of Langley have all been cannibalized, but Halfpenny's result is more geometrically disturbing than any of them.

Timothy Gyde, for whom Halfpenny designed Stouts Hill, never married and is reported to have 'kept the best society in the county',[18] yet lived a scandalous life with a series of mistresses brought up from London. One of these ladies may have protested about sitting in front of a chimneypiece like some tomb escaped from the local parish church, and the drawing room to the left of the hall is delicately feminine. Its walls have joinery panels with thin Gothick arches whose profiles are carved with ribbons tied in bows. Its chimneypiece, wooden like the embattled cornice and frieze, has writhing 'raffle leaves' in the purest Rococo forms (illus. 42). It is perhaps an early work from Thomas Paty's Bristol team as Paty is known to have worked for Halfpenny in his Bristol commissions. The dining room on the other side of the hall is Classical, so the two bays keep an uneasy balance between the styles. There is also just a hint in this dining room of Chinoiserie, as the zig-zag chain motif that runs around the panels on the walls would later be illustrated in one of Halfpenny's many pattern books, his *Rural Architecture in the Chinese*

Taste of 1752. Here again the chimneypiece is Rococo with slight Gothick touches and its is interesting that this may be the first Rococo essay of the brilliant team of joiners and plasterers which would create Bristol's Royal Fort fifteen years later. The staircase, however, is not one of Halfpenny's triumphs; the steps stagger drunkenly down in a headlong flight tucked into a corner of the stair hall.

A hillside, six miles and a motorway separate Stouts Hill from the Frampton Orangery, but to go from one to the other on a late Spring day, preferably when the daffodils are over, is one of the most rewarding experiences which eighteenth-century architecture can offer. At Stouts Hill, Halfpenny had learnt the potential of a new vocabulary, one blessedly unconfined by the rules about the relationships between windows and wall surfaces or all that unproven cant of harmonic proportions which makes neo-Palladian elevations so predictable. Then at Frampton with a virgin site, the drama of water, no earlier buildings to restrict him and only a pleasure pavilion to design, he had a unique opportunity which he took with his usual (though usually entirely misplaced) confidence.

Here, for the first time, an eccentric, stylistic movement reaches high art; it is a building of quite outstanding beauty (illus. 58). Only its diminutive scale makes the accolade of greatness seem inappropriate. William Chambers's Casino at Marino House, near Dublin and Thomas Archer's garden pavilion at Wrest Park in Bedfordshire are equally memorable and complete in their concentrated design. But while they both work within the Classical conventions, Frampton creates its own rules and its own spatial disciplines. It has a lively symmetry of unexpected forms, all set, compact and eye-catching, at the end of a long straight canal.

The walls of the Orangery are, like those of Stouts Hill, crammed with ogee windows and hexagonal glazing. The difference lies in the tight, satisfying composition of the three interacting octagons which contain them. Two face down the canal, the other, a little taller and topped by a small, impudent cupola, rises behind them and saves the Orangery from Stouts Hill's tendency to inconsequential sprawl. The curving forms of the ogees soften and contradict the geometry of the canted bays. The pavilion may well have served literally as an orangery or green house as it welcomes sunlight into its rooms from every angle. It hints at a church, wears castle pie-crust battlements and never quite admits to domesticity, but it is just this elusive, allusive character which makes it memorable. Pleasure has no precise identity, yet the Orangery makes it perfectly plain that pleasure is its function. An octagon is a favourite Classical form, ogees are Gothick, and here the two unite in a very insular Rococo. On this showing the style can create movingly beautiful buildings, which are likely always to hover on the edge of the absurd.

Applied on too grand or too repetitive a scale, as they probably were at Esher, and as they certainly were at Woodside, Berkshire, a three-storey thirteen-bay monster,[19] Gothick details look gauche. Like some zany barracks or mental home they then invite demolition. One thirteen-bay Gothick giant has survived in Ireland: Moore Abbey, Lord Drogheda's former seat at Monasterevin, County Kildare.[20] Significantly this owes its preservation to a religious order which uses it as a hospital, a grey, cold, charmless block. Rococo-Gothick design needs to be intimate and engaging, as with Halfpenny's work or Speedwell Castle, an enchanting gate-tower house dropped down casually into the main street of Brewood, Staffordshire (illus. 59). At Stourbridge in neighbouring Worcestershire a whole range of houses has taken the advantage of the canted bay but then played stylistic games with the fenestration, some Gothick, some Classical, a true hybrid of the brief Rococo-Gothick era (illus. 43). The style had no wide range of mood; it could not suggest the solemn or the tranquil; but with dash, with the right scale and the right setting it could produce the occasional cheerful marvel.

In the essential spirit of Halfpenny's frivolous masterpiece at Frampton there is a row of steps leading down from it into the long canal, as if Neptune

43 Gothick and
Classical Houses in the
same terrace at
Stourbridge,
Worcestershire.

or some Severn-side water nymph were expected to walk up and pay a visit.
For their front door Halfpenny stole another section from Langley's plate 56,
enriching its side panels a little. The interior rooms are more chastely elegant
than might be expected, but the stairs in that rear octagon swirl with a lean
economy, and for one of his chimneypieces Halfpenny has ingeniously cut
out the top and bottom sections of Langley's plate 41 and stuck them together to make it look like his own design.

The man who took the considerable risk of commissioning Halfpenny,
that loose cannon among builders, to design the Orangery was Richard
Clutterbuck. His family and the Gydes were connected by marriages and
both Clutterbuck and Timothy Gyde were lifelong bachelors, the eldest sons
of Cotswold wool merchants, but unlike Gyde, Richard Clutterbuck died
wealthy. He had been an official in the Bristol customs house who, four
years after inheriting the Frampton estate in 1727, completely rebuilt
Frampton Court in an adventurous compromise style, part Baroque, part
neo-Palladian, with errant touches of Vanbrugh in the arched chimney-
stacks. So he was a patron prepared to take stylistic risks. As the Orangery is
probably the most successful 'Rococo' exterior ever built in England, the
question naturally arises: why so far away from London and, if it was a
building of the 1740s like Stouts Hill, why so early? In fact neither of these
two Halfpenny designs is quite as isolated as might at first appear. They
were part of a whimsical fashion for the Rococo-Gothick and later for the
purer Rococo which was beginning to focus around the West Country in
general and Bristol in particular.

44 Detail of a transept at Shobdon Church, Herefordshire (1746).

Typically Kent was involved. After his bold, crude Gothick at Esher in 1733 he had been experimenting with the Rococo-Gothick. Merlin's Cave, a park building which he designed at Richmond for Queen Caroline in 1735, had a rough Gothick interior,[21] whereas the Hermitage in the same park had an interior as inventively Rococo as anything in France.[22] Then came a Gothick screen in 1739 for the Courts of Chancery in Westminster Hall and a tremendous, yet playful, canopied Gothick pulpit for York Minster.[23] That commission led to another in 1741 for Gloucester cathedral, perfectly tuned to stir the interest of Timothy Gyde in the new style. This was a choir screen of three ogee arches supported on twin Corinthian columns and encrusted with Kent's favourite acanthus cresting.[24] It carried more ogees, vases, pineapples and colonettes, pure stage scenery for a Saxon operetta and entirely inappropriate to Gloucester's lumbering Norman nave. Inevitably it would be demolished in 1820, but long before that it had given Kent another and even more unfortunate ecclesiastical commission.

This was for an entire new church at Shobdon in Herefordshire. In 1746, close to the probable date of Halfpenny's Orangery, the Hon Richard Bateman, Horace Walpole's friend 'Dickie', the Chinoiserie enthusiast, persuaded Kent to design a Rococo-Gothick church for his nephew Lord Bateman. This was to replace the most important Romanesque church in

Herefordshire which the Batemans had decided to pull down and use as a park folly, a piece of gross vandalism. Obviously a Chinese pagoda would have been dysfunctional for Anglican services so for Bateman the Gothick best expressed his eccentric nature and Kent obliged with a design disaster (illus. 44). It was erected under the direction of another of Burlington's coterie, Henry Flitcroft, in 1752–6.[25]

Shobdon is important in the history of the Rococo-Gothick for all the wrong reasons. It was essentially a one-off, an irresponsible exploration of possibilities. Everyone who visits it is delighted by its charm, no one remarks on what a dead-end the building represents. In Shobdon Kent pressed the Rococo to overtake and virtually devour the Gothick. The result is a complete absence of the numinous. It does not feel like a church. Those nine suspended and acanthus crested ogee arches that should define a sanctuary are wonderfully playful, they can be sensed as mocking real Gothic forms. 'Look!' they cry, 'No hands!', and no legs either, for they never touch the floor (illus. 45). They do not support, they simply divert the eye. The interior has been compared to a sacred drawing room and certainly it is full of engaging forms: a miniature of Kent's York pulpit, repetitious quatrefoils on the pew ends, ogees everywhere on the pews and windows, and dangling playfully from the ceiling. But it is, in the end, neither sacred nor a drawing room. Kent needed a controller and Richard Bateman, if his Chinese activities at Old Windsor, as reported by Bishop Pococke and drawn by Thomas Robins are anything to go by,[26] was an exhibitionist, obviously in no need of Walpole to convert him to an exhibitionist's style. On the Continent, in Swabia and Switzerland, Rococo builders and, above all, decorators could raise great churches that bring pilgrims to their knees, spaces alive with

decorative forms but still holy. Wrecked artistically by the Reformation, England had none of the resources of faith, as expressed in painting and stucco work, which the south Germans could command. But Kent could have done something much more functional at Shobdon even with his limited resources. It is a memorable building but no sincere Christian would ever want to copy it. Today it survives as a curiosity, amusing for agnostics but faintly sinister for all its frolicsome airs – a church out of M. R. James's *Ghost Stories of an Antiquary*, haunted by Dickie Bateman's camp laughter.

Even before this piece of mild architectural blasphemy had been realized by the dutiful Flitcroft, a young Surveyor to the fabric of Westminster Abbey, Henry Keene, had demonstrated that the functional way ahead for a religious building might well be Gothick, but not Rococo-Gothick. His chapel of 1750 for the Bishop of Worcester at Hartlebury Castle has ogee arches and quatrefoils, but its Y-tracery windows, simplified fan vaulting (in plaster) and cusped panelling behind the pews are spare and sober with no hint of Rococo levity (illus. 46). Yet Bishop Maddox's drawing room has walls decorated with airy and gracefully wilful Rococo compartments of papier mâché. At Shobdon Kent had tried to fuse the Gothick and the

47 Henry Keene's vault
at Hartwell Church,
Buckinghamshire,
before its collapse.

Rococo and failed, at Hartlebury Keene wisely reserved the styles for their
proper functions. Then between 1753 and 1755 his church of St Mary,
Hartwell, Buckinghamshire rose, Rococo only in its octagonal plan, while its
impressive plaster fan vaulting edged very near to an authentic Gothic
Revival piece by its scholarly detail and ambitious span (illus. 47).[27] Ulti-
mately even Richard Bateman would give in to stylistic correctness, reject
Richard Bentley's elegantly thin Gothick design for a cloister at his house
in Old Windsor and adopt an exquisite, far too perfect, design of 1759 in
Decorated Gothic from the awesomely well informed, deeply unattractive
German-Swiss observer of English amateurism, Johan Heinrich Müntz.[28]
Müntz had appeared at Strawberry Hill in 1755, a cuckoo in that Gothick
nest introduced to Walpole, ironically, by Bentley whom he proceeded to
supplant. Müntz was an icily accurate draughtsman who could make a
church design look as if a computer had produced it; scholarly and ambitious,
Müntz was also, if Walpole is to be believed, a lecher after kitchen maids.
With his arrival a professional was knocking at the door of the antiquaries
and the days of the Gothick, while not yet ended, were certainly numbered.

It was always in danger of being overtaken by scholarship and abandoned
by invention. Two houses in the Midlands range, Arbury Hall and Alscot
Park, both in Warwickshire, illustrate the Rococo-Gothic's precarious but

rewarding tight-rope act between charm and tedium. Arbury, Sir Roger Newdigate's house, was too long in building, it took from 1750 to the 1780s, and Newdigate was altogether too serious in his medievalism, too inclined to gather experts like Keene around him. The rooms of the house phase from the enchantingly incompetent Library to the over-authentic Saloon with its sumptuous fan vaulting and bare walls: more Gothic than Gothick, and certainly not Rococo.

Alscot was also begun in 1750 but completed in the nick of time, 1765, before seriousness set in. Its owner James West was an antiquarian, like Newdigate, but too preoccupied for many years, as Joint Secretary to the Treasury, to take his little summer residence by the Stour too seriously. The result was two distinct building periods (1750–2 and 1762–5), both blessed, not by experts, but by a genuine family of medieval survival builders, the Woodwards – Thomas, Edward and Richard – from Chipping Campden and the conservative Cotswold tradition. Their first Gothick wing for West has miniature rooms and a charming Rococo-Gothick staircase with plaster-work and Rococo scroll ironwork (illus. 60) but when West retired in 1762 he made his home a full time hobby. Then the balance swung away from Gothick to a rich but still light-hearted Rococo with three state rooms behind an engagingly gawky south front, grander in scale though still stylistically irresponsible. Alscot's new Drawing Room may, like Arbury's Saloon, have fan vaulting, but it has been squashed absurdly flat and executed in Thomas Bromwich's papier mâché. The Hall has elegantly spiny Gothick plaster arcading, a Rococo frieze and two exotic chimneypieces where Langley's simplicities have been happily corrupted by Rococo rose trails and formal busts of Shakespeare and Prior (illus. 61). The plaster overmantels have details taken from contemporary cabinet makers' pattern books, such as Ince and Mayhew's *A Universal System of Household Furniture* (1762). At Alscot the two styles have reached a perfect fifty–fifty equipoise, beyond which neither should ever have gone.

CHAPTER VI

BRISTOL – THE UNSOPHISTICATED CITY

William Kent's stimulating but ill-considered activity in the West was only one factor in the stylistic libertarianism which produced Stouts Hill and the Frampton Orangery. For some years before 1743 William Halfpenny had been working, or fretfully trying to drum up work, in Bristol which was at that time Britain's second city as measured by wealth and population. In its peculiarly provincial, intensely mercantile, sub-culture he had been to some extent shielded from the mainstream of architectural fashion. And as a pineapple can be persuaded to bear fruit in a hot-bed of horse manure, so the Rococo flourished unexpectedly in that unlikely city, a major port but situated six miles from the sea up a narrow, winding gorge and handicapped by a 45 foot tidal range (illus. 48).

Then, as now, Bristol was an oddball among English cities, a contentedly philistine place, industrial in the midst of the rural West Country. Bath, ten miles up river, had always tended to draw away the gentry and nobility leaving Bristol's élite a perverse and clubbable group of merchants which supplied that element of the unpredictable that runs through the city's history. They appear, for instance, to have discovered America some years before Columbus but, like the Portuguese, kept quiet about it because they were only interested in salted cod. Alone among England's large medieval towns Bristol had no cathedral, yet when Henry VIII gave them one, the citizens allowed the diocese to lapse several times, subsumed within the neighbouring Gloucester diocese; such was their indifference, and such the bishop's low salary.

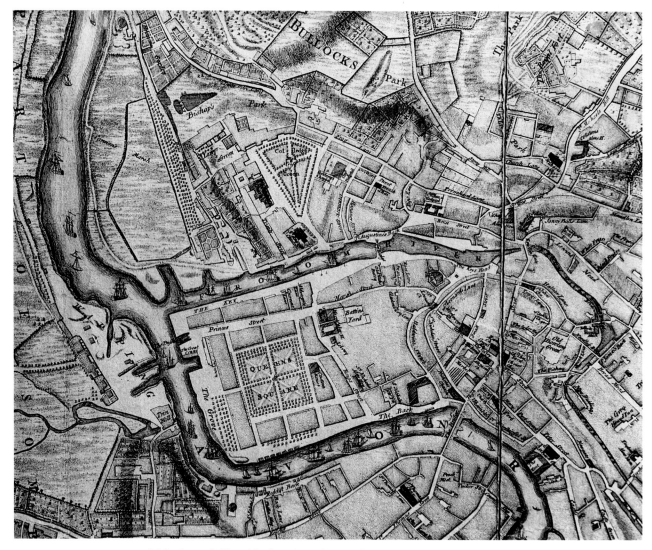

48 John Rocque's *Plan of the City of Bristol* (1743), illustrating the relationship of Queen Square with the quays.

Architecturally the city has this same record of the unexpected. In 1298 its priory church of St Augustine was rebuilt in a dazzling and completely innovatory hall church style with extraordinary vaulting. But no one ever bothered to copy it and Bristol never bothered to finish it until six hundred years later. Instead, lacking a real cathedral, the citizenry built a miniature one, complete in almost every detail, but only two-thirds the normal size. This is St Mary Redcliffe whose interior would look tremendous if only the average height of the congregation was 3 foot 6 inches. The effect is one of rich claustrophobia in a very grand toy.

In 1635 the city had its chance to equal and even surpass London in its Classicism; and blew it. The Smyths of Ashton Court, a large house over-looking the docks, persuaded someone, almost certainly an architect working in the Stuart court, to design a palatial façade of pedimented windows for their existing south-west wing. Unfortunately, though not unexpectedly, they hired a local builder to apply it and make the windows fit the rooms rather than vice versa. What could have rivalled the Whitehall Banqueting House ended up looking like a botched compromise, which is what it is.

By 1699 the City Council's habit of celebrating the banishment of a Stuart or the declaration of a new war with France by drinking two gallons (not pints) of sherry in an evening had brought them into debt. Silver trumpets had to be sold and replaced with ones of copper but that was not enough. John Romsey, the Town Clerk, raised another £1,900 by offering high civic offices to Quakers and then fining them because their religion obliged them to refuse to swear oaths, civic or otherwise. But by 1699 the Council debt still stood at £16,000 so Romsey produced another scheme for salvation. He took over the citizens' favourite recreational area, The Marsh, where they were accustomed to play bowls of an evening, and offered the land for building plots on 53-year leases, the ground rents to bring in a handsome yearly sum to pay for future drink and good fellowship. There was a rush to take the leases on what was proposed as an enormous urban square, many of the plots boasting mooring rights on the quays adjacent to their back courtyards.

Disastrously however, Romsey, who may have had a friend who owned Bristol's one and only brick kiln, stipulated in the leases that each new house should be brick built. Bristol had a wealth of craftsmen in stone and wood but virtually none in brick. As a result the city's new superior residential Queen Square was edged with houses designed in a naïve Quaker Baroque. They would have been considered old-fashioned in London and the quality of both the brickwork and the mortaring in the surviving houses leaves much to be desired, but Bristol was proud of them (illus. 49).

Within this unusual sequence of eccentric folly and an experimental excellence against the contemporary grain, Bristol's Rococo years take their natural place, and so too does William Halfpenny. It is not known where or when he was born, but it is typical of his uneven life saga that when he died in 1755 he left a son, John, who continued to work and design exactly as if his father were still alive. If William's life is traced from one gallant failure to another it appears that he was Yorkshire by birth, a carpenter by trade, but an able mathematician with a talent for writing clear, simple do-it-yourself guides for journeyman builders. He published at least 23 of these, several of them going through a number of editions as proof of their popularity and influence. In many ways he was another Batty Langley, but without Langley's London power base and consequently even more open-minded to alternative styles. In a Britain where the monarchy had been too cheeseparing or distracted to found an Academy or School of Arts, amateurs like Halfpenny took their chances.

He made his first effort at creative pilfering in 1723 by offering a design for Holy Trinity, Leeds with a spire modelled on the Mausoleum at Halicarnassus, a straight take from Nicholas Hawksmoor's St George's, Bloomsbury. This was rejected, as was another design for a bridge over the Thames. Then in 1731 Halfpenny came to Bristol hoping to flatter its citizenry into giving him work by including in his latest book, *Perspective Made Easy*, a pull-out illustration of Queen Square, their civic pride. As a bonus he also offered a design for a new Bristol Corn Exchange, a project which the city had been toying with since 1717. His Exchange would have been topped by two separate clock towers, each telling a different time, and an onion dome which changed its mind half way, turning into an obelisk. Predictably it was not built.[1]

Bristol in that year of Halfpenny's arrival must have presented an uninspiring scene. Alexander Pope described it as:

> very unpleasant, and no civilized company in it. The streets are as crowded as London; but the best image I can give of it, 'tis as if Wapping and Southwark were ten times bigger.[2]

For Horace Walpole it would be 'the dirtiest great shop I ever saw'[3]; while earlier Samuel Pepys had been shocked by the locals' consumption of alcohol and by a permanently corrupt city council, which seemed to stagger from one drunken civic orgy to another. The city's builders appeared not to have heard of Palladianism and its new houses, like those which still survive around Orchard Street, were gaunt brick boxes with the occasional grotesque mask carved on the keystones of their windows. Pent in on the level ground where the Avon and the Frome meet, the city lived within an acrid cloud of smoke thrown out from glass works, brass foundries, sugar refineries, ironworks and suburban collieries. For more than half of each day retreating tides exposed stinking mud banks, where ships lay on their sides like so many drunken aldermen. Only a skyline of fine, but blackened, medieval towers and one elegant Wren-style cupola redeemed the place; it was not, in 1731 at least, a city much interested in architects, tried or untried.

Finding no response to his little publication Halfpenny followed the course taken by many Bristolians in search of fortune. He took ship to Ireland. The links between Bristol and the other island had been close ever since Henry II, in a grand gesture, gave Dublin to the men of Bristol back in the twelfth century. That particular gift had been long rescinded, but Bristol's trade with Ireland was still flourishing and parasitic. In its nervous fear of Ireland's cheaper labour and rising productivity the British Parliament had obliged Irish traders to import and export only through England, which meant, for the most part, through Bristol. In 1731 the Merchant Venturers of Bristol had persuaded Parliament to veto a proposal to allow Ireland to import its raw sugar cane directly from America because sugar refining was a major Bristol industry and all Ireland's sugar had to come from Bristol. Irish glass could not be exported directly abroad, Irish woollens could not be imported and Irish butter was only allowed in if it was first mixed with dirt and used in the manufacture of baize. Bristol ships, some eighty to ninety in number, traded regularly across to Dublin and the southern Irish ports – Waterford, Cork, Youghal and Kinsale – carrying manufactured goods and colonial produce, taking back salt beef and pork, linen, yarn, hides and timber. Or they would pick up Irish farm produce at

Cork, go on to Portugal for wine, cross with that to America's southern colonies for sugar cane and so back again to Bristol; the merchants of Cork taking 2 per cent on the deal. With all this and the slave trade Bristol was prospering mightily, 'Here', it was said, 'the very clergy talk of nothing but trade and how to turn a penny'.[4] And of all British cities it was certainly the one with the strongest Irish connection.

Not that Halfpenny particularly benefited from the connection, but in 1732 he did design 'a horse barracks' for Viscount Hillsborough in County Down. He must have spent several years in Ireland making some professional contacts there, as in 1739 he submitted two terrible designs to the Chapter of Waterford for a new cathedral: unpleasant proposals for a squat, cross-planned structure with some Gothick tracery and other windows of Classical form with Gibbs surrounds.[5] Waterford would have been an easy port from which to take a ship back to Bristol, as he seems to have done at least once. Two outrageously individual but very enjoyable houses – 59 Queen Charlotte Street in Bristol and Rosewell House in Bath display so many of the little tricks, fussy window aprons, caryatid or 'termani' pilasters and window architraves, that feature in his pattern books, that they can be confidently attributed to him.[6] Rosewell House must have shocked polite Bath. The central window in its attic floor seems to have escaped from imperial Vienna and could, though only charitably, be described as Rococo (illus. 62). A grotesque cartouche sits on its keystone while C scrolls and crude rocaille work stream down its architraves to conclude in two cabbage-shaped rosettes. Whatever stylistic hints he may have picked up in Dublin, Halfpenny cannot have been impressed by the ruthlessly plain Protestant façades of its town houses. Rosewell House is pure Middle European, so much so as to suggest Halfpenny may have travelled abroad in the Rococo heartlands.

In 1740 Halfpenny's luck was beginning to turn. Although none of his Corn Exchange designs were accepted by the Council, the city was beginning to stir in its self-satisfied architectural torpor. Richard Bayly employed Halfpenny to add an almost conventional Palladian frontispiece to his property at 40 Prince Street and then, in 1742, Halfpenny had his first real opportunity when he took over the work on the Redland Chapel after the death of John Strahan.

The Chapel is a puzzle in more ways than one. Halfpenny was paid at such a miserable rate, agreeing on 22 May 1742 'to See the Whole Compleated for the Sum of ten pounds ten shillings',[7] that it is hard to believe that he would have done much to shape the building. On the other hand the design of the Chapel's cupola is ingenious in a very Halfpenny style, and one of his

50 Redland Chapel, Bristol (1740–3), the exterior by John Strahan, the cupola possibly by William Halfpenny.

pattern books does feature a gadrooned cap like the one which sits pertly over the octagon, vases and square base of the tower (illus. 50). He had just been disappointed when, after all his projects, the Council had given John Wood of Bath the commission to build its long postponed Corn Exchange, so he may have decided to use the Redland Chapel supervision to show the city what it had missed. Two boldly modelled blackamoor heads on the Chapel's east end are another bizarre and Halfpenny-style feature.

But it is the interior of the Chapel which is so stylistically evasive and here Halfpenny must have been in charge of the entire fitting-up process from 1742 to 1747, directing the Paty firm in its carving and plasterwork. No one would question the superb quality of the oak and limewood carving which enriches the Chapel's sanctuary (illus. 51), the question is whether to describe it as Baroque or Rococo. Fourteen broad wooden trails, each some 12 feet long, flow down the sides of the apse from cornice to dado and each trail is clustered for its whole length with an elegant profusion of ecclesiastical oddments. In among the usual fruit and flowers, far more flowers than fruit, are bishops' mitres, scrolls of the law, torches, long trumpets and cornucopia, modelled in deep relief, yet all, and this is what tips the balance of judgement towards the Rococo, all oddly stylized and subtly flattened into a harmonious union of what should be figuratively disparate (illus. 52). The Patys are said, though on no written evidence, to have based their carving skills on a

magnificent lime and pearwood overmantel once in the City Library in King Street.[8] This has all the usual Grinling Gibbons-type delicacy of dead birds, lily of the valley flowers and opening rose buds. But these great trails in the Redland sanctuary are different; they are bolder, more deliberately united in their composition, not undercut so deeply but styled to make a visual pattern when seen from the pews in the nave.

Bristol had a rich tradition of late seventeenth/early eighteenth-century woodcarving which, for want of a more precise and insular term, has to be called Baroque. The same carvers worked on church reredoses and domestic overmantels, the one in the City Library is far more likely to be local work than a Gibbons carving. A standard domestic design was of a chimneypiece, severely cut from Hotwells 'marble', which did not take fine detail. This was inset with blue Bristol Delft tiles and topped by a broad picture frame crammed with feathered corpses, pears and gourds. One of about 1725 in the Mahogany Parlour at Goldney House, Clifton may mark a half-way stage towards the Redland sanctuary's near-Rococo with oddly flattened loops of guilloche carving.[9] These recur in perhaps the most memorable feature of the Redland composition as a bold dado frieze of guilloche quite

52 Carving in the
Sanctuary of Redland
Chapel, Bristol: a
Rococo flow to
Palladian forms.

unlike any conventional Vitruvian scroll, with just the occasional acanthus
leaves curling delicately from the firmly flattened ribbons of lime wood that
make a clear rhythm proud over the dark oak. Beneath them are curtains of
wood tied up with wooden ribbons, a light feminine feature which is again
more Rococo in spirit.

The strangest feature of all in the Chapel is the altar table, so sensuous and
unholy that it has to be covered up with an altar cloth during services (illus.
63). Two boldly breasted harpies support it at either side and in the middle a
William Kent-style eagle spreads his golden wings, but not far enough to hide
the two ladies. Batty Langley illustrates similar harpy tables in his *The City
and Country Builder's and Workman's Treasury of Designs* of 1740,[10] so
Halfpenny was at least thoroughly modish in his borrowings. John Cossins,
the wealthy London grocer who built Redland Court in 1735 for his retirement, and the Chapel (1740–3) for credit in the afterlife, cannot have objected
to the harpies as his bust, and that of his wife, both by J. M. Rysbrack, look
straight down at the altar from their niches at the west end. The heads of
sixteen wondering cherubs gaze across at each other from the Chapel's north
and south walls lending the whole beautiful preaching space a curious air of
watchfulness. As a final theatrical touch, high above the harpy altar in a
semi-circular recess the hand of God is painted as if raising a curtain from
behind which blazes a celestial light. It is all as successful and functional as

Shobdon was inappropriate. It is not, however, possible to describe that enrichment of carving about the sanctuary as purely Rococo or purely Baroque, only as purely Bristol, an edging towards that confident Rococo work which the Patys would be executing ten or perhaps fifteen years later with encouragement from Dublin's example. Halfpenny's role in its design is not recorded.

It is still possible in Bristol, despite the destruction of the city's eighteenth-century fabric in the post-war years, to recreate the stylistic climate in which Halfpenny must have lived while he was designing Stouts Hill and the Frampton Orangery. The Redland Chapel records the taste of a rich and self-important old merchant, someone of the city's upper class, caught on the cusp of England's changing Classicism. Similarly, that Corn Exchange which Halfpenny had tried so hard to design, is another witness to Bristol's craftsmen-led drift into the Rococo. Its architect, John Wood of Bath, was a strict Palladian and a worshipper, only just this side of idolatry, of Inigo Jones. But even he, caught up in Bristol's insidious airs where, unlike Bath, skilled craftsmen were two-a-penny, allowed Thomas Paty's team of stone carvers to hang great limestone garlands of fruit and flowers between busts of men and heads of beasts as an exotic Corinthian frieze to his Exchange.

That was on the main street façade. In the market court behind the building Paty's team went much further, in a populist display of the birds and beasts of those continents from which the city drew its trading wealth. A whole bucolic carnival of natural life with camels, alligators, giraffes and Indians in feathered head-dresses is grouped between the market's Corinthian columns carved in bold relief, brightly painted now, as possibly it always has been (illus. 127). Can this be seen as a manifestation of Bristol's own rough proto-Rococo? Louis XV's silversmith, Juste-Aurèle Meissonier, created a soup tureen in the form of ducks, snails and artichokes resting upon cabbage leaves, onions and parsnips. It is now rightly accepted as a masterpiece of Rococo figurative work, the real world absorbed into art.[11] Were the Patys' alligators and giraffes any different? They stemmed from that same Rococo impulse to enliven Palladian Classicism with reality. Bristol had what Bath would always lack: a wealth of craftsmen in wood, stone and plaster, a social by-product of its teeming industries. There were 63 'tylers and plaisterers' on its 1754 list of freemen. So it was philistine Bristol rather than refined Bath which moved naturally towards a populist style dependent upon cheap, skilled craftsmen who were not too concerned with academic correctness.

Bristol's Guinea Street preserves this process. It is a steep little road which runs down to the inner harbour near Redcliffe church and was consequently a favourite residential area for sea captains. 10 Guinea Street was converted in 1744 from a larger house of 1718 and all the secondary decoration is Rococo. The chimneypiece frieze in its modest front parlour has bold Rococo S and C scrolls almost identical to those on the chimneypiece at Stouts Hill. In its back parlour an overmantel has been concocted by some decorator who had heard that styles were changing but had yet to work out precisely how the details should be arranged. On each side of the picture frame are slender colonettes and an upright supporting scroll of very French looking, highly stylized acanthus. These are the 'raffle leaves' that were to fill Isaac Ware with such alarm in his 1756 *Complete Body of Architecture*, but which obviously pleased the sea captain who was up-dating the house in 1744. Privateering was even more profitable than the slave trade. In 1746 the 'Southwell' privateer took three prizes in three weeks, one worth £14,000 (multiply by eighty for modern values), the 'Prince Charles' took two Greenlanders with seven whales and the 'Queen of Hungary' took one prize worth £20,000.[12] Sea captains could afford any number of new Rococo overmantels.

Down Guinea Street at number 5, in a house which he had built for himself in 1740, lived Joseph Thomas, at that time probably Bristol's leading plasterer. Isaac Ware would employ him between 1747 and 1750 at Clifton Hill House. Number 5 fell to the post-war municipal wreckers, but before it went, Walter Ison recorded a detail of the ceiling which Thomas had created for his own front parlour.[13] No mere acanthus scrolls this time but a sophisticated asymmetrical frame, jauntily set with fruit and flowers struck out at perverse angles, and perched upon one of them sat a squirrel nibbling a nut, its bushy tail perfectly reflecting the C scroll behind it, an elegant and typically Rococo device. It is unfortunate that this small passage of plasterwork has been destroyed and that it cannot be exactly dated; it is as assured in its composition as a Rococo bookplate or tradesman's card. Squirrels, monkeys and little agile animals were a favourite motif in the work of Jean Bérain (1640–1711), the French proto-Rococo artist and designer. Bérain's grotesqueries and his termini figures, half-naked boys or girls rising from sheath-like forms are always seen as an important half-way stage between the relatively formal Classicism of Louis XIV's reign and the full-blown Rococo of Louis XV. So if Joseph Thomas was ornamenting his own house with such a motif as early as 1740 that means he was already a confident Rococo artist before Isaac Ware, the Palladian, employed him seven years later. In his *Complete Body of Architecture* Ware reluctantly accepts that such termini figures must be used, 'the art will be to receive these ornaments with discretion, to adapt them to the few uses for which they are proper'.[14]

The squirrel has gone, but a greater treasure of these 1740s has survived. The great Victorian church architect Sir Gilbert Scott recorded in his *Recollections* how, as a boy, he once visited Chetwode church in Buckinghamshire and found it locked. But putting his eye to the keyhole he saw there for the first time in his life a tiny vista of very pure, etiolated Early English lancets at the east end. He was so excited that for days he could think of little else. While in no way comparing themselves to Sir Giles, the authors of this book had a similar intoxicating keyhole experience of the Rococo in Bristol. Hearing on the architectural grapevine that there was sensational plasterwork at 15 Orchard Street, one of those gaunt, basic Classical terraced houses that were built in some numbers around 1710–20 just behind the bustling quays, we went one morning to investigate. The house was completely empty and locked but there, as at Chetwode church, was a keyhole and through that could be glimpsed, unforgettably, the bend of a ramped and panelled staircase alive with a confined richness of plasterwork in that bold relief which distinguishes Rococo work from Robert Adam's later, meagre 'sippets of gingerbread' mouldings.

Some months later, when the house had been immaculately restored and had become a quietly functioning office, we got in and found a minor masterpiece of the plasterer's art, almost certainly from Joseph Thomas's own, squirrel-designing hand: a disturbing testimony to the artisan riches which must once have been a common possession of that apparently philistine Bristol middle class (illus. 3).

The 1740s redecoration of the staircase at 15 Orchard Street is not high art. It is something much more important. Here beauty was in danger of being made a common and accessible domestic property. Rococo subjects and Rococo methods had put creativity within the reach of any one of those 63 Bristol 'tylers and plaisterers'. It is the sheer profusion, not just of decorative detail, swags of roses, heaped pomegranates and pears, which is so enjoyable, but the suggestive images. The Rococo could and often did tell stories, Aesop's fables were a standard, but here in Orchard Street the plasterers hinted delightfully at a story and left anyone climbing the stairs to do the rest. French stylization and Italian figurative invention were absorbed in a cheerful artisan narrative. In among the elegant asymmetries of acanthus and rocaille are three bearded mandarins, each with a different triple-pointed hat, their moustaches entwined with the S and C scrolls. In another compartment a pretty Chinese peasant girl (illus. 53) with a dimpled chin wears a palm leaf hat from which roses and bays rise up improbably. A fat eagle spreads his wings above her and higher again, to leave no wall space

53 Woman and bird in the Chinese Rococo detail on the Stair-Hall at 15 Orchard Street, Bristol.

vacant, the perverse acanthus sprays soar up to the sloping ceiling. Next is a squirrel (illus. 64), the original Bérain motif picked up by Joseph Thomas for his own house in Guinea Street; he nibbles acorns irrelevantly below a presiding mandarin; it is fantasy-land on the way to bed.

The master plasterer, Thomas or whoever, allowed his apprentices to work the last two of the six set-pieces. Their frames are simpler, the tortuosities less confident. One pheasant is unambitious, the other has lost its tail. Lower down the stairs the dragons pecked cheekily at the fruit above them (illus. 54), here the birds simply perch. The artifice is faltering on the route to the second floor servants' bedrooms.

This modest but rewarding and inventive work in an ordinary middle-class Bristol home is arguably superior to either the formal Palladian plasterwork which preceded it or the delicate scribbles of moulded work which Robert Adam persuaded the English and, more tragically, the Irish to adopt in its place. Here the craftsman's hand, eye and individuality can be appreciated, yet the stylized framing in its sinuous confidence prevents the design from being described as naïve or untutored.

The question as to where all this Rococo inspiration came from has yet to be settled. Was it of purely Bristol inspiration or was there direct influence

54 Dragons eating peaches at 15 Orchard Street, Bristol.

from overseas to this trading city? The time has come to follow William Halfpenny on that 1732 voyage across St George's Channel to Ireland, England's tense and nervously subordinate third kingdom. Bristol did not only export sugar to Ireland and the Irish did not only export leather, linen, salted pork and dirty butter to Bristol. There was also an artistic exchange in which Ireland may have given much more than it received. In the best sense of the term, Bristol could have become for a time Ireland's cultural colony.

CHAPTER VII

DUBLIN –
THE PROTESTANT
CITY

Aside from being one of Europe's most humanely planned and accessible capital cities, Dublin's disturbing attraction for any English architectural historian is the impression which it gives of being a great and historic English city but existing in a time warp. More precisely it seems to lie in one of those alternative parallel universes that science fiction writers often invent, where everything is basically the same but subtle twists of past history have resulted in unforeseen possibilities. Here in Dublin is an England where the Reformation never quite happened, where an Industrial Revolution ran out of raw materials and where German bombers never tore out the historic heart to give city planners their dreadful openings. But for this present study the real interest in Dublin's alternative world is that here, in an apparently English eighteenth-century city, Palladian predictabilities were kept on a tight leash and the Rococo was given its natural 30-year run of gloriously inventive interior decoration.

History is inescapable in Ireland but its end products in brick and stone are more satisfying than any melancholy record of prejudice and brutality. Very briefly, to understand the flowering of the Rococo and to explain the extraordinary Protestant Herrenvolk, that Ascendancy which ran Ireland and Dublin as a gentleman's club for the whole of the eighteenth century, the best place to begin is in 1685. That was when James II succeeded his brother Charles as King of England, Scotland and Ireland, those three far from united kingdoms. Until then, under the tolerant rule of Viceroys like James

Butler, first Duke of Ormonde and a native Irishman, there had been a reasonable chance that the Catholic majority and the Protestant minority (a mere 10 per cent of the population) might come to co-exist and ultimately forget the injustices of Cromwell's brutal conquest and re-settlement. Ormonde had been reared as a Protestant but all his relatives were Catholics and his sententious aphorism: 'I am taught by nature, and also by instruction, that difference in opinion concerning matters of religion dissolves not obligations of nature' might with profit have been carved over the doors of every church and chapel in Ireland.

By the time Ormonde proclaimed James's accession to the throne Dublin's population had risen from a low of some 9,000 in the Cromwellian aftermath of 1660 to a healthier 58,000, and with 91 breweries the city was well on the road to peace-time normality. It was still a clutter of narrow streets gathered on the south bank of the tidal Liffey, a river a quarter of the width of the Thames at London, but navigable to the city centre. There were two small, ugly cathedrals – Christchurch and St Patrick's – a scatter of city churches, recently rebuilt with rough Gothic towers, and there was Dublin Castle, the seat of executive power and the Viceroy's residence when he was not taking refuge from the bad airs of the city in his country seat at Chapelizod a mile or two up the Liffey. Its first impressive urban project had been begun in 1680 and completed in 1684. This was the Royal Hospital for retired soldiers at Kilmainham designed by Sir William Robinson, the Surveyor General, in a pleasant lumbering sub-Wrenaissance style of round-arched loggias around a broad quadrangle. The trabeated ceiling of its chapel had richly worked wreaths and swags of plaster flowers[1] similar to those that could be found in English houses like Sudbury Hall, Derbyshire, or Holme Lacy, Herefordshire. Ireland may even at that point have been in danger of becoming a stylistic province of England.

James II changed all that. The beleaguered arrogance of the Anglo-Irish in the next century can only be understood, even to some extent appreciated, if King James's futile descent upon Ireland in 1689 is remembered. His brief reign from 1685 to 1688 had filled the Irish Protestants with forebodings of a Catholic take-over. Then, after fleeing London without putting up the least resistance to the invading forces of his daughter Mary and son-in-law William of Orange, James was persuaded by Louis XIV to try his luck in Ireland. He sailed into Kinsale harbour in March 1689 with a sizeable French army in support and soon had almost the whole island in his grasp with a 'Patriot Parliament' called to support him in Dublin. Only in Enniskillen and Derry the Protestant garrisons hung on, the Apprentice Boys of

Derry creating a legend by slamming the city's gates against a Catholic force.

With a well-timed political wit James declared that 'Our blessed saviour whippt people out of the Temple, but I never heard he commanded any should be forced into it'. That was little comfort to Protestant landowners when his Patriot Parliament passed an Act of Attainder confiscating the estates of every Protestant and reversing the whole Cromwellian resettlement. Mass was being celebrated in Christchurch and most of the bishops of the Church of Ireland had fled the country. These were the days that would haunt the Ascendancy and excuse every harshness of the subsequent Penal Code. In Ulster they are still remembered. They gave the Protestants a legend and a rallying point to make them a nation within a nation, a warrior state with a sense of purpose.

In June King William landed at Carrickfergus with a large Anglo-Dutch army and the Cogadh an Dá Rí, the War of the two Kings, began. William won a resounding victory on 1 July at the crossing of the Boyne. Dublin welcomed the victor, James fled back to France, but his Franco-Irish forces put up a spirited resistance in two hard fought battles at Athlone and Aughrim in 1691. By the time the Treaty of Limerick had been signed, allowing an honourable passage for the French and their Irish allies back to France, the whole island apart from Ulster had been subjected to pillage, skirmish and burning. In Dublin and in their ravaged towns and estates across the country the Protestant Ascendancy settled down to enjoy the luxury of revenge.

Their position was one of triumphal isolation, unloved, still endangered but amazingly self-righteous. In English eyes they were only a colonial garrison which owed its survival and its continuance to British troops. To pay for their privileged position their trade would be restricted, Irish patronage would be largely at England's disposal and all acts of the Irish Parliament would be scrutinized and, if needs be, overturned by the British government. As for the Catholics, the Protestants could take what repressive measures they pleased, though the Privy Council drew a line against Dublin proposals that priests should be branded and perhaps castrated. Successive acts of the Penal Code passed in the 1690s prevented Catholics from voting, holding a Crown office or sitting in Parliament. They were forbidden to buy or inherit land from a Protestant; they could not teach or enter a university; none of their leases could last longer than 31 years and, most divisive and cruel of all, if an eldest son in a Catholic family turned Protestant he had to inherit all his parents' property. For Edmund Burke it was, 'a machine as well fitted for the oppression, impoverishment and degradation of a people, and the debasement in them of human nature itself as ever proceeded from the perverted ingenuity of man'.

But it was a society much given to resounding, empty rhetoric. Jonathan Swift, the self-appointed scourge of Anglo-Irish hypocrisy, may, as his monument in St Patrick's cathedral claims, have gone where savage indignation could no longer tear his heart, but while that heart was still beating his savage indignation was turned against a very modest and acceptable proposal to extend full civil rights to Presbyterians as well as to members of his own well funded church. Nothing in Irish history is quite what it seems. There was an awesome certainty about the Protestant Ascendancy which has to be appreciated to understand the innovatory qualities of its architecture. One flicker of self-questioning and they would have been lost. If they kept their confidence and a garrison of 15,000 soldiers, at least 5,000 of them in the enormous Royal Barracks on the north bank of the Liffey, they were not only safe, they were prosperous. Both produce and domestic servants were far cheaper in Ireland than in Britain. As one visitor reported, 'there never was so splendid a metropolis in so poor a country'.[2] Agents on country estates squeezed the maximum rents from a peasant population towards whom their Protestant landlords felt no natural ties, only a nervous fear based on the recent hostilities. Dublin was the safe and increasingly sophisticated fortress city where those rents could be spent, not only on high living in a fast, fierce society where duelling was still a way of life, but on prestige projects of architecture, charity and education: anything which would assert the national identity of that artificial and basically insecure inner nation of the religious élite.

Typical of this process of building Dublin into a real capital was the extensive work undertaken by the new Surveyor General, Thomas Burgh, to make the Castle into a fitting seat for the Viceroy and Ireland's executive. Between 1710 and 1717, probably during the second viceregality of the 2nd Duke of Ormonde, who had squeezed £3,000 from the Treasury in London, the entire south wing of the Castle's Inner Yard was rebuilt in an improved version of a design which Robinson, the last Surveyor, had roughed out some years before in his usual homely but adequate manner of arched loggia, main floor and hipped roof, as at the Kilmainham Hospital. These additions allowed for an entrance hall and grand stairway up to the landing where the viceregal guard, armed with their traditional battle-axes, the formidable symbol of viceregal power, stood before the throne room of the Castle. At this stage, however, very little seems to have been done to fit up the State Rooms commanding the Inner Yard on the north side of the south wing over

55 Lye Farmhouse (*c.* 1750) acting as a Gothick lodge to Stouts Hill, Uley, Gloucestershire.

56 Opposite
The 1743 entrance
front of Stouts Hill,
Uley, Gloucestershire.

57 Chimneypiece in the
Hall at Stouts Hill,
Uley, Gloucestershire.

58 Rococo and Gothick in perfect balance on the Orangery, Frampton-on-Severn,
Gloucestershire (*c*.1750).

59 Speedwell Castle (1750) on the main street of Brewood, Staffordshire.

60 A staircase in the earlier Gothick wing at Alscot Park, Warwickshire (1750–2).

61 An overmantel in the Hall at Alscot Park, Warwickshire (*c.* 1763).

62 Rosewell House,
Bath (1735), a probable
design by William
Halfpenny.

63 An almost pagan altar-table in a Christian church: Redland Chapel, Bristol.

64 Plasterwork in the
Dublin spirit at
15 Orchard Street,
Bristol.

65 Edward Lovett
Pearce's Parliament
House, Dublin
(designed 1732), now
the Bank of Ireland.

66 Detail of a ceiling
by the Francini
brothers in the Saloon
of 85 St Stephen's
Green, Dublin.

67 Plasterwork in the
Stair-Hall of 15 Queen's
Square, Bath (*c.* 1730),
thought to be an early
work of the Francini
brothers.

Burgh's loggia, which were to become such an important feature in Dublin's social round, or the Hall (now St Patrick's Hall) on the first floor where balls and receptions were held.

Thomas Burgh was not the architect to supervise the fitting up of elegant drawing rooms. He had designed and built between 1701 and 1704 the enormous Royal Barracks to hold Dublin's permanent garrison of four regiments, and a Customs House in dated Carolean Classicism with a hipped roof in 1707. Then in 1712 he began a great new library for Trinity College, the first work that really marked out the determination of the Ascendancy to do anything that England, or in this particular case, Oxford and Cambridge, could do and do it better. A 270-feet monster of grey granite with a Long Room 200 feet in length, it lies across Trinity's splendid and generally decorative campus (illus. 68) like a severe reminder of academic disciplines. For two hundred years nothing of its kind in Europe would equal or even come near it. It signalled that Ireland had arrived among the learned nations.

Trinity Library was not completed until 1732; by that time the brief, mysteriously unchronicled, but entirely successful career of Edward Lovett Pearce would be at its peak. Brought up in Norfolk, Pearce would, if he had stayed in England, have had to struggle for commissions and, if he had found them, been tied down to the neo-Palladians and the envy of a dozen purveyors of Palladian conventions. But in Ireland young Captain Pearce, who had served in the army and studied architecture for two years, 1723–4, in Italy, was the golden boy of grand connections. As the Hanoverian succession began to look secure and a mild prosperity returned, owners of country

estates began to think of rebuilding their gutted houses and Pearce was, it
appears, ever ready to oblige with a quick plan and an elevation.

He was probably born in 1699 and died tragically young in 1733. His
mother was Irish and his father English, a general in the army and a second
cousin to Sir John Vanbrugh, who is assumed to have given the young Pearce
the architectural training which endowed him with a bold eclectic command
of a whole range of Classical styles – Baroque, Palladian, Antique Roman,
even, as this chapter will suggest, the Rococo. He died just a year after being
rewarded with a knighthood and £1,000 for designing the Parliament House,
that resounding symbol of Ireland's Protestant oligarchy in the heart of
Dublin (illus. 65); so an aura clings to Pearce. Architectural historians tend to
take advantage of his obscure life history to attribute to him any number of
distinctively odd houses in Ireland and England. But if only those buildings
that can be attributed with confidence to him are considered, the range is
impressive. Cashel Palace is a slick essay, almost a parody of William and
Mary Baroque for a conservative-minded Archbishop, Bellamont Forest,
Co. Carlow, is an exquisitely minimalist neo-Palladian three-parter, the
Parliament House is confidently Ancient Roman (illus. 69), much more so
than anything Lord Burlington achieved, his York Assembly Rooms
included. It escapes beyond mere Palladianism and anticipates the neo-
Classical by forty years. Such a dextrous stylistic sophisticate, the laid-back
young man whom a frustrated Mrs Pendarves once described as 'our *sleepy
lover*',[3] would have found no problem in giving one of the three State Rooms

in Dublin Castle, Ireland's first major Rococo ceiling. These rooms were, by their intensely public character, the one suite where the style could be absorbed, admired and copied by the entire fashionable world of Dublin.

The ceiling was destroyed by fire in 1941, but photographs record it (illus. 70). The flat central section was conventionally Palladian with acanthus rosettes, bay leaves and crossed palms in interlocking roundels, all echoed in the Doric frieze of the cornice. It was in the very deep coving that the detail was Rococo, the first version of a design that was to become a Dublin standard in one variant or another for the next thirty years. It consisted of swags of flower wreaths looped above a parallel design of gracefully curving acanthus trails. The one curious detail, which suggests that this was a precocious essay in the style, one still closely linked to French patterns by Jean Bérain or Nicolas Pineau, were the large, half-naked termini figures rising at intervals out of the acanthus clusters. Centrally placed on each long side of the coving the Royal Arms were flanked by more trails of acanthus.

An article entitled: 'Dublin Castle, Three Centuries of Development' by J. B. Maguire[4] has tended to throw doubt on the previous generally held belief that this room in the Castle, like its two neighbours, was by Pearce. Maguire had discovered plans and accounts dated 1758 by Joseph Jarratt, who became Deputy to the Surveyor General in 1753, indicating that Jarratt was responsible not only for the exterior façade of the south-east wing of the Upper Courtyard, but for the rooms along that south-facing side of the Castle and for the spinal corridor top-lit by glazed domes. This last had always been attributed to Pearce on its close stylistic likeness to Pearce's corridors in the Parliament House.

While John Cornforth, another Englishman straying dangerously onto Irish matters, was convinced that Pearce must have designed that south-facing east façade of the Castle, it has too light and smooth a Palladian Classicism to be a characteristic Pearce design and Jarratt was certainly its architect.[5] The spinal corridor is also his, copied from a Pearce original in the Parliament House with a heavy Vanbrughian feeling. As for the three supposedly Pearce State Rooms on the north side of that corridor, the fact that Jarratt included them in his plan is no proof that he designed them and Maguire does not make that claim. On Jarratt's plan the state rooms on the south side are given their full dimensions, whereas those on the north are unannotated. Figures emerging half-naked from sheaths of foliage are a typical feature of the grotesque work, originally Raphaelesque, that Jean Bérain, Nicolas Pineau and Gilles-Marie Oppenord included in those portfolios of designs which evolved into the full-blown Rococo. Jarratt is most

70 Pearce's ceiling, half-Palladian, half-Rococo (1730–3), in the reception rooms of Dublin Castle, destroyed in the fire of 1941.

unlikely in 1758 to have delved back into these prototypes, while between 1730 and 1733, when Pearce would have been supervising the work, they would have been an obvious model. Also a highly enriched, deep coving was a characteristic of French Rococo rooms of the 1730s, the flat of the ceiling being left bare.

Then in 1738 and 1739 came the Francini figurative ceilings which most accounts of Irish plasterwork accept as influential or even as seminal. This view ignores the fact that figurative ceilings such as those at Carton House, Co. Kildare, were rare and became rarer as the Rococo tide rose even higher. The present authors offer the opinion, very tentatively, being English and on Irish territory, that the Francini brothers have been given a little more prominence than they deserve.

The two brothers, Paolo (1695–1770) and Filippo (1702-79) were from the Ticino, that area of Italian-speaking Switzerland which bred any number of stuccodores and architects at this period. They had made their way up through Germany where Paolo had worked for the Bishop of Fulda, to England where they were employed by James Gibbs, who had himself been trained by another Ticinese, the architect Carlo Fontana. Their designs were usually figurative, bold relief panels of Classical subjects: Gods, Roman heads and riotous cherubs. Their first work in Ireland was the Dining Room in Riverstown House (illus. 71), just outside Cork, which the authors date to 1735. Then came the Saloon and Apollo Room of 85 St Stephen's Green, Dublin (illus. 66). In both Riverstown and the Apollo Room the plasterwork has been conceived as a substitute for paintings, the Classical subjects ranged out in plaster frames along the walls much in the manner of the earlier

72 Detail of the Francini ceiling in the Saloon of Carton House, Co. Kildare (1739).

Francini work in 15 Queen's Square, Bath (illus. 67). The Saloon at 85 St Stephen's Green was followed in the next year by a rather more ambitious composition on the loves of the Gods in the Saloon of Carton House (illus. 72), which had been recently rebuilt by the German architect Richard Castle in his typical pedestrian Palladian.

It is here that the problems begin: is this Francini figurative work Baroque or Rococo? And was it in any case of much relevance to the broad mainstream of Rococo work in Ireland of the 1740s, 1750s and 1760s? Figurative work tends to catch the eye and attracts scholarship, as in Joseph McDonnell's splendidly illustrated *Irish Eighteenth-Century Stuccowork and its European Sources*.[6] It is satisfying to be able to prove as he does that a detail on the Carton ceiling of Pluto and Proserpine has been freely adapted from Pietro Aquila's engraving published in 1685 after Giovanni Lanfranco's 'Council of the Gods' fresco in the Gallery of the Villa Borghese in Rome, painted in 1624–5.[7] Similarly he offers models from P. A. Maffei's *Raccolta di Statue Antiche* for all the Francini panels in the Apollo Room of 85 St Stephen's Green.[8] But is this interesting scholarship of much importance? The work in the Apollo Room is in every case far superior to Maffei's engravings; Aquila's Proserpine is quite unlike the Francini version and the pose of Pluto at Carton is much more tense than Lanfranco's god.[9] It is no proof of artistic merit if a stucco ceiling happens to lend itself to a doctoral thesis or offers distinctive incidents that can be captioned and photographed.

As for the stylistic question both ceilings are heavy in their detail but in them both the gods and the goddesses are framed and poised around equally heavy C scrolls and waving acanthus. The Ticinese may have been bucolic in their Swiss mountain origins but they were also Italians and Agostino Mitelli (1609–60) had been producing asymmetrical designs of animated S and C scrolls in Italy in the middle of the seventeenth century, long before the French movement.[10] On their way up through eighteenth-century Germany the Francini brothers would have had to be blind not to have absorbed something of the Rococo spirit and Rococo motifs. Most significantly on that Saloon ceiling at Carton, while the divinities and the cherubs may catch the eye, the main pattern around which they exercise themselves is that of Pearce's ceiling in Dublin Castle. The cherubs romp and swing above the loops of flowers and below them the amorous gods and goddesses recline between clumps of waving, broad-leafed acanthus. The pattern is beginning to oust the figurative element. While the pattern is not far from being Rococo in the French mood the ceiling has strong, crude, Italian Rococo elements which draw the attention away from the underlying French framework.

73 Detail of the ceiling of the Saloon at Tyrone House, Marlborough Street, Dublin (1740).

Then in 1740, only a year later than the Carton ceiling, came a major Dublin town palazzo: Tyrone House, Marlborough Street, built by Richard Castle for Sir Marcus Beresford, later Earl Tyrone in the second creation. Here the plasterwork of the Saloon ceiling, attributed inevitably to the Francinis is, apart from a few monster heads on the bandwork, entirely non-figurative. The cove is patterned with the waving fronds of broad-leafed acanthus under loops of wreathed flowers (illus. 73): exactly the design of the Castle ceiling but without the naïve grotesque figures emerging from acanthus sheaths. It is a cliché of modern stylistic texts that the true Rococo forms evolved out of designs by late seventeenth-century craftsmen-designers like Bérain and Pineau, but here, in the leap between that ceiling in the Castle and this surviving ceiling at Tyrone House, we have a perfect instance of the early grotesque work being stripped away and only the graceful curvaceous patterns remaining. If the Francini were responsible for the Tyrone ceiling, and the acanthus does seem to be modelled in their hard, coarse manner, then already in 1740 they had given in to the new non-figurative designs made fashionable, apparently by Pearce, at the Castle. One thing is clear

74 The Drawing Room, 9 Henrietta Street, Dublin (1729-31), showing the predictable Palladian decorative detail which the Irish soon rejected for Rococo invention.

about the Ascendancy society of Dublin at this early period. They were a united body, almost military in their social disciplines. The Viceroy represented security and salvation. He might only appear for brief visits from England but in his absence his spirit hovered over the Castle and the social round of balls and 'afternoons' held in its State Rooms continued. If the Castle went Rococo then – 'Left wheel! About turn!' – the rest of polite Protestant Dublin would follow.

If Pearce was responsible for that ceiling his own conversion is the more remarkable. At Bellamont Forest (1730) the ceilings are as crisply and conventionally Palladian as its marvellously pure exterior demands; while the interiors of 9 Henrietta Street of 1729–31, designed either by Henry Simmonds or possibly by Pearce himself, are so richly yet chillingly correct that they could be used as a model for Palladian detail with every sign of the plasterer's own invention and interpretation banished (illus. 74). To stand in its Stair-Hall is like experiencing the pages of a French illustrated manual, Antoine Desgodetz's *Les Édifices antiques de Rome* for instance, realized in perfectly moulded plaster. Whether or not Pearce was responsible for those interiors, he was the designer of its unsatisfactory and most un-Dublinesque exterior which, with its plat and sill bands and its round-arched window, stands out like a sore thumb against the gaunt minimalist restraint of the rest of the street. But then, in a typical Pearce mystery, comes the question: did he also design that gaunt minimalist restraint, as exemplified in the houses next door? Why do those plat and sill bands, which in a city like Bath would link every house into a street unity, first falter and then stop dead on the next but one house down from Number 9? Was it precisely here in Henrietta Street that Dublin's peculiar elegance, of bare proportions, white plaster window reveals to reflect the sunlight inwards and nothing else, except the door surround, was born? That extreme minimalism has to be seen as the essential Dublin Rococo exterior but it deserves an architect instead of being left with a mere general public consensus as its originator.

At Tyrone House, Irish designers had opted, through a German Huguenot architect, Richard Castle, and Italian stuccodores, for the patterns of S and C scrolls waving in a permanent Rococo wind. At Russborough, Co. Wicklow, is another Saloon ceiling of the middle 1740s attributed reliably to the Francinis. Here the same satisfying rhythm of the broad-leafed acanthus below loops of flowers fills the cove and the grotesque figures have been reduced to a few cheerful cherubs. In another sign of Rococo vitality, one absent from the Tyrone ceiling, the acanthus fronds reach out like predatory tropical creepers to overlap the compartment boundary onto the flat of the ceiling. Russborough's plasterwork will be discussed in detail in a later chapter on Irish country houses.

Joseph McDonnell describes this diminished role for figurative work as 'surprising';[11] but it is only surprising if Pearce's ceiling in the Castle is ignored. Pearce had infinitely more prestige in Ireland than the two Swiss craftsmen, and Dublin Castle was a far more impressive address than 85 St Stephen's Green or even Carton. There is always this danger of scholars becoming fixated upon any plasterwork that can be given an impressive Italian provenance. A scholarly pedigree is no proof of contemporary popularity. Indeed the very neo-Classical feeling of the panels lining the Apollo Room in 85 St Stephen's Green is an indication that in its time it would have been considered old fashioned and out of touch with Rococo vivacity and patterning. To discover the reaction of polite society in the late 1750s and 1760s to this early Francini work it is only necessary to go next door to 86 and find that in the 1760s Rococo patterning was triumphant.

What kind of society took to this Italo-French style so many years before the English had even half begun to conquer their nervous distaste for its perverse elaborations? And where did the craftsmen come from to seize the initiative from the Francini brothers and fill the Dublin ceilings with ever more ingenious and daring improvisations of acanthus, rocaille and natural forms caught up in fantasy life? No society in the United Kingdoms had been so directly threatened by the French. Only in Ireland had French troops marched, fought, been forcibly billeted on Protestant homes and, on occasion, looted them. Yet it was in Ireland in the great country houses like Russborough, Curraghmore, Co. Waterford, and Desart Court, Co. Kilkenny, and in literally countless first-floor reception rooms and stair-halls of the pre-1770 Dublin terraces that this Italo-French style was welcomed so enthusiastically. Tame Palladian details, on the other hand, were abandoned abruptly, even though they related to those English in the island next door who kept the city secure for its Protestants, so why this cultural treachery?

One obvious possibility was that many of the individual plasterers were Catholics. To a surprising degree it seems to have been left to them to negotiate the acceptability of a particular design regardless of what was being created in the room next door. Each plasterer would have his own stock of moulds, a limitation in itself, and his own particular skills in modelling, skills originally acquired, though no doubt later improved, in one of Dublin's art schools. If the teacher in the school had been French, or trained in France, then French designs would have been taught, and if the young student happened to be a Catholic or one pretending to a Protestant conversion for the convenience of the training, then the French would not have been the villainous enemy but the lost ally in the last conflict. The role of the Dublin Society's Schools will become increasingly relevant in this tracing of the Rococo. But the Society itself was not founded by a group of fourteen shrewd, well intentioned Protestants until 25 June 1731, and they did not begin to subsidize an existing art school, run by Robert West in George's Lane, by paying the fees of talented boys to study under him, until 1740.[12] Before that time notices in the *Dublin Daily Advertiser* suggest that the masters of private drawing schools advertising for students were either French or had a bias towards French instruction and that their instruction was directly relevant to plasterwork.

The *Advertiser* for 24 August 1736 offered 'Proposals for opening a Drawing School in the nature of an Academy or School of Genuine Designing by John Esdall, Painter, at his house in Crow Street. It is well known', it continued, 'that Drawing is the Mistress of all the Manual Arts and Masonry, Carving, Stucco-forming, Jewellery, Furniture and Damask weaving'.[13] A little later in the same year and in the same journal (25 November), Pierre Monade Lesat, describing himself as: 'Painter and Medalist, Member of the Royal Academy of Paris hereby advertises the Nobility and Gentry that he will teach Pupils . . . to draw from Nature, copy Curious Pieces . . . at the easiest rates.'[14] There could hardly be a better definition of the basics of Rococo design than that of 'Curious Pieces', combined with drawings 'from Nature'. From very early on in the century it was apparent that art teaching in Dublin was strictly utilitarian and commercial, training that would lead to success in a trade whether as a plasterer, a joiner, a silversmith, a jeweller or a fabric designer. That was Dublin's strength, its teachers taught art forms which would relate directly to ordinary life rather than to the production of a few highly priced artistic masterpieces to be hung on the walls of the super rich. Not only were food and domestic servants relatively cheap in Ireland, so too were the services of skilled plasterers trained in current French art. Robert West, the teacher ultimately most favoured by the Dublin Society, claimed to have trained in Paris under François Boucher (1703–70) and Carle van Loo (1705–65), though no record of any formal apprenticeship has been found. These teachers will account for the scatter of Rococo interiors created before 1740 by Irish plasterers. Clearly, when the Dublin Society moved in on this field of design, its committee members believed that they were responding to an existing luxury market. Dublin was fast becoming one of Europe's capitals of high living and Parisian fashions, regardless of whatever military threat Paris may have posed in the recent past. Confidence had become an Anglo-Irish habit and the style of the enemy was now the *dernier cri* of Dublin Castle.

CHAPTER VIII

THE PLAYGIRL
OF THE
WESTERN WORLD

The lifestyle of the Dublin élite which patronized these craftsmen and raised, as a matter of course, complex works of art in friable plaster over their reception rooms, demands respect for an uninhibited dedication to selfish pleasure. They not only patronized a Rococo art, they lived it out. If there was ever in the eighteenth century a true *douceur de la vie*, one easy and elegant yet informed, it was in Dublin in those middle decades when confidence was returning and nationalism was still subdued. Historians are rightly anxious to present a balanced view, so they report the heavy drinking, the street violence, the habit of settling the slightest of disputes by a duel; and, of course, the life of the poor in town and country was wretched. They lived precariously from famine to famine in ragged squalor, supporting the glittering edifice of gaiety and fashion above them by their miserable wages and their diet of potatoes and skimmed milk. But the edifice did really glitter and the gaiety was seductive. In Ireland, for the Protestant Ascendancy at least, this was a true golden age. Society was united in its loyalties, tightly bound about the Castle and the occasional presence of the Viceroy and his lady. Everyone knew everyone else, met often, sang, ate, drank, played cards and, above all, danced together, secure in a busy round of entertainments, ordering their clothes and planning the menus from one function to another. With ridottos, balls, charity concerts, church musics, plays, the occasional light opera, a pattern of 'at homes', receptions, presentations and Vicereine's 'drawing rooms' there was a wonderfully ebullient rhythm to Dublin high life, the rooms were always crowded and the dances rationed out for lack of space. Behind the set piece events there were impromptu parties and picnicking, a relish for conversation and comment, that distinctive Irish note of malice which gave an edge to the complacent selfishness of it all. The English Privy Council made the real rules so there was an irresponsibility to the intellectualism. Dean Swift might write his critical *Drapier's Letters*, but it was his printer not Swift who was sent to prison for them. There was also a strong sense of country matters behind the urbanity. Alternating with the winter season were the long summers away in lonely country houses and sylvan bishoprics. It was an aristocracy of country squires puffed up by grand new titles, delightful by its high spirits and curiously permeated with worldly churchmen.

Here, when it was at its height, with Pearce's superb Parliament House just occupied and the immense length of Trinity Library newly opened to its students, came Mrs Pendarves, born Mary Granville but best known for her happy second marriage as Mrs Delany. To say that she was formidable would be to miss her charm, yet her social poise has been described as 'historic' because she was accepted in her lifetime as representing the feminine ideal of her century: Jane Austen's several heroines rolled into one and realized in the flesh before Austen had written a word. She was hailed by Edmund Burke as 'the highest bred woman in the world, the woman of fashion of all ages',[1] while her second husband, Dr Delany, Dean of Down, could only express her in Solomon's words: 'fair as the moon! clear as the sun! but terrible as an army with banners!'[2] (illus. 75).

This prodigy and self-appointed social observer, England's answer to Madame de Sevigny, sailed over from Parkgate to Dublin in the 'Pretty Betty', paying five guineas for the best cabin and landing in mid-September 1731. She was thirty-one years old, entirely unsubdued after an appalling seven-year marriage to an ugly libertine old enough to be her grandfather, and being born a Granville she was very well connected, not only to Lord Carteret, the Viceroy recently retired after a seven-year stint of firm and unusually hands-on rule at the Castle and later raised in the peerage to become Earl Granville, but also to the new Viceroy, Lionel Sackville, Duke of Dorset, who would serve another long term: eleven years in all with a break between. So she had instant entrée to the Castle and, as the guest of the very wealthy Bishop of Killala (Killaloe), Dr Clayton, later Bishop of Cork and then of Clogher, she moved easily within Ireland's influential ecclesiastical aristocracy, those well salaried pilots who gave a religious justification to the whole illogical structure of the Ascendancy.

75 Joseph Brown, *Mrs Pendarves as a young woman*, engraving from an enamel picture given by Erskine Sandford Esq. to the Baroness de Bunsen.

Quite why Mrs Pendarves came out to Ireland initially for a six-month stay which expanded to eighteen months has never been made perfectly clear. She claimed at one time or another to have turned down the hands of Lord Baltimore, Lord Weymouth and Lord Tyrconnel, not to mention several wealthy commoners. But since Baltimore had asked for a trial marriage before committing himself, Weymouth was homosexual and Tyrconnel was deeply foolish, she may have been shrewd to wait twenty years for a kindly cleric. Much of her hold upon her contemporaries arose from a strict morality tempered by sweetness; Hannah More and George III were equally impressed by her. For the purposes of this book she timed her visits to Ireland perfectly at two strategic points in the rise of the Rococo. In 1731 she was in time to meet and even flirt with Edward Lovett Pearce himself, and on her second, much longer stay, she entertained and dined with Lord Chesterfield. She was a purely Rococo woman in her personal taste, equally delighted by grand balls and peasant festivities on the green, an early enthusiast for the

Picturesque, devoted to shells, the rocaille motif of Rococo art, forever collecting them to decorate grottoes, and snipping coloured papers to create artificial flowers of precise botanical accuracy.

She had selected her host for a lengthy Irish visit very shrewdly. The Bishop of Killala's town house on St Stephen's Green was one of Dublin's finest. There he and Mrs Clayton, his ambitious, stylish, yet often surprisingly easy-going wife, the daughter of Ireland's Chief Justice, presided among the statuary, virtues, busts and the paintings which the Bishop had picked up on his Grand Tour. He was a true Prince of the Church yet, with a typically Irish paradox, his only cathedral was a modest tabernacle of 1670 that had neither choir nor organ and was set on the wild sea shores of County Sligo, four hard day's travelling from Dublin and a world apart from its sophistication.

'*Magnifique*' was Mrs Pendarves's reaction to her new home.[3] It had only just been completed by Richard Castle, the man destined soon to succeed Pearce as Ireland's leading architect after Pearce's early death from an 'imposthune' in 1733. 'The chief front of it', she claimed 'is like Devonshire House',[4] a description which proves she had a poor eye for accurate architectural detail as it was only a fine three-bay town house. Castle had a complex stylistic pedigree. He came from an area of Germany where many French Huguenots had settled and a Palladianism akin to the English version was popular, so at least Devonshire House and the Bishop's house were both loosely Palladian. He rarely took much interest in the interior decoration behind his bland, competent façades. With a woman's eye Mrs Pendarves approved the gold coloured damask of the furnishings and the lavish cuisine: 'They keep a very handsome table, six dishes of meat are constantly at dinner, and six plates at supper', and overall she found 'a universal cheerfulness reigns in the house'.[5] But that was to be her general impression of the Anglo-Irish: 'There is a heartiness among them that is more *like Cornwall* than any I have known, and great sociableness'.[6] She soon found that her habit of English reserve was beginning to crumble, 'Our spirits ought to have their full career when our inclinations are innocent', she noted priggishly.[7] The demure widow of that first autumn month who retired exhausted after three country (contrée, with pairs of dancers facing each other) dances was soon looking forward to a fortnight at a country house where six couples would dance every night, usually until one in the morning.

A few interiors of Bishop Clayton's house have survived surprisingly within the present 80 St Stephen's Green, now Iveagh House, a generously proportioned Victorian building created in 1862 for Sir Benjamin Lee

Guinness by uniting 80 and 81. One ceiling has four pairs of tiny birds billing[8] and the Morning Room has a narrow frieze of flower baskets. With these motifs which were soon to become so popular, the Clayton house has a claim to be the first Rococo interior in Dublin, contemporary with, though much less bold than, that State Room in the Castle. It is, therefore, irritating that while Mrs Pendarves's description of the interiors comes very close to indicating early Rococo effects, she never quite clinches the proof. Every Wednesday, she relates, 'Mrs Clayton opened her apartment and admitted all her acquaintance'.[9] The letter, written like most of her correspondence to her beloved sister Ann in Gloucester, explains which rooms in a town house were 'public' apartments and would, therefore, have had rich plasterwork. 'First there is a very good hall well filled with servants'. Many visitors remarked on this profusion of domestics in Irish houses. Dr Madden, the reformer of the Dublin Society, complained that domestic wages were so low that the gentry collected servants in the same way that they bought pots and pans. 'Then', Mrs Pendarves continued, 'a room of eighteen foot square, wainscoted with oak, the panels all carved and the doors and chimney finished with very fine high carving, the ceiling stucco'. In a contemporary French boudoir the boiseries would be carved from French oak panels. Had Bishop Clayton anticipated Chesterfield House in London by almost twenty years and indulged himself in the authentic article? Such of the Bishop's panelling as survives is simple raised-and-fielded. Mrs Pendarves's mention of virtues and busts sounds more in the mood of the early Francini work – Classical figures in panels – of 1738 in 85 St Stephen's Green than full-blooded Rococo frivolities. There were 'marble tables between the windows and looking-glasses with gilt frames'. The next room was 22 foot long and 22 broad, 'as finely adorned as damask, pictures, and busts can make it, besides the floor being covered with the finest Persian carpet that ever was seen'. Such was the state kept by the bishop of one of Ireland's lesser dioceses. A function of the largest room in these houses was to act as a dance floor. Mrs Pendarves believed that six couples and no more, usually to one fiddler, in sets of country dances was the ideal. So the patterns of the ceilings in these first-floor rooms would be echoed by the complex figures of the couples dancing beneath them. Once Jean Bérain had broken away from compartmented ceilings and made links between the cardinal points and diagonal points of the decoration, the patterns themselves would make a repeating but unified dance. Last in these apartment rooms came the Bishop's bedroom, 'large and handsome, all furnished with the same damask' and apparently open to the inspection of the guests who, with Mrs Pendarves presiding over a card table, stayed on until ten thirty.

Strict Sabbatarianism was not a feature of the Church of Ireland. Receptions were held on Saturday and Sunday evenings to introduce the English visitor and then on Monday 'we are to go to the Duchess of Dorset's to pay our court'.[10] The Vicereine was at home receiving in 'three rooms, not altogether as large as those at St James's, but of a very tolerable size'.[11] This was that suite of State Rooms gutted in the fire of 1941 and now replaced by one long, dull reception room next to the Throne Room. One contained that important Rococo ceiling but the Pendarves description only relates, 'In the farthest room', the Rococo room presumably, with the richest decoration, 'there is placed a basset table at which the Duchess of Dorset sits down after she has received and made her compliments to the company. It is very seldom any ladies sit down to basset, but quadrille parties are made in the other rooms'.[12] Mrs Pendarves played neither of these card games but wandered confidently up and down chatting to acquaintances.

Previous Vicereines had held a ball once a week, the Dorsets, however, had decided that a ball only on public days would be enough. The Duke danced energetically at Dublin's public ridottos, but the Duchess was inclined to headaches, being 'of a quiet spirit'.[13] Visitors to Ireland remarked that 'the Lord Lieutenant [the Viceroy's official title] and his wife were treated with greater state and reverence than the King and Queen in London'.[14] Being English and not German would have helped. Viceroys were either prominent Whig politicians like Lord Carteret, whom their rivals had found it convenient to isolate from the Cabinet in London, or wealthy Whig aristocrats like the Dorsets, figureheads who valued the honour and the dignity. For the Anglo-Irish they represented England, authority and protection in a potentially beleaguered state, with the promise of those regiments quartered in the Royal Barracks.

The military were popular, parades and reviews were commonplace, and on the next Friday the Claytons and their guest attended a morning review in Phoenix Park: 'One regiment of horse and three of foot, who all performed their parts well. The Duchess of Dorset was there in great state, and all the beau monde of Dublin.'[15] This solidarity was usual, the Ascendancy never forgot that Ireland was an armed camp and that Dublin's barracks were the largest in Europe. As for the Vicereine, even if she attended a christening as sponsor and substitute for the Queen, she travelled the streets with a troop of cavalry and guards, the viceregal Battle-Axes. Mrs Pendarves was delighted by Phoenix Park and 'a delightful wood, in the midst of which is a ring where the beaux and belles resort in fair weather', remarking that 'Nobody's equipage outlooked our's except my Lord Lieutenant's, but in every respect I must say Mrs Clayton's *outshines* her neighbours, not that that is easily done here, for people understand not only living well, but politely'.[16] At times the writer seemed almost in awe of her hostess, torn between admiration for her 'bon ton' and Christian disapproval of her worldly ways.

A first experience of a ball at the Castle had 'French dancing in abundance'.[17] Mrs Pendarves danced three country dances and then was summoned to supper where there were 'Three large tables beside the Duke's, covered with all sorts of provision disposed very well. I never saw so much meat with so little confusion'.[18] The Duke's birthday ball was particularly interesting because, 'The room where the ball was to be was ordered by Capt. Pierce, [Pearce] finely adorned with paintings and obelisks, and made as light as a summer's day'.[19] That was St Patrick's Hall, which Mrs Pendarves calls 'the old Beef-eaters hall'. A contemporary illustration of the occasion exists showing the roof covered with newly painted wreaths of flowers linking roundels (illus. 76). Pearce's wall hangings, described by the Duke in a letter to Lady Suffolk as 'canvas painted in perspective',[20] appear from the illustration to have rows of half-naked Atlantes rising from pedestals with the Pendarves 'obelisks' and appearing to support the roof. The link between these and the similar half-naked figures springing from the acanthus scrolls in that end state room is further indication of Pearce's authorship of the early Rococo ceiling.

Society's appetite for pleasure and constitution for absorbing it was remarkable. On St Cecilia's day there was a concert of music in St Patrick's cathedral – Corelli, Purcell and Blow – which lasted six hours from ten in the morning until four in the afternoon. Then, immediately after dinner, came a ball at seven held by Lord Mountjoy to honour the Dorsets:

> There was four-and-twenty couple, 12 danced at a time, and when they had danced 2 dances, the other 12 took their turn. No lookers-on but the Duchess and Mrs Clayton, who thought it beneath the dignity of a Bishop's wife to dance.[21]

At eleven everyone followed the Duke and Duchess upstairs to eat and then returned to dancing until four in the morning. Yet Mrs Pendarves was up again at nine o'clock, put on 'genteel dishabille' and went to the Parliament House, Captain Pearce's gleaming new granite palace of democratic oligarchy, to enjoy the debates and discussion until eight in the evening. The letter gives a fascinating account of how that impressive bicameral structure also

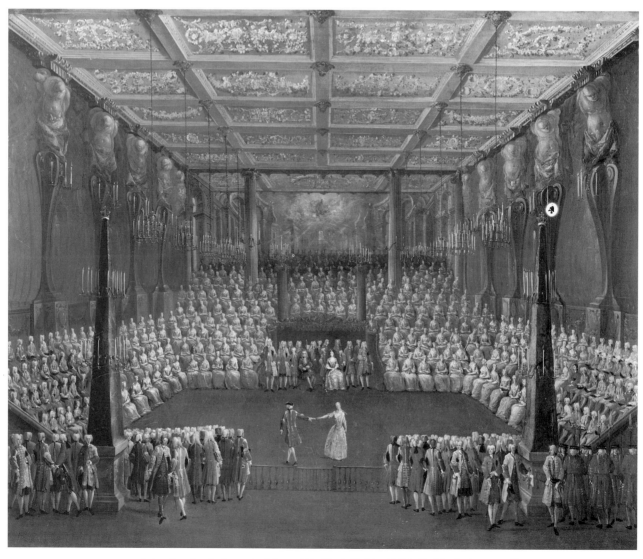

76 Attributed to Joris van der Hagen, *The King's Birthday Ball in Dublin Castle*, 1731, oil on canvas. The room is decorated as Mrs Pendarves must have seen it. Pearce's decorations are visible along the upper walls.

functioned as yet another Dublin resort of pleasure. In the late afternoon a gentleman 'brought us up chickens, and ham, and tongue, and everything we could desire'.[22] Did they actually picnic in the public gallery of the octagonal House of Commons? Then at an adjournment they were 'conveyed, by some gentlemen of our acquaintance, into the Usher of the Black Rod's room, where we had a good fire, &., and meat, tea, and bread and butter. Were we not well taken care of?'[23]

As Christmas approached the Castle threw a tremendous supper for 700 with 'a holly tree, illuminated by an hundred wax tapers; round it was placed all sorts of meat, fruit and sweetmeats', a spectacle which caused a near riot, 'the hurly burly is not to be described; squawling, shrieking, all sorts of noises'.[24] Her account casts doubt on the claim that it was Victoria's Prince Albert who introduced Christmas trees to the English.

The emphasis upon food at all these occasions is insistent: 'lamb, pigeon pye, Dutch beef, tongue, cockells, sallad, much variety of liquors and the finest syllabub that ever was tasted' would be followed by two hours of dancing at which 'the master of the house fiddled and danced the whole time'.[25] That was on one winter's day; the next day there was more food: 'plates of all sorts of cold meat neatly cut, and sweetmeats wet and dry, with chocolate, sago, jelly, and salvers of all sorts of wine', then 'fiddles were sent for, (a sudden thought). We began before eleven and held briskly to it till half an hour after two . . . we were eight couple of *as clever dancers* as ever eye beheld, though *I say it that should not*'.[26] But then in a bewildering assumption of concerned sentimentality, Mrs Pendarves could observe and relate to her sister: 'The poverty of the people as I have passed through the country has made *my heart ache*, I never saw greater appearance *of misery*, they live in great extremes, either *profusely* or *wretchedly*'.[27] To appreciate the eighteenth-century's refined sensibility it is necessary to take note of that brief 'heart ache' and at the same time to savour those syllabubs.

The Dublin season came to an end, but instead of going home Mrs Pendarves, clearly enchanted by the high spirited society of the place, decided to follow the Claytons out to their remote diocese where the Bishop for a few sunny months serviced his scattered flock of Protestant gentry in a land of alienated Catholic peasants. This is perhaps the most interesting, certainly the most surprising, sequence of the Pendarves correspondence, for instead of complaint, shock and dismay the tone of her writing rises to a cross between a recall of Theocritus's *Eclogues*, the shepherd songs of an ideal Arcadia, and an anticipation of Synge's *Playboy of the Western World*, the rough poetry of the Celtic west.

The Pendarves' resilience and adaptability is completely unexpected. She took the 'cathedral' in her stride: 'a good parish minister and *bawling* of psalms is our method of proceeding!'[28] Her delight in the savage scenery of the Atlantic coast is a revelation of how far back in the century the sources of Wordsworth's responses to Nature go. 'It is impossible to describe the oddness of the place', she wrote, 'the strange rocks and cavities where the sea had forced its way . . . it raised a thousand great ideas'.[29] She had found a nut wood and a hill with a natural grotto at its top and there she settled down to decorate it with the shells she had gathered from the wild beaches, the first of many shell grottoes which she was to create in Ireland, setting up a national fashion for them. A picnic was held with 'a "*swilled mouton*"',[30] a sheep roasted whole in its skin, and scorning the accompanying vegetables she devoured nothing but roasted flesh.

At Killala fair Mrs Clayton rolled up in her coach 'drawn by six flouncing Flanders mares', more like some Celtic queen out of legend than a bishop's wife, and there were races along the sands. 'Every man rode his neighbour's horse without saddle, whip or spur. Such hollowing, kicking of legs, sprawling of arms, *could not* be seen *without laughing immoderately*'.[31] For Mrs Clayton's birthday all the celebrations were outside the house with 'dancing, singing, grinning, accompanied with an excellent bagpipe, the whole concluded with a ball, bonfire, and illuminations; pray', she quizzed her sister, 'does *your Bishop* promote such entertainments at Gloster as ours does at Killala?'[32] In a curious way Anglo-Irish society was both more nervously embattled and ruthless than English society and also more extrovert and informal. In a sense they were a frontier people, pioneering not among hostile Indians but the hostile native Irish and catching some of their spirit.

Always there is this thread of the dance which runs through alfresco life in Sligo as much as in Dublin: 'we expect a famous piper and haut-boy, and then we shall foot it again most furiously'; 'after dinner a fiddler appeared and to dancing we went, ding dong'. At Mrs Mahone's 'we danced and sang'; 'at two we went to dancing again'. 'Sir Thomas Prendergast dances with great spirit, and in very good time'; 'in the evening we have a merry tribe at home to eat oysters'.[33] What, one wonders, has happened to Burke's 'highest bred woman in the world'? Or did he mean that a really well-bred woman could cope with all sorts and conditions of life, adapting with appropriate good nature to any environment? There is some danger in seeing the whole eighteenth century in terms of Palladian formality and neo-Classical perfection, and forgetting the long Rococo decades lying between when people were more at ease and art followed them in this easiness.

On their way back to Dublin after this Episcopal holiday the party called at Mr Wesley's Dangan Castle in Co. Meath, the Duke of Wellington's boyhood home. Mr Wesley had been that master of the house at Butler's Town who had 'took his fiddle and played to his daughter's dancing'. At Dangan he had let his gardening fancy run in a nautical direction with three straight canals in a park set with a temple and statues of Apollo, Neptune, Proserpine, Diana and Fame. On one canal was a large model of the King's yacht 'Carolina', in the second a barge called after the 'Pretty Betty' and in the third was a miniature yawl, all three capable of taking passengers. 'We carry our music on board', Mrs Pendarves wrote in happy reminiscence, 'hoist our flag, and row away most harmoniously'.[34] She recorded many more such occasions in the next six months, another whole winter season of Dublin before she returned to the other more sober and less Rococo inclined island. But it seems appropriate, in this her first term of Ireland, to leave her there singing in the boat on Mr Wesley's canal at Dangan. It exemplifies the spirit of the country in those years: ideal, escapist, certainly self-indulgent, but also optimistic, playful and open, a society which had already chosen as the central symbols of its domestic art-form – birds, waving leaves, baskets of flowers and laughing children.

CHAPTER IX

LORD CHESTERFIELD AND DUBLIN – THE CICERONIAN VICEROY

When Mrs Pendarves returned to Ireland in June 1744, she and the country were both becoming middle-aged and serious. The Dublin Society was moving towards the establishment of its own technical schools of art and design with a pronounced French and Rococo bias, while the lady had become, in 1743, and against the wishes of her family, the wife of Dr Delany, sixteen years her senior, Chancellor of St Patrick's Cathedral, Dublin and soon to be advanced in an alliterative promotion to become Dr Delany, Dean of Down, a ruined cathedral in Ulster. Mrs Delany's dancing days, while not quite ended, were now severely limited: there would be no more merriment into the small hours. On 10 January 1745 she could only record:

> The little rout is over? we had four hours of smart, clever dancing; and broke off a quarter before nine; supped, and were all quiet in our nests by twelve, and the Dean seemed as well pleased with looking on as we were with our dancing.[1]

That 'looking on' was a little ominous. Far more evenings would be spent reading Shakespeare, playing the harpsichord or 'after supper I make shirts and shifts for the poor naked wretches in the neighbourhood'.[2] There were, however, real compensations, for the last twenty years her new husband, who had been a friend of Pope, had been devising what must have been Ireland's first garden in the Rococo spirit around her new home. One of Mrs Delany's first tasks was to give her sister a full account of it. She admitted that to write such a description 'puzzles me extremely', but still tried her hand at conveying its charming complexities in a letter of 19 July 1744. As in so many gardens of the Rococo, the homely and the bucolic – 'our hayrick', 'a wall of good fruit' and 'a bowling green' – featured alongside the eclectic structures. She had

> a very large handsome terrace-walk, with double rows of large elms, and the walk well gravelled, so that we may walk securely in any weather ... About half way up the walk there is a path that goes up that bank to the remains of an old castle (as it were) from whence there is an unbounded prospect all over the country; under it is a cave that opens with an arch to the terrace-walk, that will make a very pretty grotto. At the end of this terrace is a very pretty portico, prettily painted within and neatly finished without; you go up a high slope to it, which gives a mighty good air as you come up the walk; from thence you go on to the trees and with bushes, that look so naturally that you would not image it the work of art. There are several prettinesses I can't explain to you – little wild walks, private seats, and lovely prospects. One seat particularly I am very fond of, in a nut grove, and 'the beggar's hut', which is a seat in a rock; on the top are bushes of all kinds that bend over, it is placed at the end of a cunning wild path, thick set with trees, and it overlooks the brook, which entertains you with a purling rill.[3]

In its casual charm, its response to the natural features of the site, its viewpoints and its seats, the juxtaposition of Gothick castle and Classical temple, above all in the way it served the ordinary pleasures of the day, this was a garden which Pococke would have relished.

Unfortunately Pococke was Lord Chesterfield's acolyte, a member of an opposing political party. Mrs Delany automatically disliked him because he was a rival to her husband for ecclesiastical preferment and, in any case, she found him a bore at the dinner table. Her hopes of social advancement in Ireland were optimistically set on her husband being offered the linked posts of Bishop of Kildare (another ruined cathedral) and Dean of Christ Church, Dublin, so the arrival of the new Viceroy, the Earl of Chesterfield, master of all such patronage, was awaited with some nervous apprehension. Mrs Delany had been born a Granville and Lord Chesterfield had very recently brought about Earl Granville's political downfall. Chesterfield, while already appointed, was still occupied with diplomatic affairs of state in The Hague. Ireland was soon to enjoy one of its heavyweight viceregalities, but he would not have time for Dublin until late August 1745.

It is easy to mock and underrate those Irish Protestants of the Ascendancy, but for all their faults of hypocrisy, repression and pride, Protestants did tend towards good works as their justification: Mrs Delany to her shirts and shifts for the naked and the Dublin Society to education and the sharing of advances in agriculture and manufactures. Thomas Prior had been the leading figure of those fourteen men who founded the Society in June 1731 with a committee of arts to meet fortnightly and admit 'artists, tradesmen and husbandmen to assist and inform the members in such arts and improvements as shall be thought useful'.[4] A prime aim was to bring 'the several mechanic arts in this kingdom'[5] up to the standards of other countries; and each member was supposed occasionally to address the others on some improving topic.

All this was well intentioned but very amateur, and it was Dr Samuel Madden (1686–1765), a clergyman and squire of Co. Fermanagh, not Prior, who drove the Society forward, between 1731 and Chesterfield's arrival in 1745, to become a potent force in the Irish establishment. Madden published proposals in 1738[6] urging the gentry of Ireland not only to patronize the fine arts themselves but to bring over foreign artists to encourage the Irish in their manufacture of the decorative arts: carpets, fabrics and earthenware. At the heart of his proposals, and the key to their eventual success, was his scheme for 'encouraging by proper praemiums, those politer arts, which are in a manner strangers to our country; I mean Sculpture, Painting and Architecture . . . Since we must have luxury', Madden allowed, 'we should encourage that kind of it which has the most of pleasure, and nothing of vice in it; which will give Bread and Industry to our Natives'.[7] Pleasure linked with improvement was central to the Rococo mind-set.

He followed this pamphlet up in 1739 with exact and practical proposals for these premiums to be offered particularly for sculpture and modelling. From being an island famed for learning and merit, he raged, Ireland was now 'a Nursery of lazy Bigots and Beggars'. Why should not 'our good *Catholics*' divert the money they spent on prayers for relief in Purgatory to the carving of commemorative statuary? Most Protestant proposals of this century contrived a hidden anti-Catholic slant but Madden was still broad-minded enough to urge annual awards as given 'by the *Popes* at the Academy of *St Luke* at Rome and by the *French* King at Paris'.[8] These were Continental and not British exemplars and an interesting instance of Ireland reaching out, even through its Protestant leaders, towards a European and Catholic dimension.

Madden put fire into his proposals by offering to fund the prize-giving himself and to involve the Society by suggesting that the votes of its members would be required before awarding any premium. He wound up splendidly with the promise that:

If this delightful design be once establish'd here . . . I shall make no question, but in a few, a very few years, we shall have an Academy for Painting and Sculpture, set up even in this Western desert of the world, forsaken and neglected as it is. We may then hope to see some of the great Masters of Italy settling here, and founding Schools for these Noble arts, and convincing the World that Barbarism and a *Gothick* taste are not forever to be the shameful lot and reproof of poor *Ireland*. Poor *Ireland*! I say, that ought to receive at least this one blessing from her Poverty.[9]

This was empty rhetoric of course, the great masters of Italy never materialized, but it was a necessary overstatement in order to persuade his fellow committee members to support a scheme which really had more modest, commercial aims. These Madden premiums were to prove nothing more nor less than hidden investments in Irish capitalism, and in view of Dublin's subsequent wave of decorative plasterwork Madden's emphasis upon sculpture is most significant.

Madden's proposals were accepted in February 1739; in 1740 the premiums were advertised in Dublin and London, five years before London's Society of Arts was even founded or able to follow Dublin's example. The first premiums were awarded in January 1740 to get the scheme off to a quick start. A woman, Susanna Drury, took a first prize of £25 for four meticulous gouaches of the Giant's Causeway. Sculptures included a chimneypiece with boy cherubs, a typical Rococo artefact, and a Hercules in clay ripping a lion apart. Joseph Tudor, who won one premium prize for landscapes this year and another in 1746, was soon to be the painter who introduced the Dutch landscape style to Ireland; so from the very start the Society's premiums were central and influential in the Irish cultural scene. John Haughton, later a carver and designer at Carton, won sculpture prizes in 1742 and 1743; George Ensor, who would go on to complete the Rotunda Hospital after Castle's death in 1751, was given a prize for a house design in 1745, Castle being one of the adjudicators. The Society was introducing an elder generation to its successor.

These Society members were mercantilists, committed to the theories of the French Enlightenment: that a country's prosperity would increase if it could cut back on imports by improving its own manufactures and increase its exports by the same means. Technical education leading to technical advances was to be the key, hence the Society's wish to set up its own technical school teaching drawing skills which would be directly applicable to industrial design. This explains Lord Chesterfield's enthusiasm for the Dublin Society. He too was a mercantilist and will have made Richard Pococke his

77 A proto-Rococo overmantel design by François Mansart (1715).

chaplain and given him a bishopric, not because Pococke was a great traveller, but because he worked to set up Protestant Charter schools to create educated artisans. As for the French Rococo bias of the Society's school, that was inevitable. Just as the Art Nouveau of the nineteenth century was often referred to as the 'Style Moderne', so the Rococo was seen in its time as the wave of the future, the 'Genre Pittoresque', partly ignoring, partly reshaping an outworn Classicism (illus. 77). It was more closely related to the real life of birds and flowers, overtly decorative and high-spirited, aesthetically challenging also with its sinuous, abstract frameworks of design. To be modern, to be prosperous and to make a fashionable reference to France, the Rococo was the natural choice for Chesterfield's town house when he could return to London, and for the Dublin Society when it came to the decoration of their own town houses. It offered a riot of feminine decorative detail and charm to counter the extreme functional austerity, masculinity even, of those regular, anonymous brick façades. In that hopeful mid-century, mercantilism and the Rococo were natural partners.

As soon as the premiums began to be awarded it became evident that Robert West was the most talented and successful of the drawing instructors in Dublin's several private schools. In 1747 all eight of the young prizewinners were, so *Faulkner's Dublin Journal* noted, 'taught by Mr West who keeps a School in George's Lane and is the best Master for drawings we ever had amongst us'.[10] None of his work survives but one of his students, Martin Archer Shee, a later President of the Royal Academy, described West's chalk studies as 'masterpieces of drawing execution'.[11] West was not a Dubliner but the son of a Waterford alderman. He had dropped out of the Parisian art scene, possibly on account of a nervous breakdown. Married with several sons, one of whom, Francis, was to succeed him as figure drawing master, West never painted in oils, but always demonstrated in chalk, the medium of his students. His method was simply to make a study of one of the younger boys and then set the others to copy it. From John O'Keefe's claim that West drew in the style of Guido Reni it sounds as if he aimed at the soft rounded effects of Boucher which he had picked up in Paris. This could account for at least one strand of design in Dublin's more figurative plasterwork. One premium winning entry in 1754 was 'a group of Boys playing with a basket of flowers',[12] a very Rococo theme and another indication of Robert West's artistic bias. By that time he had become the official master of the Society's own school.

On 31 August 1745 two viceregal yachts and an attendant ten-gun frigate brought the Earl of Chesterfield to Ireland as its new Lord Lieutenant, 'Stunned as I am', he wrote that evening, 'with the noise of cannon, drums and trumpets'.[13] He complained a few days later of 'the silly forms and ceremonies I have been obliged to go through',[14] but was in reality delighted by the pomps and power of it all. No king, it was said, ever sat in Westminster with half the state of a Viceroy in Dublin. When they came to open the Irish Parliament they even wore the robe of state which the luckless James II had left behind in his haste to avoid his victorious son-in-law after the Battle of the Boyne. Chesterfield had spent a political career in opposition, carping and sniping at authority. Now he was authority, unhindered by a cabinet or a crown, the virtual dictator of a country in wartime, but a dictator brought up on the precepts and ideals of Cicero and Plato (illus. 78). It was his one chance in a lifetime of critical detachment and he took it with a relaxed and confident authority. As one of his contemporary admirers wrote: 'Cicero, whom he had constantly before his eyes as an orator, became also the subject of his imitation in his government'.[15]

No Viceroy of Ireland was ever given the title of the 'Great' or the 'Good'; it was not in the nature of either the office or of the divided people, but Philip Dormer Stanhope, 4th Earl of Chesterfield, is generally conceded as having been the most popular and respected man ever to have held Ireland as the

78 Joseph Wilton, Bust of Lord Chesterfield, 1757, marble.

King's deputy. If the stylistic term had been invented in the eighteenth century he might have been known as the 'Rococo Viceroy' for he was an ardent and uncritical Francophile. With any stylistic movement there is always a natural tendency to look for a hero figure, a fountain-head of influence. Chesterfield, pleasantly ugly, laid back and witty, genuinely devoted to justice, good government and prosperity through industry, was the perfect aristocrat in the right place at the right time to stand as patron of the Irish Rococo.

Dublin was charmed by him; he was fair, he was firm and he was always accessible for consultation and advice. His period of office coincided almost exactly with the second Jacobite Rebellion, when Catholic Ireland was expected to spring to arms at any moment as Scotland fell to Prince Charles Edward and London was in a near panic. Chesterfield never for a moment lost his cool composure. There was to be no closing of Catholic chapels, no lynch law or raising of amateur regiments. Instead he played his bawdy appreciation of female beauty to perfect advantage. Asked if there were dangerous Papists in Dublin he named Miss Ambrose, a celebrated and lovely court Catholic, as the only one he could think of, addressing her with the extempore verse at an Orange ball:

> Say, lovely Tory, why the jest
> Of wearing orange at thy breast
> When that same breast betraying shows
> The whiteness of the rebel rose.

and, then with the even less proper:

> In Flavia's eyes is every grace
> She's handsome as she could be
> With Jacob's beauty in her face
> And Essau's where it should be.

As a practised spin doctor he urged the soldiers of his guard to press for a rise in pay like their officers, assuring them of his support, and he let it be known that he hoped to be considered not as the Lord Lieutenant of Ireland but as the Irish Lord Lieutenant. While strengthening the coastal defences of the south he urged his Protestants to be 'as much on your guard against Poverty as against Popery, take my word for it, you are in more danger of the former than of the latter'.[16] From the first he lent his weight to the improving effect of the Dublin Society, expressing warm friendship for Thomas Prior and Samuel Madden, enduring all the latter's appalling verses and dedications because he valued the premiums and Madden's concern for Irish industry. If only his letters to these two men had made an occasional reference to French design and lavish stucco work it would clinch his Rococo associations, but all Chesterfield's practical interest seemed centred on improving the quality of Irish paper and Irish bottle glass.

Sometimes he tended to despair of Irish irresponsibility: 'You think less of two or three years hence than any people under the sun', but when he was back in London he wrote nostalgically, 'I will own that I thought I could, and began to hope that I should, do some good in Ireland. I flattered myself that I had put jobbery a little out of fashion, and your manufactures a little in fashion, and that I had in some degree discouraged the pernicious and beastly habit of drinking, with many other pleasing visions of public good'.[17] This may read like a lament at failure, but it was while he held office, in March 1746, that the Dublin Society was placed on the Civil Establishment with a £500 grant and later, in 1750 but through Chesterfield's influence exerted from London, that the Society was legally incorporated with a Royal Charter. In his viceregal term the Society first proposed premium prizes for boys and girls, making awards to the under-fifteens on 15 May 1746, after the first supervised art examination ever to be held in Ireland. As a direct result of this success the Society declared: 'it is intended to erect a little Academy or School of Drawing and Painting, from whence some genius may arise, to the benefit and honour of this kingdom'.[18] By 1748 twenty-eight candidates for premiums were drawing the Rape of the Sabines and a statue of Antinous in the examination. Finally, in 1750, Robert West's school was absorbed into the Dublin Society Schools with premises in Shaws Court, Dame Street and its own collection of casts and busts. On the first floor West taught figure drawing, in a back room on the second floor James Mannin, a Huguenot, taught ornament and landscape. These two strands of design were to run through Irish plasterwork.

From contemporary accounts it seems that the activities of the Society's drawing schools became something of a social focus for an art-starved population. Lords, gentry and even Viceroys would look in of a morning to observe the work of the students seated around a long table drawing either from a cast of the antique, an anatomy figure or a nude model, 'a fine person', paid at the handsome rate of four shillings an hour. The boys' entries for the premiums were actually pinned up on the walls of Pearce's House of Lords for the peers' appraisal. Also on the walls of that chamber, as an even more impressive reminder of the Society's influence, were hung two tremendous trophies of Protestant power, tapestries of the Relief of Londonderry and the Crossing of the Boyne. They had been woven by John van Beaver, a £10 premium winner of 1743.

In support to these more picturesque and visible activities the schools' text book was Dodsley's *Preceptor*, published in 1749, a strictly practical set of rules for 'Painters, Engravers, Architects, Engineers, Gardeners, Cabinet-makers, Carvers, Embroiderers, Statuaries, Tapestry-weavers and many others concerned with designing'.[19] Along with the usual instructions of figure drawing Dodsley urged students to copy prints, advice which many designers of Dublin ceilings took to heart. Lesson four (illus. 79) taught the drawing of flowers, fruits and birds, the staple motifs of Dublin ceilings, and flower pieces were the favourite exercise of James Mannin, the French teacher of ornament and landscape. So between Dodsley's citation of the work of Le Brun, de Fresnoy and de Piles as exemplars, and the two French-trained teachers, West and Mannin, the Gallic bias of applied ornament in Irish plasterwork, cabinet making and silverware of the middle eighteenth century is easily explained.

London's equivalent of the Dublin Society Schools was the Academy which William Hogarth had set up fifteen years earlier (1735) in a converted Presbyterian meeting house in Peter Court, just off St Martin's Lane. Unfortunately all records of this academy have been lost and its nature and functioning has had to be reconstructed by conjecture from a few notes by George Vertue. Apparently Hogarth intended it as an 'Academy of Painting and Sculpture' and 'for the study of Drawing'.[20] Unlike the Dublin Society Schools which were founded by the city's establishment with the express purpose of improving technical education, the St Martin's Lane Academy

79 Birds from Robert Dodsley's 1748 edition of the *Preceptor*.

was founded by an artist for artists. However, the list of its teachers as recorded by Vertue suggests that to make the Academy a profitable concern Hogarth had included a strong technical element in its syllabus. Francis Hayman, 'History Painter', Louis François Roubilliac, 'Statuary', Mr Wills, 'Portrait Painter Treasurer', were balanced by the more practical Hubert Gravelot, 'designer', George Moser, 'chaser', and Mr Yeo, 'seal engraver'.[21] Hogarth is generally supposed to have shared the Academy's direction with Isaac Ware for three years in the late 1730s, and it is probable, though not proven, that James Paine, an architect uneasily suspended like Ware between the Palladian and the Rococo, studied at the Academy.[22]

In a brilliantly creative account of Hogarth's Academy, Mark Girouard traced how Hogarth's friendship with Jonathan Tyers, the proprietor of the Vauxhall Pleasure Gardens, allowed him to infiltrate teachers from his Academy – Hayman, Moser and Roubilliac in particular – into the design and building works of the gardens.[23] But whether this was to the advantage of the Rococo cause in England is questionable. Unlike Dublin, London never accepted that its town houses should, to be fashionable, have Rococo interiors. The grand courtyard at Vauxhall was not Rococo in styling but a fantasy hybrid, part Chinese, part Gothic, part Moorish, while Moser's decorative treatment of the Vauxhall central Rotunda and Foyer resulted in heavy Salamonic columns and a pleated tent-like roof which could have inspired no imitation in the reception rooms of polite society.

80 Hogarth's *Analysis of Beauty* (1753), Plate 1, with various examples of the 'Serpentine Line of Beauty and of Grace'.

Hogarth himself, for all his early involvement in what seems to have been an active group of 'Genre Pittoresque' enthusiasts, is a difficult, even a frustrating figure to place in any account of an English Rococo. His theoretical writing, the *Analysis of Beauty*, begun around 1745 and published in 1753, reads like a gospel for the style with its author an ardent and persuasive advocate for sinuous lines, C and S scrollwork and delicious complexities of design. 'Simplicity without variety is', he declares, 'wholly insipid'.[24] The aim of the artist should be a fusion of 'FITNESS, VARIETY, UNIFORMITY, SIMPLICITY, INTRICACY and QUANTITY – *all which co-operate in the production of beauty, mutually correcting and restraining each other occasionally*'.[25] But after backing every horse in the race by that collection of qualities he committed himself more boldly to 'enjoyment in winding walks, and serpentine rivers . . . the *waving* and *serpentine* lines'.[26] He defined 'Intricacy of form' as 'that peculiarity in the lines, which compose it, that *leads the eye a wanton kind of chace* and from the pleasure that gives the mind, intitles it to the name of beautiful'.[27] So 'Intricacy', a very Rococo quality, was the first of the six artistic virtues. In abstract form he saw this quality best expressed in a sinuous curve wrapped around a solid cone; in real life 'the most amiable in itself is the flowing curl; and the many waving and contrasted turns of naturally intermingling locks ravish the eye with the pleasure of the pursuit, especially when they are put in motion by a gentle breeze'[28] (illus. 80).

Nothing could be less Palladian than this. He mocked the austere pomps of Palladian façades, praised Christopher Wren's St Pauls, which Lord Shaftesbury had despised, and enjoyed Gothic Windsor Castle for its 'hugeness . . . tho' void of any regular order'[29] and even allowed Westminster Abbey 'a consistency of parts': clear evidence of a Gothick–Rococo alliance in taste.[30] But all this was theory not practice. Hogarth's paintings, with a few doubtful exceptions, represent an absolute antithesis to the Rococo spirit as the style was interpreted on the Continent and in Ireland. His vision of the human condition was central to his paintings and that vision was, according to individual viewpoints, either deeply depressing or harshly realistic.

The essence of Irish and European Rococo art was escapism, a projection of an aristocratic ideal. It took the normal physical world of human bodies, clothes, flowers, musical instruments, birds and animals as its material, but then perfected them in an elegant stylization and order. As the Rococo churches of south Germany brought Heaven down to earth, so painters like Fragonard, Watteau and Boucher, designers like Pineau (illus. 81), Oppenord and Cuvilliès created images of perfection and spaces where a perfect life could be lived out and loved in a complex refinement of rooms, with graciously

81 A buffet design by Nicolas Pineau (*c.* 1730), illustrating the decorative leap since the earlier Mansart design (illus. 77).

Dessein de Buffet pour une Salle à manger in-
ventée par le Sr. Pineau, Architecte a Paris.
Entwurff eines Credenz-Tisches in einē Speiss-Saal
inventirt durch Sr. Pineau, Architect in Paris.

dressed and undressed women, at alfresco meals in natural yet flawless sylvan surroundings (illus. 82). In their insular Irish way the happy, irresponsible high society of Protestant Dublin shared this vision of the Continental Rococo, questing in their reception rooms after the same ideal, sinuous beauty, ignoring the squalor on the streets and the utterly disenfranchised Catholic poor. The Robert Wests, Bartholomew Cramillion, John Ensor and Henry Darley were their versions of Pineau and his followers.

Hogarth's approach to life and art was the exact reverse. Where the French artists gilded life, Hogarth first piled mud on it and then spat at it. His paintings concentrated life's dishonesties, hypocrisies and treacheries in a moral, educational programme which was essentially Puritan – man is a fallen creature, show him his vices in a pictorial form and there is a possibility of reform. It is interesting to observe in retrospect how Protestant Ireland ignored unpleasant truths (there was only one print shop in the whole of Dublin) while Protestant England relished its own ordure, eagerly buying the prints and engravings of Hogarth's great moral sequences. But it was the states which had lost themselves in an exquisite Rococo ideal: France, Ireland and fissiparous Germany, which came to a painful reckoning with bloody revolutions at the end of the century, while England's social

82 John Rocque's engraved 'View of the Royal Palace at Richmond' (1736) from *Vitruvius Britannicus*, IV (1739), with the English aristocracy behaving as if they were in a French Rococo painting.

fabric held triumphantly together, aristocrats, bourgeois and workers, in a patriotic and relatively contented whole.

One part of the price for England's social cohesion was its lame response to Rococo art, and one reason for that lame response was Hogarth's mocking vision of the moral degradation behind apparently refined society. His celebrated pictorial narratives: *A Harlot's Progress*, *The Rake's Progress*, *Marriage-à-la-Mode* and *The Election*, are deeply depressing and cynical. Country girls end in gaol, diseased and dying, husbands cheat wives, wives play false to their husbands, clergymen are hypocritical lechers, doctors are greedy quacks, funerals are farces. At least three-quarters of the faces painted by this inventor of the 'line of beauty' are ugly, with snout-like noses, sly eyes, predatory hands and deformed bodies. Who would guess from Hogarth's version of a parliamentary election that England in his day had the most helpful approach to representative government of any state in Europe, or that it would soon try and ruin corrupt colonial administrators like Warren Hastings?

There are glimpses of an ideal Rococo world in those pseudo-Palladian rooms which Hogarth painted: the despairing, epicene beauty of the young earl sprawled out on his chair, faultlessly attired in black, gold and white in

After the Marriage, 1743, that wise dog in *The Painter and his Pug* of 1745, the enchanting *Graham Children* of 1742, all frills, curtsies and music. But for Hogarth it was almost a religion to be Anti-Gallican. Across the Channel where C and S scrolls reigned supreme and refinement was, for the fortunate few, an absolute, all Hogarth could see were greedy friars, ill-clad scrawny soldiers and a superstitious priest dispensing the Mass to a foolish flock kneeling on the cobbles of a street. That was his *Calais Gate, or The Roast Beef of Old England* of 1748. By a perverse twist, if anyone did more to block the taste for Rococo frivolities in England than Lord Burlington it was his sworn aesthetic enemy William Hogarth. That potentially great painting of *The Wedding Dance* (1745) could so easily have been his poetic masterpiece: revelry of the upper classes in a vast room lit by candlelight, but significantly he left it unfinished. If he should be remembered for any social warmth it should be for *The Shrimp Girl*, *Captain Coram* or that entirely unrefined explosion of crude C and S scrolls: *Strolling Actresses dressing in a Barn*, an engraving of 1738 which is probably the version of Rococo art nearest to English preferences – knickers, bosoms, howling babies and a heap of tawdry theatrical props. In the England of Fielding's *Tom Jones* and *Joseph Andrews*, an irreverent land of malicious cartoons and wickedly funny, anonymous pamphlets, the Rococo would always labour under the handicap of humour and gross reality.[31]

In Ireland the Rococo laboured under no such handicap of earthy associations and comic cynicism. In Dublin there was the same link between the artists and students of the Society schools and the city's pleasure garden as there was in London between St Martin's Lane and Vauxhall. However, Dublin was able to combine the airy spirit of Rococo frivolity with the pious charity of a lying-in hospital while ignoring the general social degradation of the city upon which its upper and middle class society was founded. Dublin achieved a hospital, but its most striking architectural gain from the project was a Christian chapel, rather than the pleasure gardens sited immediately behind the hospital buildings. Lord Chesterfield's moral impetus can be clearly traced in this, Dublin's most outstanding social achievement of the century, the founding by Dr Bartholomew Mosse in 1751 of the maternity hospital, known since later additions as the Rotunda Hospital. It was not only an architectural ornament to the city but combined its charitable function with the role of Dublin's premier night spot, the capital's equivalent of London's Vauxhall Gardens. In this dualism of good deeds and gaiety Mosse's Hospital and gardens reflected Chesterfield's equally dualist regime at the Castle. On the one hand he had banned his own favourite vice, gambling, and spoke often and severely against the Irish vice of heavy drinking. Yet on the other, throughout the tense months of the Rebellion, when Edinburgh had fallen and Mrs Delany for one was fluttering with alarm at the rumour of a Scottish invasion fleet off Belfast, Chesterfield kept up the full traditional round of viceregal entertainment: Friday balls, afternoon drawing rooms and frequent intimate dinner parties and breakfasts. In keeping with his mercantilist beliefs he let it be known that he would look favourably on ladies who wore dresses of Irish design and Irish fabrics. With his gallant reputation the instruction proved irresistible and Lady Chesterfield set a good example. Predictably Mrs Delany claimed that the initiative was hers:

> On the Princess of Wales's birthday there appeared at Court a great number of Irish stuffs. Lady Chesterfield was dressed in one and I had the secret satisfaction of knowing myself to be the cause, but dare not say so here; but I say, 'I am glad to find my Lady C's example has had so good an influence', the poor weavers are starving – all trade has met with a great check this year.[32]

The point which Chesterfield, not Mrs Delany, was making, in addition to 'business as usual', was that good government in a Protestant state need not be divorced from joy and innocent pleasure: exactly the principles on which Dr Mosse would proceed in the subsequent five years.

Chesterfield left Dublin for ever in May 1746 walking, in a characteristic populist gesture, through the streets to the boat, arm in arm with his wife who, as a bastard child of George I, may have given additional regal lustre to his term of office. The poor of the city crowded the dockside begging him to return again and Lord Orrery wrote that 'Lord Chesterfield's influence, like the departing sun, has left a warm and serene sky behind it'.[33]

One person in Dublin who would not have been sorry to see that sun departing was Mrs Delany. Back in December there had been another general post of Irish bishoprics, and the see of Killala, in that far western country where she had been so happy fourteen years before, had become vacant. On the very day when Lord Chesterfield appointed another man to the coveted diocese he invited, with exquisite cruelty, the Delanys to dinner at the Castle tête-à-tête. Not a word of explanation, anger or regret was exchanged, only 'the Dean and my Lord Lieutenant fell into a very agreeable and entertaining conversation, chiefly of poets and poetry'. But to her sister she confessed, 'Now I know the rage boils'. Thereafter she recorded, 'The great folks in the Castle continue to show great favour, but we pay them little attendance, no more than not to be remarked as backward'.[34] When her husband died he would still only be Dean of Down.

Mrs Delany would not have long to wait for Chesterfield's own career to

83 The Saloon at
Chesterfield House,
Mayfair, London
(1748–9): Isaac Ware's
reluctant capitulation to
the French.

run into the buffers. He had returned to England, still technically the Viceroy, praised on every side for a successful term. That consummate political manipulator, the Duke of Newcastle, always underrated because of his amiable, bustling profile, persuaded him to resign Ireland and serve under him as second Secretary of State. The old King, long hostile, had become reconciled and would soon offer the Earl a dukedom which he would refuse. Frederick, the Prince of Wales and natural focus of the parliamentary opposition, was another admirer. When King George died there was every probability that King Frederick would make Chesterfield his First Minister.

Within five years everything went wrong and in those years any chance of the 'Genre Pittoresque' becoming the generally accepted decorative style of England was lost. First Newcastle made Chesterfield look weak and ineffective as a Secretary of State by ignoring his advice and frustrating his patronage. Content to bide his time Chesterfield resigned the seals in February 1748. He had a new hobby, his London town house, begun in the Spring of 1747, and until well into 1750 he was supervising every detail of Chesterfield House. This could and should have been a resounding Rococo statement based upon what he had seen developing in Dublin before he left, a house to seduce all fashionable London into imitation. Instead it was a deliberately ambivalent stylistic statement, part Palladian, part pure French. Chesterfield had chosen Isaac Ware as his architect so the house was to be a stylistic demonstration piece by the supposedly arch Burlingtonian and Palladian Ware – a case of the enemy's architect won over to the opponent's cause. Its exterior was rigidly Palladian and inside, the 'Great Room', Library and Breakfast Room all had firmly compartmented Palladian ceilings which defied any artistic invention. But the boiseries of the Ballroom and Drawing Room were authentic French work by French craftsmen with all the abstract frivolity of Parisian design. The plasterwork drops in the Hall were as fine in high relief as were the great flower garlands in the coving of the Ballroom, while the ceilings of both Ballroom and Drawing Room were pages taken by Ware from François Cuvilliés's *Livre des Plafonds Irreguliers* (1738). Now that the house has been demolished it is not easy to make informed judgements, but it seems to have had some feeling at least in its plasterwork of Dublin's freedom, invention and figurative life (illus. 83); but stylewise it was an uncertain credo, an unconvincing hedging of bets.[35]

In order to enjoy a lavish garden and generous grounds Chesterfield had sited his house out in the comparative wilds of Mayfair, a district so criminal and lawless that the Earl had to be escorted back from his evenings of

gambling by a squad of servants armed with blunderbusses; guests naturally ran the same risks. Nevertheless it was impressive and would have made a prestigious base for a king's First Minister. But then, inconsiderately and unexpectedly, Prince Frederick died, overturning the entire pattern of political calculations and expectations in the country. Frederick had certainly been in a position to add his influence as heir to the throne to that of Lord Chesterfield and swing London round to the Rococo, if that had ever been his intention. The Palladian was flagging, Robert Adam had yet to devise his Neronian neo-Classicism, the 'Genre Pittoresque' could have slipped neatly in to fill a stylistic void. But what precisely had Frederick's inclinations been and how considerable a figure was he in those years before his untimely death?

For twenty-six years as the unemployed and underfunded heir to the throne he had been a loose cannon on the decks of power, the unpredictable factor, causing Sir Robert Walpole many an uneasy moment and resort to shifty devices. Wholly German in his upbringing, Frederick was wrenched away from the palace of Herrenhausen at the age of 22, to England, a move from quasi-viceregal status to constitutional impotence. Detested by his parents, George II and Queen Caroline, he lived in the shadow of their beloved younger son, 'Butcher' Cumberland. Wildly popular with the common people Prince Frederick was seen, hopefully, as Bolingbroke's Patriot King in waiting, courted by opposition peers, frustrated and blackguarded by every government supporter. In that long enforced idleness Frederick played to the gallery: sometimes the genial sportsman racing his yacht down the Thames, captaining the Surrey cricket team or sweating at royal tennis; sometimes the Firbankian aesthete relaxing in a Venetian barge down a Gloucestershire river or consulting a wise woman in the depth of Norwood Forest to improve his gambling fortunes. Nothing about this most unpredictable of Hanoverians adds up to a consistent whole character.

As far as his social profile goes he was an eminently Rococo figure. He adored his children and pursued the natural life as defined in Rococo terms. But this 'Rococo Prince' built an austerely neo-Palladian White House as his favourite country seat at Kew and patronized William Chambers, that least Rococo of neo-Roman classicists. Those Chinese pavilions raised to attract Frederick's patronage to Vauxhall Gardens in 1751 were not in any sense Rococo. On the other hand William Kent, who had designed that frigid White House, devised for him a convincingly casual picturesque garden with Classical terms and a pavilion at Carlton House in the heart of fashionable London.[36]

Always there is this ambivalence. The Prince acted as a solvent, both to contemporary taste as the Palladian drive faded and to constitutional thinking as

Whigs of the *ancien régime* cast about for new political garments. He was an emotional Jacobite, devoted to Van Dyck replicas and Van Dyck collars, forever pestering George Vertue for biographical details of King Charles I and his picture collecting. Yet the Prince could still appeal passionately to be allowed to lead the army that crushed Scotland at Culloden. Those middle decades of the 1730s and the 1740s were as uncertain in direction as Frederick himself. He was the perfect image of his time, an ardent botanist, amateur astronomer, artistic Francophile in a country almost permanently at war with France, not so much a 'Rococo Prince' as a Prince who radiated eclecticism. To create Frederician vibrations Lord Cobham began the revolutionary gardens at Stowe, Lord Egmont built a giant moated castle in mid-Somerset.[37] Frederick's whole time in England, his politics, his patronage, his exuberant eclecticism and his basic reverence for the arts of France, read like a pre-run of the life of his grandson, the Prince Regent.

An exhibition, 'Princes as Patrons', toured England in 1998 illustrating the art patronage of Princes of Wales from King James I's Henry onwards, and it has to be said that Prince Frederick's patronage made only a feeble showing. On the credit side he bought a small Brueghel the Elder of a *Flemish Fair*, Claude's *Seaport*, now in the National Gallery, and a number of miniatures by Isaac and Peter Oliver, including Isaac Oliver's celebrated *Portrait of a Melancholy Young Man*. A Gaspar Dughet of Jonah being swallowed by the whale during a terrible storm while lightning strikes a castle on a cliff and horrified onlookers gesticulate on the shore revealed a surprising taste for romantic horror. On the other hand a Eustach le Sueur of about 1650 but very like a neo-Classical David, suggested that Frederick may have had a macabre sense of humour as it illustrated Caligula depositing the ashes of his mother and brother. As Frederick hated both his mother, Queen Caroline, and the Duke of Cumberland, he would cheerfully have deposited the ashes of both with every pious pomp and ceremony.

Between 1729 and 1736 Frederick employed Philippe Mercier as his painter and librarian. A painting commissioned from Mercier by Frederick, *The Music Party*, with the Prince scraping earnestly away at his cello and another, a companion piece by Wootton, *The Shooting Party*, showing Frederick and his friends surrounded by dead birds and live spaniels, are both undemanding mementos with token caricature faces, charming enough but not serious studies.[38] Van Dyck's wistfully beautiful double portrait of Thomas Killigrew and Lord Crofts together with *Head of a Man in Profile* by Annibale Carraci and the before mentioned Isaac Oliver indicate some feeling in the Prince for the sadness of the male condition. This is a little unexpected in the owner of a Charles Cray barrel organ playing ten tunes from Handel operas and topped by Melchior Baumgartner's vulgar mille fiore and rock-crystal casket of 1664.

None of this is definitive taste. *The Shooting Party* has a heavy Rococo frame of guns and powder flasks by Paul Petit, but it was the Neptune silver-gilt tureen with all its attendant sauce boats and entrée dishes which gave the exhibition's most revealing insight into the quality of English Rococo craftsmanship at this period. In an appreciative critical study, Martin Gayford described the Neptune set as 'wonderful . . . ebullient rococo pieces of goldsmith's work'.[39] This is true of the top sections of the tureen, but these were pieces of French and Turinese silver by Paul Crespin and Andrea Boucheron, only put together in London by Nicholas Sprimont in 1742–3. It was painfully obvious that where English silversmiths were involved in shaping shepherds or various shellfish, the standard of modelling immediately sank to that which can be observed in any twentieth-century shop selling sports trophies for dart or local football championships. This confirmed a suspicion which has grown over the years from appraisals of Continental and English silverware of the eighteenth century. English craft standards were very low and the facility of French Rococo silversmiths like Meissonnier was quite beyond them.

This does not reflect on Prince Frederick, but it does offer a perspective to contemporary levels of English Rococo arts and crafts. If the Neptune tureen was all that a Prince of Wales could command then English silverware was insular indeed, as was the Wootton painting. The truth about Frederick and his influence is probably that he was an average, cricket-playing, theatre-going, duck-shooting man. He may have been gently melancholy as a result of estrangement from his royal father and mother, and was certainly interested in his royal Tudor ancestors. He bought George Vertue's copy of a portrait of the (melancholy?) boy king Edward VI. Where old masters were concerned he purchased, as if trying to recreate Charles I's picture collection, five Van Dycks, four Rubenses, a Veronese, a Titian and a Tintoretto; but where contemporary paintings were concerned his tastes were second rate. In a great age of French Rococo painters he patronized Philippe Mercier, who was barely third rate, and employed Joseph Goupy to copy old masters, which makes his Van Dycks and Rubenses suspect. Wonderful French Rococo silverware was available, but he bought Sprimont's composites.

Frederick's best known act of patronage was his commissioning in 1732 of that most royal of state barges, crested with golden dolphins, scallop shells and lion's heads, its cabin a pilastered pavilion.[40] Every detail of the barge could be described as Palladian, but it was the Palladian of William Kent who, despite Lord Burlington, veered towards a Rococo richness all his creative life. That ambiguity is the most a 'Rococo Prince' can be offered.

In England there is always this tendency to give more significance to royal figures than they really deserve. Frederick was a genial mediocrity with antiquarian tendencies. After his death a few of his courtiers, men like George Lyttelton, the builder of Hagley, went Rococo, but in his lifetime Frederick was, if anything, becoming a patron of Chinoiserie. Frederick's death and Chesterfield's subsequent relegation to the political sidelines may have injured the Rococo's chances of general popularity in England, but it had absolutely no effect upon Dublin and Ireland. There, regardless of unpopular mediocrities like the Earl of Harrington who followed as Viceroy, the taste and influence, industrious, positive and benign, of Chesterfield continued to reign in a Rococo island with a Rococo capital.

CHAPTER X

RENAISSANCE
ON THE
NORTH BANK

In the year when Lord Chesterfield left Dublin, 1746, the Apollo ceiling in 40 St Stephen's Green, later known as Tracton House, was raised, acting almost as a starting pistol for all the hundreds of fine passages of Rococo plasterwork that were to be created on both sides of the Liffey over the next three decades. After the demolition of Number 40 and two subsequent moves, Apollo now hangs over one of the refurbished state rooms of Dublin Castle (illus. 84, 96). A photograph of a rescue operation, when a slightly later work was saved at 15 Dawson Street, will illustrate the structural trauma and the inevitable damage sustained by frail plaster in such a process (illus. 85). But the medium is a forgiving one, cracks are soon filled and delicate mouldings reshaped. Now on the outskirts of Dublin a whole stockpile of these Rococo master works waits for some appropriate new or old building to rehouse them. Several of the very finest ceilings have already been re-hung in other rooms of the Castle, the Viceregal Lodge and the Bank of Ireland.

The survival of this fine Apollo ceiling is doubly fortunate because, in addition to its quality, it bridges very neatly the gap between the figurative Italian style of the Francinis – the soft pornography of the classically educated – and the French, Bérain-style compositions which, being rather more abstract, could be seen as more appropriate to moral Protestant households. Being so accessible and so stylistically strategic the Apollo repays a brief analysis as virtually all subsequent, more committedly Rococo, ceilings

84 The Apollo Musagates ceiling from Tracton House (1746), now in Dublin Castle.

worked around the same axial lines and compositional constraints. It is compartmented, though only very lightly, and the mouldings, apart from the inevitable swags of flowers which are sharply defined bravura pieces, are relatively soft in definition. The cardinal axes of the outer, French compartment are occupied by tiresome diaper work contained within coarse acanthus scrolls, the worst kind of Bérain device. It is the diagonals that count in both outer and inner compartments. In the outer they are maintained by four long trophies of the Arts, taken straight from plates by Jacques Dumont le Romain, published in the 1730s. These are just the kind of trendy French models which the teacher, Robert West, is likely to have been drawing to his students' attention.[1] None of this French work dares to overlap the multi-sided lozenge of the inner Italian compartment. Here, nude and completely at ease, Apollo Musagates, patron of those diagonal Arts, lolls back on billowing clouds in a subtle contraposto composition of complementary hidden diagonals – billowing cloak to extended left leg, raised lyre to descending zodiacal arc. Here in the competition between the two styles, figurative and abstract, the Italian wins hands down by its confident eroticism. But Tracton House was in the old enclave of superior residences around St Stephen's Green on the south bank of the Liffey, figurative territory pioneered by the Francini brothers as early as 1738. For a time in the early 1750s the best Rococo work was being executed on the north bank.

This north–south divide of the capital's architecture was another of Dublin's deviations from a London-type growth pattern. While London developers edged west, scorning the south bank as an adjunct of low, commercial Southwark, Dublin, divided by a much lesser stream, sometimes taken for a canal, virtually ignored the Liffey as anything more than an obstacle to

be bridged. Its quays could so easily have been lined with regular terraces and town palazzos but they have never been handsome, apart from James Gandon's two great buildings, his Custom House and his Four Courts, added later in the century. With two cathedrals, the Castle (illus. 97), Trinity College and most of the old churches, the south bank should logically have been the most fashionable area. In 1745 its claim had been further strengthened when the Earl of Kildare, a Fitzgerald, head of one of Ireland's two leading families, began to build his town palace to Richard Castle's designs at the end of Molesworth Street. Leinster House, as this became when Kildare was elevated to a dukedom, should, with the predictable grandeurs of its Palladian façades and some delicate but unremarkable Rococo interiors, have set the seal upon south Dublin.

Dr Bartholomew Mosse's hospital changed all that. The north side of the river had been largely Gardiner territory. Luke Gardiner was a self-made man, a banker-developer, Privy Councillor and a deputy Vice Treasurer of Ireland. Henrietta Street had, in 1730, been his first enterprise and now in the 1740s he had begun to widen some of his early streets by pulling one side of them down to create finer vistas and a wider field of fire should any possible rebel rising need a quick response. Riots were still commonplace in the religiously divided city: the Protestant weavers of the Huguenot quarter taking on the Catholic butchers of the Ormonde Market. Penalties in combat were standardized. Weavers caught by butchers were hung up to bleed with a hook through their lower jaw. Butchers caught by Weavers had their hamstrings cut. Trinity students fighting alongside the Protestant weavers were only hung up by their trouser belts if the butchers captured them. They were, after all, gentry, so the rules were different. This bloody violence was of a piece with the streets' outward austerity; the Rococo interiors balanced the spiritual equation. Airy delicacy lay within, but outside the only ornaments were the doors and the window reveals of white plaster for reflected lighting. North Dublin was in danger of becoming a city of arid brick grids until Dr Mosse came with his hospital.

Dr Mosse was an idealist with a flair for publicity and a most winning human warmth. He had opened a small maternity hospital in 1745, the year of Chesterfield's arrival. This was the first in either Ireland or England and it prospered. By various lotteries, ridottos, concerts and public entertainments Mosse scraped money together and leased in 1748 a large plot of land in the middle of Gardiner territory at the north end of the present O'Connell (then Sackville) Street. His aim was to build a new lying-in, to use the contemporary term, hospital which would double as an architectural masterpiece.

85 A ceiling from 15 Dawson Street, Dublin (*c.* 1755) being removed for storage.

86 A general view of the ceiling of the Chapel in the Rotunda Hospital, Dublin (1755–8).

Behind it on a large, square of sloping land Mosse planned Dublin's equivalent of London's Vauxhall Gardens, a pleasure ground for music, refreshment, walking and dancing. The revenues from the grounds would support the hospital and the land around the grounds would become the city's most desirable residential area, the plots rising in value as a consequence.

Everything worked out precisely as Dr Mosse intended. Dubliners contributed generously to the scheme and Parliament helped out with a substantial grant. It was regrettable that Richard Castle, a close friend of Mosse, had to be the designer of the hospital building, but with its stumpy tower it has at least more drama than Leinster House on the other side of the city (illus. 98). The foundation stone was laid in 1751, Castle died a few months later and George Ensor took over the building work; the tower is to Ensor's design and the one feature distinguishing the Hospital from Leinster House, a twinning that was probably deliberate on Mosse's ingenious part. But in typical Dublin fashion the Hospital's real distinction was internal: a spacious and, for the Protestant Church of Ireland, daringly ambitious, chapel on its first floor.

This un-Irish, un-Protestant interior struggles dramatically to combine three styles – a Palladian base, a billowing Baroque roof (illus. 86) and a scattering of Rococo details on its galleries. The whole insistently allegorical space is approached by a staircase covered with a wonderfully suave ceiling of flowing acanthus in the Tyrone House tradition (illus. 87). A visit to the Chapel is still a most unusual social and aesthetic experience. Nurses pass briskly and pregnant women sail heavily along the corridors, there is inevitably a subdued sense of surgical drama and all the regular hospital smells of disinfectant. Then, through a dark, heavy door, Dr Mosse's vision opens up, of religious faith as the proper concomitant to efficient midwifery and caring nursing. It is a little like walking from a confused and busy London street into Wren's St Stephen's Walbrook, but Wren, his father being a vicar, knew the aesthetic and liturgical limits within which the Church of England was prepared to work and St Stephen's, with all its immaculate spatial geometry, never oversteps them. Here in Mosse's Hospital Chapel there is no such feeling of decorative tact. True, there are no saints' images to disturb Protestant sensibilities, but the whole impact of the ceiling is one of Catholic triumphalism. Over the Communion Table, as if it were an altar where the Sacrament was reserved, two very small cherubs suspend on an extremely heavy plaster curtain. Under its folds kneeling and adoring angels look down at the bare table. Topping the staid Venetian window, where Christ, or at least some major apostle, should rise in majesty, the Holy Lamb stands

87 Robert West's ceiling
to the Stair-Hall
leading to the Rotunda
Chapel, Dublin.

quietly, an inappropriate farmyard creature with a rich canopy and a dangling lambrequin above it.

It is the ceiling which equivocates so tantalizingly between late Baroque and frivolous Rococo. Its compartmentation is heavy and sinuous, full of movement and alive with fluttering cherubs. Semi-circular areas are set at each rounded corner of the central undulant lozenge. At each cardinal point two caryatid angels on long sheath-like pedestals tether down the central compartment (illus. 88), while the semi-circles touch down impatiently at the corners with vine wreaths and volutes as if struggling to lift the staid lower spaces of the Chapel up to Heaven. Most un-Dublinesque of all are the fully three-dimensional allegorical groups sheltering under the caryatid angels. Charity, over the Communion Table, nurses three children; Hope on one side has her anchor; Faith on the other holds cross, Bible and plummet of righteousness while crushing under her cruel foot a fox, surely Catholicism!

88 A detail of the
ceiling in the Dublin
Rotunda Chapel
showing blind Faith,
the fox and attendant
angels.

The man who initiated all this impressive activity was a Huguenot, Bartholomew Cramillion, brought in by Dr Mosse to evoke some at least of the splendours which Mosse had obviously enjoyed and admired on his extensive continental travels. Cramillion agreed on 1 August 1755 to execute the stuccowork for 300 guineas. This must only have covered the ceilings for on 29 December 1757 he signed a second agreement for the stucco of the altarpiece, being paid another £200.[2] But who designed it all? That roof with its caryatid angels could easily be a memory of Frederick the Great's 1747 pavilion palace of Sans Souci at Potsdam, an internalized form of San Souci's caryatid supported dome. Con Curran's research has virtually proved that Cramillion had connections by blood and by marriage with Huguenot linen merchants settled in Ulster;[3] but that does nothing to explain the sources of the Chapel. Other plasterwork in Dublin tentatively attributed to Cramillion bears no relationship to the Chapel's decoration. Dr Mosse was such a vibrant, positive personality and a man of so many parts, a business man, musical, artistic, a late night party-goer with a real talent for friendship, and his Chapel is so unique in Dublin that it is tempting to attribute some role in the general design of that ceiling to him: Carolo Maria Pozzi's Baroque compartments (illus. 89) supported by Bérain's proto-Rococo termini figures. It

89 Ceiling design by
Carolo Maria Pozzi
(*c.* 1710) from Robert
West's collection.

was Catholic art harnessed loosely to Protestant iconography by a doctor with a great delight in humanity and children.

So many carvers, plasterers and craftsmen soon to be dominant in the Dublin building scene were employed in the decoration of the Chapel that it functioned as a practical adult education centre for the subsequent arts of the city. William Lee, Hugh Kelly, McCulagh, Ferdinand Ward and Robert Hallam all worked there between 1751 and 1756. But the name of the plasterer chiefly associated with that broad acanthus work over the staircase to the Chapel has to be kept to the last, because of a most unfortunate coincidence of nomenclature that reads more like the plot of Shakespeare's *Two Gentlemen of Verona* than a sober treatise on the Rococo. Before December 1756, by which time the Hospital was nearing completion, Mosse paid out over £534 to Cramillion's main assistant, Robert West.

This was not Robert West the artist-teacher of the Dublin schools nor, according to all research, was this plasterer-builder Robert West even remotely related to his artist namesake. Yet the artist West taught French Rococo design and the plasterer West created French Rococo plasterwork, he even used designs from Boucher who had been the artist West's master in Paris, or so the artist West always claimed. The situation of the two names is so improbable as to be embarrassing, but it has to be accepted.

Robert West, this plasterer-builder, will feature often in subsequent chapters, presiding, as his building enterprises prospered, over a team of plasterers whose members varied from house to house and over whose designs their employer kept only a loose and sometimes unsuccessful control. West was made a Freeman of Dublin in 1752, three years before he began work at the Rotunda. His brother John was made a Freeman in 1758 and John's son, Robert became a Freeman in 1795. While the family's ancestry has not been precisely traced, it is assumed that they were descended from an old line of Dublin artisans. A John West was made a Freeman in 1639, while Richard West, plasterer, and Edward West, bricklayer, were admitted in 1681.[4]

Often changing his residence and never marrying, West died in 1790, but no commissions are recorded to his name in the last twenty years of his life, which is curious. To become a Freeman of the city he would have had to have been a Protestant, though there was nothing unusual in that. Between 1700 and 1750 78 plasterers achieved Freeman status and another 46 were made between 1750 and 1800. Interestingly, between those last two dates, there are records of 30 plasterers who were not Freemen; these may have been Catholics. What was unusual was that the Protestant West made the Catholic plasterer and designer, Michael Stapleton, the executor of his will. The stylistic implications of this improbable partnership will be considered in a later chapter.

What brings the artistic tastes of West, a key figure in Dublin's brilliant renaissance of plasterwork, to life is a fascinating bundle of prints and engravings in the Architectural Archive.[5] These were bequeathed to Stapleton by his dying friend and bought from Stapleton's descendants for the National Library. So here is invaluable proof as to which foreign artists and designers impressed West and which he considered valuable enough, long after they had become fashionable, to leave to Stapleton.

There are indications that these designs were collected by West early in his working life. None of them relates closely to the more mature and flowing Dublin Rococo work of the 1760s, such as West's rooms at 86 St Stephen's Green. The four designs by Jean Bérain are obviously early influences with their termini figures rising out of sheath-like forms (illus. 90): links to both that lost Pearce ceiling in Dublin Castle, to the caryatid angels on pedestals in the dome of the Rotunda and to the seductive termini women over the Stair-Hall in West's masterpiece, 20 Dominick Street.

Then there are ten designs by Pineau, faint in their printing but containing many vignettes of groups, which have been used for some of Dublin's liveliest ceilings. These are described as 'Nouveau desseins de Plafonds inventés par Pineau et qui peuvent s'executer en sculture ou en peinture',

Berain Invent .   Iacob Weishoff sculpsit .   Ieremias Wolff excud: aug. Vind printed 'A Paris chez Mariette'. One in particular[6] features in its oval frieze or cove small dragons, rocaille work, sphinxes and children playing with a goat, splashing in a wine press and shooting a wolf with a gun: themes picked up by whoever designed the Dining Room ceiling to 9 St Stephen's Green. But all these Pineau designs restrict their ceiling enrichments to coves or friezes. This was the French practice. Only once or twice they sketch tentatively a slight star form for a centrepiece or a few random C scrolls, so West did not take up the usual custom of covering the whole ceiling with a design from these prints. The more generous patterning must have come either from English or Italian influences.

Several West collection prints are English Rococo designs by Glazier, published in 1748, priced sixpence each. These are figurative but with the usual acanthus work and scrolls. Being woolly and vague in their execution and printing they seem more appropriate for silverwork and unlikely subjects for a master plasterer like West to have collected. His four or five dual-image prints of mirrors, overmantels and furniture by Thomas Johnson, dated 1752, would have offered easier, more linear models to follow (illus. 91).

The most interesting items in this seminal collection are six very large and boldly drawn Baroque ceiling designs by Carolo Maria Pozzi (illus. 89). He was producing his designs in the early decades of the eighteenth century with their pronounced, and often double, cornices and lozenge-shaped corner and central compartments, all animated with cherubs. They are a likely source, or inspiration at least, for the great ceiling of the Rotunda Chapel. The interesting questions, to which there can be no sure answers, is why were the Pozzi designs in West's collection? Who actually suggested the broad framework for the design of the Chapel ceiling? Did West, a master builder as well as a plasterer, suggest Pozzi as a model, and was Cramillion then left to execute the figurative work poised on those broad mouldings and in the four corners? Or did Cramillion simply leave the Pozzi designs with West as a memento, and for us as a puzzle? Were the Pozzi sheets perhaps souvenirs from Dr Mosse's European travels, visual sources which he passed on to Cramillion or West in order to set their creative imagination working? That would be the most satisying answer.

Everything which Dr Mosse touched seemed to turn to music and enchantments, he was a typical Rococo figure: joyful, uninhibited, practical and life enhancing. The pleasure gardens behind the Hospital were an immediate success. By 1761 there were 500 subscribers, each paying a guinea a year. The concert season lasted from nineteen to twenty-one weeks with three concerts a week, held from noon to 3 pm in Spring and from 6.30 to

90 Grotesque design by Jean Bérain (c. 1705) from Robert West's collection.

91 A 1752 design by
Thomas Johnson from
Robert West's
collection.

9.30 pm on Summer evenings. There was high class social walking on Sunday evenings and not quite such high class social walking on weekdays. Mrs Delany only referred to 'Ireland's Vauxhall' to recount a public battle which took place there, so she claimed, between a gentleman and a street walker lady who had no business to intrude. But that could have been sour grapes from a house-bound Mrs Delany as the programme of events, ridottos, four oratorios a year, Handel's *Artaxerxes*, balls and card parties, could have been designed to delight her youthful tastes. Lord Mornington, whose house in Merrion Street will be noticed later for its superbly crafted plasterwork, played there after 1757 with his Musical Academy and Lord Charlemont, for whom William Chambers would design the Casino at Marino, sang the part of Peachum in Gay's *Beggar's Opera*.

Quick to take advantage of the rocketing ground values of his new Rutland Square overlooking the pleasure grounds on its northern, eastern and western sides (the Hospital occupied the southern), Dr Mosse formed a building consortium with John Ensor and Henry Darley to build three particularly grand and splendidly appointed town houses behind Dublin's usual unrevealing brick façades. One of these, Number 5 in Rutland, re-named Parnell, Square, has been gutted by redevelopment, but the other two, now numbered 4 in Parnell Square and 9 in its southern arm of Cavendish

Row, are of great significance as Robert West was in charge of their plaster-work.[7] His work here, carried out 1756–7, bridges the gap in his extraordinary learning curve between the fine but wholly conventional ceiling over the Hospital's Stair-Hall, a work similar to the Saloon ceiling at Russborough, and his amazing stylistic eruption at 20 Lower Dominick Street, a little to the east of the Hospital, in 1758. Even Dominick Street would not be the end of Robert West's development, but it has to be seen as the high point of his career when he allowed several plasterers of his team to go their own way and thereby achieve the Sistine Chapel of Dublin Rococo in the Stair-Hall.

Number 9 Cavendish Row is the more conventional and probably the earlier of West's two surviving interiors from 1756–7, the house where he personally kept a close control of the ceiling designs. But in the interval between the ceilings of the first-floor front and back rooms his elegantly curving broad acanthus took courage and learnt to fly. In the front room the leaves wave decorously in the outer compartment (illus. 92), only touching the inner at the cardinal points. In the back room, while the compartment boundary survives, it is almost lost under a dance of leaping, overlapping acanthus. The diagonal and cardinal points are all underplayed and West is clearly beginning to see the ceiling as a whole complex symmetry (illus. 93). Only the swags of flowers still impose some rhythmic discipline.

Then at 4 Parnell Square a kind of chaos is threatened; West was loosening his grip on the design process. His acanthus still command the cavernous Stair-Hall with a splendid leafy rhythm at the frieze, ceiling and mid-stair level; but either the four fine rooms of the house, two on each main floor, were designed by four different plasterers or some schizoid and improbable genius moved from room to room in the house's quite brief building period designing in unrelated styles. In the first-floor front room masks are ineptly scattered among loose rose trails on the ceiling and more masks alternate with fat roses and intrusive double brackets on the cornice. The other three fine rooms are different again, one confident with flowers in pots and elegant busts of little boys, one with flower swags and corner urns (illus. 94), another with a broad ring of daisies and a rounded square of fruit. Each suggests a different plasterer. By 1756 the schools of the Dublin Society had been active for seven years turning out a steady stream of young men familiar with French designs, and some at least of these had become plasterers, so West and other Dublin builders could call upon a pool of skilled workers when a house had to be decorated for a quick sale and profit. But did West arbitrate over the designs these new men could offer? Did Mosse or Ensor or a potential purchaser have any say?

Number 4 Parnell Square offers some preparation for 20 Lower Dominick Street by this diversity but nothing for the shock of the Dominick Street Stair-Hall. Rising to the right directly out of the Entrance Hall this is the puzzle and delight of the house. In these relatively early days of Dublin's tourism it is still possible to enjoy the city's supreme decorative experience alone, at leisure and for free. Inevitably this cannot last and in one sense it should not last, for it is a treasure of far greater imaginative reach than McCormac's much visited Romanesque chapel on the hill of Cashel. Every school child in Dublin should, at some appropriate educational stage, be taken to 20 Lower Dominick Street to see what Irish craftsmen were capable of, not in the remote medieval past, but in the eighteenth century of tyrant landlords, famines and the Protestant Ascendancy. They should, ideally, visit the house when it is perfectly lit and preferably unfurnished, with no distracting commentary on the social life of the upper classes to divert their attention; for this is a shrine of concentrated art, a series of spatial experiences not merely a house, and it needs to be enjoyed as it was when Robert West handed it over in 1758 to its first owner, the Right Hon. Robert Marshall, all white and bare and alive with invention.

The interiors represent no unified masterpiece of domestic planning such as Robert Taylor was devising in these years at Harleyford Manor, Bucking-

93 In the first-floor rear room of 9 Cavendish Row, Dublin (1756–7), the West team of plasterers are venturing to overfly the compartment boundaries with confidence.

94 Heavy detail from
the hall-floor rear room
of 4 Parnell Square,
Dublin (1757).

hamshire and Barlaston Hall, Staffordshire. Dominick Street contains four
unequal and unrelated episodes of genius, descending in quality from the
brilliant Stair-Hall to the poetic first-floor Drawing Room, the uncertain
ground-floor front room and lastly the unrestored first-floor back, or Venus
Room.

The Stair-Hall is nothing like as large as those of West's earlier three
houses yet it has the pretensions and the spatial effects which could easily
carry the grand stairs of an Italian palace like Caserta (illus. 100). Half an
hour is not too long to spend absorbing its distractions and its multiple
effects. Even then the memory of how its groups inter-related soon grows
confused. It is quite unlike any other room associated with West, though
the Stair-Hall of 86 St Stephen's Green has details by the same plasterer, and
the projection of the ornament in one room at Malahide Castle and in the
Red Drawing Room at Newbridge Hall approaches, though never equals,
the sixteen-inch projection of the flapping crane birds of Dominick Street
(ilus. 99). Richard Williams, a pupil of West, is known to have worked at
Newbridge and, in default of any other name to credit for this master work,
Richard Williams, working to a design by Bartholomew Cramillion, is the
likeliest suggestion: a last flourish of Baroque theatricality in Rococo Dublin.

Cramillion may have been at least consulted here. His Baroque-Rococo

95 The Stair-Hall of
20 Lower Dominick
Street, Dublin: detail of
musical trophy and
palms.

Rotunda Chapel ceiling rotates around four semi-circles loosely anchored to the corners by wreaths and to the cardinal points of the square by angels rising out of long sheaths. All its relief is very bold with many free-standing figures. The Stair-Hall ceiling at Dominick Street rotates around eight semi-circles loosely anchored at the corners by women's busts rising out of long sheaths and to the cardinal points of the square by flower trails (illus. 95) and acanthus, so both ceilings relate loosely in design to those Pozzi engravings in the collection West left to Stapleton. No other Dublin ceilings have these rhythms, but while the Dominick Street semi-circles rotate about an exact circular compartment, the Chapel semi-circles touch an undulating lozenge, and where the Chapel's free-standing figures are human allegories symmetrically placed, those at Dominick Street are ho-ho birds or cranes which have escaped from their usual roosts on Rococo mirrors and perch unpredictably at various levels of the stairs and the landing (illus. 101).

When that has been said everything else is bewilderment: a bewilderment of birds, flapping, peering and preening, of musical instruments and musical stands, of the 'termini' women trapped on their sheaths and around all those, cornucopia, flower wreaths and drops with a few acanthus for good measure, all in bold relief and rich detail. But the birds are not confined to the ceiling; four twinned sets of them have come down to roost on rakishly elegant C scroll perches. The most beautiful, because it is the most asymmetrical, of these pairs greets the visitor climbing the stairs. Here the two perches are wilfully set at different levels (illus. 102; 105) with delicate commas of plasterwork trailing away at inconsequential angles below and curving up above to overfly the cornice via one of the music stands which are part of the hall's mysterious imagery. So much of Dublin's figurative plasterwork can be interpreted in the light of Caesare Ripa's *Iconologie* (1593), the illustrated edition of 1645, published in Venice, but this Stair-Hall is too individual and whimsical for that. It is a royal aviary with captive women.

A door on the left of the landing leads into the Drawing Room and an enchanting sanity. This would have been socially the most superior room in the house and the focus of the most privileged entertainment. Here the walls below the rich Corinthian cornice have no perches and the superb ceiling celebrates feminine fertility with groups of naked cherubs at play, straight copies from François Boucher's *Premier Livre de Groupes d'Enfants.* Joseph McDonnell has traced borrowings from Boucher in plaster and wood elsewhere in Dublin[8] and it seems reasonable to suggest that the other Robert West had recommended the sources to his students. Around the cherubs much lighter C scrolls delicately twine out to heavier rocaille work at the corners, the birds that fly among the rose trails are doves, none of the giant ho-ho birds from next door have intruded, even the violins are diminutive. What gives the ceiling its grace and charm is the absolute absence of any compartmentation, possibly the earliest Irish incidence of such freedom.

With all these Rococo, as opposed to Adam-style or, in Ireland, Michael Stapleton, ceilings, it is a point of contention as to how much of the work was done by freehand modelling and how much was produced by moulds. Andrew Smith, who was restoring the Drawing Room ceiling on two of the authors' visits, was of the opinion that almost everything was freehand. The authors incline to moulds, at least for the acanthus and for many of the flower trails. Andrew Smith has done restoration work at Newbridge and supports the theory that Richard Williams had been involved in the Stair-Hall of Dominick Street.

Liam Daly, a skilled craftsman encountered on one visit, offered some revealing insights into the practicalities of restoration work. He had been associated with Dominick Street for many years and recalled the orphans and their depredations. When he had to reconstruct some of the giant birds on the stairs he began with twisted coat hangers as armatures, wrapped crumpled chicken wire around these, and then formed the crude shape from newspaper which had been dampened to bring out the paraffin wax in the

96 Apollo Musagates in Dublin Castle, posed in a composition of hidden diagonals.

97 The entrance pavilion of Dublin Castle (1750s).

98 The Rotunda Hospital, Dublin (begun 1751). Windows on the first floor of the central block light the Chapel.

99 One of the birds on the Stair-Hall at 20 Lower Dominick Street, Dublin (1756–8).

101 The clasp over the string course in the Stair-Hall of 20 Lower Dominick Street is a stylized music stand.

100 Opposite
The compartmented ceiling over the Stair-Hall of 20 Lower Dominick Street, Dublin, with plasterwork by the Robert West team.

103 Merrion Square, North Side, Dublin: bland façades to a chain of lyrical Rococo interiors of the 1760s.

102 Opposite
A royal aviary with captive women on the Stair-Hall of 20 Lower Dominick Street.

104 Over
The Stair-Hall of 86 St Stephen's Green, Dublin (1765), a late work by Robert West.

print. More subtle details were then built up with a mixture of cowdung, horsehair and plaster, exactly as in the eighteenth century.

The Parlour on the ground floor immediately under the Drawing Room would have been the Morning or Breakfast Room where ordinary visitors were received. It is distinguished by its use of a Chinese fret to connect quite crudely modelled women's heads, cockatoos and parrots with the usual flower trails (illus. 106). Ireland never became as infatuated with Chinoiserie as England and here the Eastern reference is unauthentic. Indeed the fret could easily be a borrowing from Bérain bandwork. At the rear of the house on the first floor is the Venus Room, the best Bedroom which would, if Mrs Delany's account of reception is believed, have been used as one of the rooms for the entertainment of visitors on an 'At Home' day. Unfortunately it is still so encrusted with centuries of overpainting that it is impossible to judge its quality fairly. The ceiling appears to have simple and quite crude Rococo scrolls around a centrepiece of Venus and Cupid, this last very small but a figurative throw-back to the Francini brothers. Robert West was also the builder of the house next door, and there the plasterwork is urbane, impersonal and French in styling. Bristol at this period had up to seventy plasterers on its records and contemporary Dublin had at least a hundred working all over the city, which would easily account for the diversity of style so far observed.

On this evidence Robert West seems to have been a plasterer who worked his way up through a series of ceilings based principally on broad waving acanthus. He had acquired a repertory of moulds which could be used to lay the flowing outlines of the ceiling quickly, the details and delicate variations being filled in afterwards by hand. West may have learnt his trade at Tyrone House as early as 1740 and on the Russborough Saloon around 1742–3. By the time he came to the ceiling of the Rotunda Chapel stairs he was confident but still limited as to invention, and this limitation shows in his work at 4 Parnell Square and 9 Cavendish Row, even though by that time he was growing increasingly contemptuous of rigid compartmental confinement. He had been working over at least a two-year period alongside Bartholomew Cramillion. At this time he had come into possession of his Pozzi drawings as well as those by Pineau and Bérain. While he still tended to use conventional cornices of the Classical orders with their correct enrichments, he was now wide open to other new ideas: Italian Baroque as well as French Rococo for the broad spaces of main ceilings. When he took on 20 Lower Dominick Street he had become more the builder-contractor than the plasterer, a man with capital to risk but with a team of craftsmen plasterers whom he could

106 The Breakfast
Room ceiling of 20
Lower Dominick
Street, Dublin:
Bérainesque strapwork
with Chinese birds.

105 Opposite
Two birds perched on
the landing of 20
Lower Dominick
Street, Dublin.

trust to absorb the possibilities of these new designs which he had been collecting. This would explain the extraordinary stylistic disparity of the Dominick Street rooms. There were perhaps four men working in the four separate rooms, inspired by four different designs from West's collection. McDonnell has traced the Boucher, the other sources have proved more elusive. It is unlikely that West himself, the broad acanthus man, was personally responsible for any of the work in Dominick Street, he seems rather to have offered the models for adaptation and then to have had the confidence to preside over a multi-talented group in a positive detachment.

CHAPTER XI

WIDE STREETS AND
AN EMBARRASSMENT
OF RICHES

Does a great period of decorative art, such as Dublin enjoyed in the Rococo decades, reflect in any way the contemporary spirit of a nation? A photograph of Lower Dominick Street (illus. 107), taken before the clearances and municipal rebuilding schemes of the last forty years, conveys the resolutely unrewarding outward face of those Protestant grandee houses and the apparently deliberate, rather than economically enforced, contrast between their interior exuberance and their utterly undemonstrative elevations to the street. If it were possible to return to the city as it stood in 1770, before James Gandon's Custom House, Four Courts and Inns of Court gave poetry to the waterfront, distinction and drama to its skyline, Dublin must have appeared an oddly twentieth-century and soulless urban complex. Apart from its old core of narrow streets between Trinity College and the two cathedrals, its new streets, north and south-east, presented a grid of almost featureless brick uniformity.

For a militantly Protestant city alive with high-living bishops it was strangely indifferent to building those churches which would have given it the vertical elements so necessary to counter the horizontality of Georgian classicism. St Stephen's, the pepper-pot at the end of Upper Mount Street's attenuated vista, was not built until 1825, and the only really resounding Gibbs-style church steeple, St George's, did not go up until 1803–13. In the old centre, St Werburgh's was eventually given a spire in 1768, only to have it pulled down deliberately by the authorities in the early nineteenth century

because it overlooked the Castle. Dublin was essentially a garrison city in
potentially hostile Catholic territory; in times of riot towers and spires would
offer strong-points for snipers. The way in which massive Classical buildings
like the Post Office and the Four Courts were to function in the twentieth-
century civil wars seems to prove that the Ascendancy was not being unduly
nervous in the eighteenth century.

This faceless, ground-hugging nature of mid-century Dublin does also
raise questions about the Rococo generally as an architectural movement.
Palladian Bath and Robert Adam's neo-Classical Edinburgh could both rise
easily to grand façades of the orders on entirely domestic buildings. Rococo
Dublin notably failed to achieve such a face. Visitors were usually impressed
by the width of its streets and Dubliners were themselves given to self-
congratulation on the subject. The Wide Streets Commission set up by Act
of Parliament in 1757 was only an official response to an existing public
demand. It was as if spaciousness, not only in the width of the streets but in
the length – 300 to 400 feet (91–121 m) – of the rear garden and premises,
was a sufficient mark of outward affluence. Canted bays, the mark of Rococo
design in England, were common enough in Dublin's backs, but virtually
non-existent on street façades. Everywhere there was this wind-blown open-
ness. Sackville Street (O'Connell) is 154 feet wide (47 m), Lower Dominick
Street 74 feet (22 m), Gardiner Street 85 feet (26 m); even with twentieth-
century traffic levels ever rising, Upper Merrion Street in the heart of the
administrative quarter is usually a wide open desert of tarmac which demands not so much a pedestrian crossing as an expedition to traverse it. But
consciously noble façades, columns, pediments and ashlar facing are, by

English and Scottish standards, miserably lacking. Instead, that bland repetition of pink brick, sharp-edged and lightly poised (illus. 103), extends on all sides and down all the uniformly horizontal vistas. Bath's speculative builders had been achieving terraces with palatial fronts since the 1730s and even mercantile, bourgeois Bristol contrived a unified terrace, Albemarle Row, in 1762; but Dublin's speculators contented themselves with small ventures, apart from one late and abandoned scheme for a square at the top of Upper Gardiner street. There was never any thought that lively, poetic interiors should be matched by a frivolous elevation. In that sense it was a Protestant Rococo.

The dismal political background to Dublin's Rococo years, the period from 1746 to 1770, may explain in some measure the almost exclusively internal nature of its architecture in the capital, though country houses like Dunboyne Castle and Dowth Hall, both with exotic Rococo interiors, are in their exteriors nothing more than raw chunks of Dublin street architecture cut off and dropped down gracelessly in smiling countryside. There was something oddly sour and grudging about the Ascendancy's response to outward show. It was as if the effort required to furnish Trinity with not just one but multiple grand, columnar elevations, infinitely beyond anything which contemporary English universities could show, had exhausted the whole country's requirement for pomp. Or was the Rococo spirit essentially one of casual domestic joy rather than outward dignity?

After Lord Chesterfield's light-hearted and up-beat viceregality a profitless schism developed between the Executive and the Legislative arms of government, a rift, in effect, between the controlling English and the increasingly confident Anglo-Irish. In the eighteenth century a country tended to be made, or in the case of Poland and Ireland, unmade, by the integrity and sense of patriotic purpose of its aristocracy. A majority of the Irish House of Lords were Protestants, of quite recent creation, ennobled carpet-baggers. In an unfortunate twist, Lord Chesterfield's honest management of the state had left a surplus in the Treasury and for many years this created a running battle between Parliament and the Castle. The Viceroys were obliged to claim the money for the Crown to reduce England's national debt, while Parliament was determined to keep it in Ireland. The Earl of Harrington, Chesterfield's lacklustre successor, endured a miserable four years of financial wrangling and political agitation as the Protestant Irish, increasingly assertive, rocked the boat of state which they would have been well advised to keep on an even keel. A surge of prosperity had followed the ending of the war in 1748; the Dublin building boom of the 1750s, when so many rich

Rococo interiors were created, was a sign of it. Like the American colonists across the Atlantic, the ruling Irish began to fret against English control as soon as the French enemy had been countered. After being pelted with whisky bottles in a public theatre, a dramatic sign of public affluence, Lord Harrington retreated to England. The Duke of Dorset, who had been a safe pair of hands in his first viceregal term, was sent out again in 1751, hopefully to calm an obstreperous city.

He failed. The Lords Justices, the so-called 'undertakers', who ruled Ireland during the long viceregal absences, made Dorset ineffective. The Ponsonby family, whose head was the Earl of Bessborough, had grown too influential by marriage to two daughters of the Duke of Devonshire during an earlier viceregal term. Now they intrigued for the Speakership of the Commons, and the three Lords Justices: the Primate, Archbishop Stone, Speaker Boyle and the Chancellor, never worked as a team. Dorset retired with relief in 1755 and the Duke of Devonshire's heir, the cold, arrogant Marquis of Hartington, was sent out to succeed him in the hope that he could control his Ponsonby brothers-in-law. Ill-advisedly Hartington, who was a widower, asked one of his Ponsonby sisters to do the honours for him at the Castle. Only eight months later his father died and, as the new Duke of Devonshire, he became anxious to escape the tensions of Ireland and return home. Speaker Boyle retired in 1756 and John Ponsonby succeeded him at last as Speaker. Soon he, the malcontent Earl of Kildare and Bessborough joined the commission of the Lords Justices creating an unenviable situation for the next Viceroy, the Duke of Bedford, who endured, from 1756 to 1761 – the greater part of the Seven Years War – an Ireland of sniping journalism and a truculent Parliament.

At that point Ireland began to reflect the political instability which the blundering of the new King, George III, had produced in England. Five Viceroys followed in quick succession between 1761 and 1767, two of them, Viscount Weymouth and the Earl of Bristol, never even crossed the Irish Sea. But in 1767, coinciding roughly with the decline of the Rococo and the rage for the new Adam style, Lord Townshend took office. Thereafter Viceroys were expected to live in Dublin throughout their term and no longer treat the honour as a biennial inconvenience distracting them from real life in London. So the twenty-odd years of Dublin Rococo were those when a spirit of detachment from England prevailed and the earlier subservience to the decrees of London had been replaced by contention and resentment. By 1750 the population of the city had risen to 120,000 and 3,000 new houses would soon be going up. Ireland's ruling Protestant minority was growing restless for real self-government, an illogicality considering their continuing dependence upon a large English garrison, but Irish nationalism had yet to become a threatening force. The Rococo appears then to have been an inward sign of a misplaced outward confidence, and possibly a mark of detachment from the Palladian fashions across the water. Whatever its inspiration may have been, Irish plasterwork of that period represented the first major episode in European art which the island had produced since its book illustrations of the Dark Ages.

It is easy to understand why those illustrated books loom so much larger in Irish self-awareness than does Rococo plasterwork. Religious associations apart, the books can be contained in darkened galleries, cleverly lit and surrounded by dramatic enlargements, all at eye level or a little below. On payment of one entry fee an entire Celtic art form can be comfortably absorbed. But to gain even a partial impression of the several variant strains of Dublin plasterwork, their richness and individuality, means knocking at the doors of, at the very least, twenty private houses. Even then these houses have usually been converted into multiple office tenancy. Rooms have been divided, lift shafts sever superb overdoors, secondary ceilings have been hung, often garish decorative painting has been applied to patterning which would always have been better left white or off-white, to allow the shadows of the boldly raised Rococo work to make its own subtle impact. Perhaps most alienating of all is the height of the plasterwork. To study it properly a portable chaise longue with a head rest would be required. English cathedrals attempt to solve the problem by laying large horizontal mirrors on stands. Dublin offices are too full of word processors and board meetings to have the space or the time for such visual aids.

This chapter will attempt to convey the five or six main strands of Dublin's Rococo, but the only way to suggest how rewarding and important these ceilings are in a European context is by comparisons. A week spent in their investigation and enjoyment is as satisfying and memorable as the equivalent time spent enjoying Palladio's villas on the Brenta or touring for a week the Romanesque churches of the Saintonge. Somehow the Irish Tourist Board should find a solution to the problems of accessibility as well as of care. Dublin's Rococo deserves to be put firmly on the cultural agenda of the educated visitor, to become a 'tourist must' like the cave paintings of the Dordogne, the Baroque churches of Swabia or the Manoeline of Portugal. Those stored ceilings could be returned to public view. Lisbon has a wonderful museum of *azulegos* in a deconsecrated convent. Somewhere in one of its barracks, hospitals or locked Protestant churches, Dublin could create an equivalent for its plasterwork.

The rigid geometry of Palladian compartments, as evidenced in the early houses of Henrietta Street and the House of Lords seems to have held very little appeal for Irish plasterers. On the one hand they had the nude gods and goddesses of the Francini brothers' Italian style and on the other the treillage and the dance of grotesque motifs, diagonals to diagonals, cardinal points to cardinal points, of the French Bérainesque designs. More appealing than either, as earlier chapters have indicated, were the flowing patterns of acanthus work. These acanthus would change gradually over a twenty-year period to leaner, more abstract forms of rocaille work, thin writhing pie-crust shapes edging away from free-form invention towards the entirely predictable scroll work, elegant enough in its way, but tedious, of Michael Stapleton, Ireland's interpreter of the Adam style.

Before that decorative dead-end Dublin plasterers had two decades in which to create cultural crosses between the Italian and the French, to absorb the mature sophistications of the continental Rococo as introduced by Cramillion and then to devise an Irish Rococo of their own. The first hybrid form was conceived either by plasterers who had worked under the Francinis but reacted against their neo-Classical solemnities with grace and humour, or by the Francinis themselves designing in more florid Baroque compositions once they had escaped from the confines of premature neo-Classicism and Palladian predictability. This resulted in an enchanting cartoon world of big chubby cherubs (illus. 108), amorous deities and moralities, all disporting against a dense framework of ribbons and acanthus. The Hall and reception rooms of 9 St Stephen's Green and the Saloon and Library at Kilshannig, Co. Cork have the most overwhelming examples of this mode. Its essence is fleshly, a coarsening, an earthy commentary on its sources which it is tempting to describe as typically Irish, a refusal to be overawed by exemplars. The cherubs of the seasons, set around the figure of Fortitude in the Dining Room of Number 9 are comic masterpieces. One huddles over a winter fire like an old man, another simpers in a mirror like a society belle, another muscular baby beats out metal on an anvil. Their designer could clearly turn his hand to any subject but chose to limit himself to cheerful mockery, a very Rococo choice. In the same house where these delightful ceilings were being hung, plasterers were still working on the walls in the dated and inappropriate manner of the early Francini work in 85 St Stephen's Green and in Riverstown House, Co. Cork, treating plaster not just as a frame for a picture but as the picture itself. The scenes from Classical legend so created are amusing conversation pieces but fortunately this naïve deployment of the medium never became popular in the city.

108 Cherubs of the Seasons from the Large Drawing Room ceiling of 9 St Stephen's Green, Dublin (c. 1756).

Venus wounded by Love, probably the best known of all Dublin's ceilings, should be included in this cartoon school of design as it is a soft focus parody of Hendrick Goltzuis's engraving of that name.[1] Intended as a piece of mild pornography to divert the off-duty hours of a La Touche banker, it has found its way, after the demolition of the La Touche premises, to the Directors' Dining Room in the National Bank of Ireland. With clever lighting it photographs superbly, but seen, as it were, in the flesh, either its new siting is too lofty or its relief was always too shallow for the *di sotto in sù* (seen from below) illusion to work well. The plasterer had a penchant for plump mounds and he distributed them impartially on Venus's breasts, right hand, left leg and stomach, on Cupid's cheek and belly and on two attendant love birds. The swans at the four corners of the composition are meltingly beautiful but again, too shallow in relief; the best Rococo work requires peaks and ridges to define by its shadows. John and Peter La Touche, the banker's sons, were favourite pupils of Robert West at his private school, winning premiums in 1746 for drawings praised, significantly, for 'spirit, life and softness, being good copies of original prints and pictures'.[2] West's role in the selection of the Goltzuis as a model is likely to have been decisive.

Six ceilings, three rescued from the demolition of Mespil House on the Dublin outskirts, two, or more accurately two-and-a-half, at Belvedere House in Co. Westmeath and the one Aesop ceiling which has always been in the Viceregal Lodge, are so exquisitely refined and so allusively German

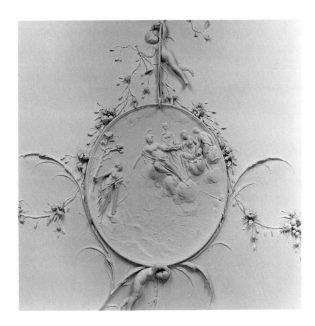

in their Rococo styling that they are usually attributed to a foreigner. McDonnell believes that they were created by Bartholomew Cramillion, author of the Rotunda Chapel ceiling. They certainly have the sophistication of that last, but it is difficult to relate the heavy mouldings and insistent Baroque compartments of the Chapel with the airy lightness of the six ceilings. Cramillion is known to have arrived in 1755, to have worked at the Rotunda until either 1759 or 1760 and then left Ireland in 1762 for ten years. A central date for these six would appear to be 1751–2. That was when Mespil House was built for the physician, Sir Edward Barry, and probably the year when Nathaniel Clements built Phoenix Park Lodge, which was the original core of the Viceregal Lodge. Theories that such ceilings may have been added eight or nine years after the houses were built are never convincing as that would require major refitting operations in almost new buildings. When Sir Edward wrote in 1751, 'My little villa begins to ryse above the ground, I shall be as happy there as Pliny was at Laurenti. Then as I have been a slave to the town I shall think my garden and park an Elysian Field where I can freely breathe airs of my own',[3] he was creating a perfect retirement home superbly appointed, not a shell for future contractors in which to work.

Two of these ceilings, Apollo with the Arts and Sciences and a Minerva bringing the Arts to Hibernia (illus. 109), are now in the State Rooms of the Castle. While both are very fine they appear to be the work of two different

110 Air from the
Ceiling of the
Elements, Mespil
House (*c*. 1752), now in
Áras an Uachtaráin, the
old Viceregal Lodge.

111 Opposite
The Aesop ceiling in
Áras an Uachtaráin
(*c*. 1752).

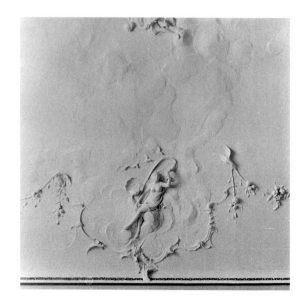

plasterers. Minerva is sharply moulded with a peaked and linear definition; the other is far softer in its moulding, the Apollo head almost melting back into the surface and the design of diagonals, corner trophy to corner trophy, is Bérainesque and quite unlike the composition of the Minerva. While it is just possible that a skilled craftsman might design two ceilings in the same house in two different styles, it is most unlikely. The finest of the three Mespil ceilings, Jupiter presiding over the four Elements and Seasons (illus. 110), has joined Aesop at the Viceregal Lodge and by a happy accident it looks as if two ceilings by the same plasterer, but originally raised in two different houses, have now been brought together. In these two ceilings more than in any other of the six there is a strong south German influence. The tenderly executed groups of Aesop animals and elemental figures (illus. 111) are not as encrusted with garlands as the figurative groups which Johann Baptist Zimmermann created on the 1734–9 ceilings of the Spiegelsaal of the Amalienburg at Schloss Nymphenburg, near Munich,[4] but the Dublin plasterer seems at one time to have either worked alongside the Zimmermann brothers or observed their French-inspired German Rococo appreciatively.

The two-and-a-half ceilings over the Dining and Drawing Rooms and Hall of Belvedere House are very close in styling to the Aesop and Elements ceilings but more tentative in their moulding, airier, as if the plasterer had not yet the confidence to raise shadows by his reliefs. Any attempt to date them involves some mildly prurient discussion of Ireland's outstanding eighteenth-century sex and incest scandal. Robert Rochfort, Lord Belfield, married

Mary Molesworth, a daughter of Viscount Molesworth, the wealthy Dublin property owner. She is supposed to have played him false with Arthur, the younger of his two brothers, in 1743, and compounded the insult by telling him that one of his sons was actually sired by Arthur and 'she had no pleasure with any man like that she had with him'.[5] In her old age, when she had managed to outlive her dreadful husband, she strenuously denied the story, but at the time everyone accepted it and Arthur's flight to England suggests that it was true. Its relevance to the dating of Belvedere House and the plasterwork is that her husband shut her up in his old family house, Gaulston, and took up his own residence in Belvedere, quite a small two-storey villa with Rococo semi-circular bays at each end, built for him surprisingly by the usually staid Palladian, Richard Castle. The interesting question is whether Belvedere was built after the scandal as a permanent home where he could escape from his wife's memory, or whether it was built even earlier, 1740 is sometimes suggested, as a pleasure house, five miles away from Gaulston and delightfully situated on the banks of Lough Ennell. If it dates from 1740, or even from 1744 after the trauma, the house, and presumably the ceilings, are not only very fine, but very early in the Rococo period. Cramillion is supposed to have been brought over to Ireland by Dr Mosse in 1751, which would make him an unlikely designer for the ceilings, though, it will be recalled, Con Curran suggested an Ulster Huguenot connection for him.[6]

Rochfort was made Earl Belvedere in 1756 and lived on in great state at the house for many years, almost forgiving his wife on one occasion but then hardening his heart and tightening the conditions of her confinement. Belvedere is a small house, but even so he employed seven footmen and four *valets de chambre* in laced clothes. Dining there in 1773, Sir James Caldwell praised the food and the plate and noted the presence of Lord Newton 'by many degrees the handsomest boy I ever laid my eyes on'.[7] The plasterwork at the house is elegantly feminine to the point of being effete, which would seem to suit the Earl's character. Jupiter in the Hall is very close in modelling to Jupiter in the centre of the Mespil 'Elements and Seasons' ceiling, so both are clearly by the same plasterer; the skittish perversity of the rocaille work and the way in which all the ceilings are enclosed within curvilinear lozenges also points to one designer. An advancing maturity of composition in the main elements would suggest that they were designed in the sequence of Belvedere House (1740–6), Mespil House (*c.* 1751–2) and Phoenix Park Lodge (*c.* 1753).

Whatever their chronology their beauty is haunting; they are miniature heavens of dream-like reference to the usual Cesare Ripa iconography.

112 Detail from the
Dining Room ceiling of
Belvedere House,
Co. Westmeath (1740s).

Water and Air, personified by naked female figures on the Elements ceiling, are particularly fine. The modelling of them is quite distinct from the smooth, rounded outlines of the 'cartoon' ceilings, sharper, more peaked and shadowed for all their tiny scale. Dangling leaves and frets hang everywhere and Mark Girouard wrote of 'scrollwork that flickers and crackles like flames around the edge of the ceiling'[8] (illus. 112). In them there is no element of parody, even the cherubs are wistful studies of real life babies, they suffer with the emblematic Seasons on which they perch, they do not laugh at them as the cartoon cherubs do. Over the Belvedere Dining Room the artist-plasterer began, with his flying dragon balancing a bowl of fruit, to invent a fantasy world and then opted out with a few clouds and cherubs. But then in Aesop and the Elements he raised the domestic art of ceiling design to a pitch of escapist realism with an undulant symmetry of rocaille and garlands: high art in every sense of the word. These, together with the 20 Lower Dominick Street Stair-Hall, are Irish plasterwork at its best.

There was much more to come but nothing quite as memorable, and whoever modelled these six ceilings, whether Cramillion or several unknowns, appears not to have worked again in Ireland. With such skills and

113 The rocaille-work ceiling in the first-floor Drawing Room of 26 Merrion Square, Dublin (*c.* 1767).

such creative imagination they could hardly have remained inactive, though ceilings like that on the first-floor Drawing Room of 26 Merrion Square, North Side (illus. 113), reflect his influence. One curious feature of Irish Rococo work is that it never developed into one coherent school of design. Like wallpaper, it seems to have been varied and selected to satisfy individual tastes. In that sense Robert West was the archetypal Dublin plasterer, turned builder-decorator.

It would be satisfying, since there was such a clear movement throughout the Rococo years in Dublin from broad leaf to ever airier and more feminine, delicate rocaille work, to prove that the lady of the house was a dominant factor in design. Unfortunately, Mrs Delany, who should have thrown light on this issue, tends to suggest that her husband decided the plasterwork. Speaking of the Library at Delville, 'The Dean', she wrote, 'has made an addition at the end of it . . . it is to be all of stucco, and adorned with pilasters'.[9] When wall-papering was involved she was in charge; for her bedchamber: 'blue and white linen and blue and white hangings, this has taken up a good deal of attention', and for her work room: 'the paper I have chosen is pearl colour caffoy paper; the pattern like damask: the pictures look extremely well on that colour, and the crimson damask window-curtain and chairs will suit very well with it'.[10]

In the popular mind Dublin plasterwork generally, and West's work in particular, is rightly closely associated with birds. The Stair-Hall at 20 Dominick Street is chiefly responsible for this, but oddly those querulous cranes or ho-ho birds which feature so dramatically there were never copied, perhaps because they were too vulnerable to damage. Other birds have a much longer history as motifs in Irish plasterwork. A pioneering eagle, his wings spread wide, is flying up in the lantern vault of Edward Lovett Pearce's Bellamont Forest, built in the early 1730s. Nothing would seem more natural than for a ceiling designer to conceive his rectangular space as a sky and to give his flower baskets and wreaths birds as supporters. In fact the staid Palladian ceiling rarely took the obvious course. Henry Dogood added a flight of swans to the Library ceiling of Pembroke College, Cambridge in 1690 but, faced with the *di sotto in sù* problem, modelled the birds quite literally from underneath, resulting in an immodest group of flying hens with horrid feathery bottoms. The Hall ceiling at Belvedere House has a parrot perched improbably on a cloud, an early Irish instance; the flying dragonette in the Dining Room is more at ease because it has something to carry.

The grotesque work of Jean Bérain and Claude Audran (1658–1734) often includes birds and dragons, so these are the likeliest sources of that commonest of Dublin frieze motifs: the battle between eagles or eagle-like birds, and flying dragons or wyverns. There is also the possibility that someone had read that Spenserian stanza describing the aerial combat which occurs when 'a gryphon seized of its prey, through widest sky making its airy way', encounters an 'arimpasion' and has to defend its dinner. Initially Robert West avoided birds: by the time he came to 20 Lower Dominick Street they began to take over. But the West plasterer who raised the ceiling of Dominick's Parlour-Breakfast Room and went on in about 1761 to create the gloriously confused, over-rich and ill-composed plasterwork in the Hall of 56 St Stephen's Green, kept his birds subsidiary to the aediculae and band work containing allegorical figures of the months from Claude Audran's *Douze Mois Grotesques* of 1726.[11] A few years later, when probably the same plasterer decorated the Stair-Hall of 19 Dawson Street, he had abandoned the birds completely, flattened the profile of his mouldings and achieved, quite accidentally, a delightful Chinoiserie effect by the geometric play of Bérainesque band work.

Somewhere between 1758 and 1761 West had lost his two best plasterers and, when he surfaced again working on the exceptionally rich and various decorative schemes of 86 St Stephen's Green, that very strange bird, the seagull-eagle, had emerged. As Curran has pointed out, Rococo plasterers were more inclined to the actual than the ideal, it is a source of their freshness, and while Dublin was short on eagles there were ugly, raucous seagulls squabbling and scavenging in strident flocks on all the mud banks and tidal reaches of the Liffey.[12] Their flight patterns, that peculiar gymnastic twist of the neck, have been captured exactly over the stairs of Number 86, then cleverly stylized to make linking patterns with acanthus leaves. At Dowth Hall, Co. Meath, West copied, sequence for sequence, his supremely confident and sophisticated panelled treatment of the front parlour of Number 86. All around the walls of the Dowth Drawing Room alternating broad and pilaster panels offer the perfect Irish answer in plaster to the boiseries of a great French Rococo town house. In the broad panels, richly modelled trails of vine leaves hang above trophies of musical instruments or twinned clusters of gourds; in the narrower pilaster panels, that curvaceous abstract form, a question mark of acanthus caught in a high wind, expresses the essential gleeful asymmetry of the Rococo. On tall, gilt pier glasses golden pheasants respond to the white birds in the plaster frieze. But in the middle of all this harmony, central to the ceiling, is a monstrous Dublin seagull-eagle, suspending the chandelier in its hooked claws and fending off an attack by five small birds who have appeared out of the clouds. It is life in the midst of elegant suaverie. Next door in the Dining Room, perhaps a year later yet nearly an entire style distant, Robert West is betraying his latest allegiance and allowing his friendship with Michael Stapleton, the Irish 'Adam', to take over. Here there is yet another Apollo ceiling, apparently in the Rococo tradition, with the God's head and his lyre surrounded by radiants. In the four diagonals are the well tried Rococo motifs of flying birds carrying rose trails; but between them, twining in anorexic curls, the acanthus have been reduced to a wiry Adam elegance covering all the rest of the ceiling.

Assuming that West was working here for the 6th Viscount Netterville at the end of the 1760s, then the Drawing Room would be about 1768 and the Dining Room, 1769. One more year and the Irish Rococo would be finished. It is often supposed that West gave up when Stapleton's designs triumphed, but it is far more likely that West, the natural stylistic chameleon, dabbler in all designs, committed to none, went over completely to Stapleton's camp. Here was a new style with a London cachet. It guaranteed elegance and it could be applied mechanically from shallow moulds. By following a permutation of some 111 set forms drawn from antique Roman decorative details and Raphaelesque grotesque work,[13] the individual craftsmanship and invention required for Rococo plasterwork was made to seem old-fashioned and expensive. West, like all the other Dublin builders, settled down to churn out the thin husks and predictable looped rinceaux trails of the new style as he had begun to do in Dowth's Dining Room. Why else would he have remembered Stapleton trustingly and generously in his will if he had not been converted to his young friend's innovations? As late as 1765, in 86 St Stephen's Green, the prototype for much of Dowth's decorative work, the birds had been swooping in the acanthus trails of the ceilings, dragons and birds were battling it out on the friezes, monkey-faced leaf forms were peeping maliciously out from trails on the Stair-Hall walls (illus. 104). But emaciated elegance must have been beckoning him away from vitality and invention, he was becoming a traitor in denial of his own best work.

This stylistic ambivalence, this balancing on the cusp, is a feature of most Dublin Rococo work of the 1760s. Number 12 Merrion Square, North Side, has plasterwork in its Hall of 1762 which is virtually Baroque still in its projection and exuberance. Even the flowers of its metopes strain out and peer down like Disney animations, denying the usual rigidity of the Doric. Its flower swags are wedding bouquets in their projection and seagull-eagles squawk (illus. 114) down with wide open beaks. Yet in the first floor the mood changes completely, a gracious charm of abstract twining takes over the ceiling and the modelling is far less demanding. Number 26 in the same

wonderful row of houses has, as mentioned earlier, a front room of rocaille work carried to the limit of abstract, pie-crust form, but the overdoor leading into it has a carefully observed eagle reaching down to support trails of flowers correct in every detail above broad leafed acanthus as lush as anything of the mid-1750s (illus. 115), yet Number 26 must be as late as 1767. Two other interiors, the vast Red Drawing Room at Newbridge Hall and the smaller of the two drawing rooms at Malahide Castle are as late, or even a year or two later, but their aerial combats, gourds, flowers and acanthus are quite uninfluenced by Stapleton. Richard Williams, who is known to have worked at Newbridge and who was obviously responsible for the one room at Malahide, treated his Rococo forms with a bucolic vigour. His fruit and flowers bulge out of their friezes and he has used the same bold ice-cream cornet mould for his dragons' tails and for his cornucopia. The friezes of these two rooms are such a decorative battleground that one strain of the Irish Rococo has to be termed the robust bucolic. In the Hall of 12 Merrion Square, North Side, the Doric triglyphs still managed to impose a certain discipline on the errant blossoms between them, but at Malahide the frieze is a free-for-all of near three-dimensional aggression. Melons bulge, gourds extrude, grapes and wheat ears dangle and at every few feet these terrible birds riot and grapple with victimized gryphons, or are they arimpasions?

Was it this undisciplined exuberance which led to Ireland's quite abrupt abandonment of the Rococo in 1770, or did the style commit suicide, moving

from the human figurative of the Francinis to the abstract, from acanthus scrolls through to ever more emaciated rocaille work? The graciously effete ceilings of Merrion Square, North Side, lead naturally through the 1760s to the shallow husks and mere tracery of Michael Stapleton's work on the square's South Side. At Dunboyne Castle, a few miles west of Dublin, the two principal rooms of about 1767 have Rococo and Stapletonesque forms twining around each other uneasily, just as in the Dining Room of Dowth.

There was one other Rococo strain which could have led to revulsion and a drive towards simplification. It is best described as 'plasterer's virtuoso', one where the ceilings and friezes are so delicately overwrought and the forms, whether bird, leaf, fruit or flower, so elaborately interpenetrated that the response has to be one of amazement that the medium could be worked with such skill, rather than one of delight at the beauty of it. Kenure Park, a large house on the northern outskirts of Dublin, was the prime example of this virtuoso strain. Empty and rotting for many years it hung on the conscience of the city's cognoscenti like a lead weight. There were photographs

115 An overdoor at 26 Merrion Square, Dublin (*c*. 1767) severed by a mirrored lift shaft.

116 A ceiling, now
demolished, from the
last Rococo years at
Kenure Park, Dublin
(*c.* 1768).

in the *Irish Times* of magnificent but crumbling eagles, acanthus friezes of
impossible subtlety (illus. 116) with raw bricks, broken laths and daylight
showing beyond them. What could be done about such a treasure of Irish
craftsmanship? The answer was demolition and another housing estate.
Would the Greeks have replaced the Erectheion with a block of luxury flats?
Kenure had the wrong cultural vibrations; it was not associated with an
acceptable period of national resurgence. In its absence the Convent of the
Holy Faith at Glasnevin has ceilings of almost the same obsessional perfec-
tionism with its lunatic gardens of plasterwork still securely suspended over
the heads of the nuns.

Number 24 Upper Merrion Street (Mornington House) is inner Dublin's
best example of this virtuoso Rococo, a house where the style has been
acceptably refined by aristocratic good taste. Converted now into a superior
hotel, Number 24 has been linked up with three neighbouring houses and
safeguards a particularly rich series of interiors. Its Stair-Hall has an intensely active abstract frieze of doubled oval acanthus trails, in its rear
Drawing Room the sheer quality of all the conventional forms is unavoidable: doves, parrots and cockatoos flutter about and every strand of
wicker-work on the flower baskets is exactly delineated (illus. 117). Then in
the Dining Room the virtuoso plasterer has invented flaming cabbage forms
and a Catherine Wheel centrepiece of eight whirling flower trails that snake
out towards the burning vegetables. It may sound amusing, but it is more

117 Ceiling detail from the first-floor rear room, 24 Upper Merrion Street, Dublin (1760s).

awesome in its evidence of time taken and technique mastered than humorous. Like the great Irish ceilings, it projects an imagined world of its own, but whereas the others – the six, the 20 Lower Dominick Street Stair-Hall and Drawing Room, the Red Drawing Room at Newbridge – are comprehensible, the Dining Room at Mornington House is literally disappearing up its own self-created vortex. Standing under it, the notion of a less demanding decorative style, one which could be taken for granted, like canned music in a restaurant, seems almost appealing.

The time for Robert Adam and Michael Stapleton was very near. It would be dramatically satisfying if there had been bitter antagonism between the practitioners of the inventive, free-hand Rococo and the flat Stapleton work, applied for the most part from moulds. In reality commercial pressures took their natural course: a fashion changed, London still had its prestige and if the new Robert Adam forms could be raised faster and at less cost in manpower then Dublin's builders would make no defence of the richer native style.

CHAPTER XII

THE IRISH COUNTRY HOUSE AS A COMMENTARY ON THE URBAN ROCOCO

I f, as is often suggested, eighteenth-century Ireland was culturally a Dublin city state, then the pattern of the Rococo's development in Irish country houses should logically follow that of Dublin town houses. The heavy Francini-style figurative work should give way, after the first shock of its bravura wall panels and god-encrusted ceilings, to more native Irish linear designs drawing from French rather than Italian sources. There should be sinuous acanthus scrolls and flowery wreaths refining themselves away through the 1760s with ever leaner and more attenuated rocaille work. But country house reality is much more complex. Distance from Dublin seems to have mattered; the grand Francini manner hung on much longer, as being more appropriate to a rural aristocratic image and lifestyle; the Baroque fought back against the airy Rococo.

Between 1921 and 1960 Eire, caught up in an exciting tide of Catholic and peasant nationalism, was reinventing Irish history, and so many country houses were burnt or demolished that it is no longer easy to make generalizations about their plasterwork. If, for instance, Desart Court, a house of about 1733 in Co. Kilkenny had survived, then Jean Bérain would not seem such a remote French influence on Irish design as he does now. Summerhill in Co. Meath, another early house and one of great size and distinction, was gutted in 1922 and pulled down in 1957, but its Rococo interiors must have been at least as influential as that well-known Saloon ceiling in Carton, Co. Kildare. So the chains of connection are broken. This chapter will, however, attempt, by a brisk survey of eleven houses that have survived, to suggest at least the complexity of Rococo fortunes in the Pale and out in the more distant counties.

As Eire prospers economically and moves eagerly into a context more European than Atlantic, official attitudes have mellowed. A number of these eleven houses are owned by the state or by corporations and are open to the public. Others are privately owned and there the authors have trespassed on the kindness of their fortunate residents. Few architectural pleasures are quite as intense as that first nervous turning up the drive of a large Irish house, uncertain what to expect: a convent, a mental home, a prosperous stud farm, rich Americans, descendants of the original Angevin conquerors or a ruin haunted by amiable farm dogs. Sometimes there are improbable towers and a Gothicized façade half-veiled in drifting rain, sometimes a radiant Corinthian hall chaotic with spring-cleaning, at other times again a cash desk and a well-informed curator; only the Rococo is the constant.

The dating of Irish houses is notoriously obscure. In their *Buildings of Ireland* series Alistair Rowan and Christine Casey, a notably scholarly team, often fall back on vaguenesses like 'mid-eighteenth century' or offer '*c.* 1760' for the plasterwork of Belvedere, Co. Westmeath, though the house was designed by Richard Castle in 1740. It may, therefore, be foolhardy to suggest a list of dates for plasterwork, but since this survey of the eleven is intended to be chronological such a list is unavoidable and here, though most vulnerable to criticism, it is:

Riverstown House, Co. Cork	1734–40
Newbridge House, Co. Dublin	1737–65
Russborough, Co. Wicklow	1741–51
Belvedere, Co. Westmeath	1740–6
Barmeath Castle, Co. Louth	1758
Glasnevin House, Co. Dublin	1760
Dunboyne Castle, Co. Meath	1764–6
Kilshannig, Co. Cork	1765–6
Malahide Castle, Co. Dublin	1768
Dowth Hall, Co. Meath	1767–9
Castletown Cox, Co. Kilkenny	1769–72

There is, of course, the reliably dated Rococo work of 1759 by one of the Francini brothers on the Stair-Hall of Castletown Conolly in Co. Kildare. This is conventional swirling acanthus but whichever of the Francini brothers,

Paolo or Filippo, worked at Castletown Conolly it was the other brother, probably Filippo, the specialist in figurative as opposed to decorative work, who was employed at Riverstown House. Even by Irish standards the exterior of Riverstown is unpretentious; it has more the appearance of a canal warehouse which has sprouted canted bays than that of a bucolic retreat for Dr Jemmett Browne, the Dean of Ross, which is what it was. Sometimes the plasterwork and the canted additions are dated to 1745 when the Dean became Bishop of Cork, but here, since the Francini brothers were working on the new Classical cathedral at Cork in 1735, an earlier date is preferred. By his outward walls the Dean was a minimalist but internally, by his plasterwork, he was a spiritual Republican. The Dining Room at Riverstown is one of the great rooms of Ireland, not in its dimensions, for it is modest, but in its unrelenting emphasis upon civic virtues and noble living. It is easy to see why, when the house seemed to be in terminal decay, Con Curran, the apostle of Ireland's eighteenth-century plasterwork, persuaded the state to have casts of the Dining Room panels made and used to decorate Áras an Uachtaráin in Phoenix Park, for they express the very essence of Republican strengths. Modelled on P. A. Maffei's 1707–9 edition of Agostini's *Gemme Antiche Figurate* they record in bold relief of candle-cream coloured plaster, Marcus Curtius for Roman valour (illus. 118), Aeneas for family loyalties, Liberty, Ceres, Fides Publica, Cincinnatus and Roma Aeterna herself, armed and formidable.

The room is richly domestic, its woodwork almost black but the overdoors subtly gilded (illus. 137). Dean Jemmett Browne was an heir to that influential generation of churchmen who had made and unmade kings in 1688 and experienced their religion through Virgil and Cicero rather than the Gospels. Consequently he chose to dine in an heroic setting of Republican Rome in a simple house of no outward pomp. No room could be less in tune with the usual frivolous Rococo spirit than the Dining Room, and yet it has just to be classed as Rococo. Between the austere neo-Classical panels run drops of Bérainesque strapwork with hanging flower bells while C scrolls support and top the panels and surround the mirrors. This is how the Rococo could have developed in a sterner society, a masculine room where Marcus Curtius, set like St George over the chimneypiece, dominates all the other qualities. On the ceiling, in a plain oval frame, Filippo Francini has simplified Poussin's *Allegory of Time saving Truth from the assault of Envy and Discord*: Dean Browne's self-justifying comment on the rightness of the Glorious Revolution of 1688 (illus. 138). If ever a Rococo room deserved a noble Roman and Palladian setting it is this one, yet the house is astylar,

118 Caius Martius rides into the mouth of Hades to save Rome from Hell-fire, from a panel in the Dining Room of Riverstown House, Co. Cork (1735–6).

homely and completely devoid of any Classical ornaments; a large green-house flanks the entrance drive and all around it the new commuter suburbs of Cork are springing up. The Irish Georgian Society, that remarkable group of true patriots, who were for several dark decades the effective guardians of Ireland's real artistic heritage, rallied to help Riverstown's present owner and together they have rescued the house from decay, a very Protestant monument.

Newbridge House at Donabate on the coast a few miles north of Dublin is yet another achievement by a Protestant churchman. It was built for Dr Charles Cobbe in 1737, shortly before he became Archbishop of Dublin, Church of Ireland bishops preferring to spend their generous incomes on their houses rather than on their churches. As they held literally half the power of the kingdom it seemed natural to them to live like lords. Newbridge lies in curious country, dry yet maritime; its park is planted with grey green ilexes; ivy and ramping brambles have covered the lower trees so that the landscape seems weed-conquered and half dead. But the house has that rarest of attributes, a bright Rococo façade polychromatic and sprightly with dark golden granite and white limestone dressings, more Serlian than Palladian with its low-key central feature of four Ionic columns. By the time John Aheron brought out his *General Treatise of Architecture* (Dublin, 1754) this Serlian preference for coy and inconsequential central notes to elevations appears to have become a mark of Irish Classicism. The house has been attributed to Richard Castle in the past; it has now, however, been convincingly suggested that George Semple, a Dublin architect and friend of Archbishop Cobbe, designed Newbridge.[1] This would explain its multi-coloured un-Castle-like entrance front (illus. 139) and mean that Newbridge was actually that rare creation, an Irish Rococo house designed by a native Irish architect.

Behind that cheerful front is the usual chaos of additions. Newbridge's long building period, extending over several decades, has resulted in it reflecting accurately the fluctuations in Dublin Rococo. The ceiling of the Library, originally a drawing room, is an early handsome Bérainesque essay on the Four Seasons within bold compartments, not remotely Francini in design, pre-Francini in fact. It has a fluent central star, four cameo busts and every quarter piece is richly varied. As there is nothing quite like it in Dublin it is tempting to attribute its ordering at least to Semple. The Archbishop's Study has a modest C scroll ceiling that could be almost as early as the very different Library ceiling. In the Dining Room frail, airy 'Merrion Square North' trails of 1767 acanthus wisp around the ceiling and, though only lightly, the walls. But then someone, as if in a fit of impatience at their fragile uncertainty, ordered a plasterer to pick up the guilloche and Greek key patterns of the new furniture and slice them boldly onto the walls, creating a stimulating 'Empire' effect.

The Red Drawing Room at the back of the house is a very grand apartment, part-ballroom, part-picture gallery. It was added in 1763–4, just before the Archbishop's death in 1765, by which time his son, Colonel Thomas and his wife Lady Betty, a sister of the Marquess of Waterford, had virtually taken over the house and were spending lavishly on redecoration. The room has been mentioned earlier, in the context of Robert West and 20 Dominick Street. Richard Williams, 'Williams the Stucco' of the household accounts, was one of the team of plasterers who had sometimes worked for Robert West.[2] Williams was paid £39.15 in 1763, apparently for his work on the Red Drawing Room, and then a mere £9.13.4 the next year for the artistically superior octagonal Cobbe family pew, raised to a lordly height behind three round arches at the back of Donabate parish church half a mile away to the north. Without wishing to take credit from Williams, three plasterers and designers seem to have been active in and around Newbridge House at this late period. There was one creating on the flat of the Red Drawing Room ceiling appropriately heavier versions of the acanthus curlicues, rocaille and flower wreaths of the Dining Room and another, probably Williams, was designing a ferocious battle between seagull-eagles and fork-tailed dragons, destroying each other among the heavy leaves and wreaths of the frieze.

Finally there was the minor genius of the Donabate pew (illus. 119). An octagon above a deep cove is a naturally flattering spatial unit, the pew has adopted it and over its complex ceiling have been laid the longest and most languidly graceful acanthus trails in Ireland. There has been no meagre scrimping on the details of the foliage but an asymmetrical maze of leaves has been set nodding back over themselves, all mingled with the melancholy coroneted swans of the Cobbe family arms. Glimpsed from the nave it is a luminous visual delight; enjoyed from within it evokes the Lady Betty era wonderfully with four red velvet benches set around its sides as if for a card party. The pew is nearer in spirit to the staircase of the Royal Fort in Bristol than anything else in Rococo Ireland. Both spaces allow a natural growing form, in one the vine, in the other the acanthus, to take over and impose its own discipline of design.[3]

Russborough, the next of the eleven, is a house quite different in atmosphere to Newbridge. It is so beautiful, possibly the most beautiful Palladian house outside Italy (illus. 140), and so sodden with art treasures collected by Sir Alfred and Lady Beit, that it can hardly afford to be relaxed or charming. Quite how Richard Castle achieved such an inspired and entirely satisfying design, remembering his many other mediocre houses, is a problem. The answer is probably that a Palladian design only works if it has the standard three distinct sections of building, if the quadrant arms connecting them are handsomely spatial in depth and if the whole composition contrives not to seem seriously bulky. Russborough satisfies on all three requirements. Even though it is some seven hundred feet (212 m) from entrance arch to entrance arch of its flanking 'farmyards', the side pavilions have Castle's characteristic 'low-browed' effect at their roofline. This keeps them unthreatening for all their length, while the central block, though in reality a palace, contrives to retain that typical Irish bungalow look. It is achieved by Castle's clever stress upon the porticoed reception floor, his subjection of the basement and an attic recession of the chamber floor. Finally, to complete the Arcadian ideal, there is the landscape which this proud length of glittering silver granite overlooks: a pictorial composition realized on a scale even Claude never attempted with an entire mountain range in the background, a large lake in the proper middle distance and great trees set about the foreground of an enormous green lawn beyond the ha-ha.

Internally the first surprise, or perhaps shock is a better word, of Russborough's Rococo is the coarseness, almost the vulgarity of its plasterwork and the way in which each room is roofed not so much with a flat ceiling and a cove as with an intensely decorated dome. The delicate twirls and spirals of the average Dublin town house are no preparation for this. But then Joseph Leeson, the brewery heir who became the 1st Earl of Milltown, began his house in 1741 before Dublin's chief plasterers had developed their style. He made his own design way forward independently, influencing and eventually being influenced by the Francini. It is unfortunate that the first rooms on the guided tour are, decoratively speaking, the latest in the house. By the time he came to them the Francini were no longer working for him but Leeson seems to have given in, or been converted to their style, after his long battle with them in earlier rooms. He had come to accept that the Palladian was an interior style proper only to municipal offices and had absorbed the Francini's intoxicating Rococo-Baroque. Then, with the brothers departed, he had been left with the Sorcerers' apprentices, their Irish trainees, more Franciniesque than their masters. The first reception rooms of the tour are the work of these apprentices, hence the shock.

Joseph Leeson came to his interiors with all the dreary English preconceptions: Lord Burlington's absurd notion that the heavy, coffered ceilings of Roman public baths were ideal to roof afternoon tea rooms in a damp northern island. Leeson's partial salvation was that he had heard, via Carton and St Stephen's Green, that the Francini brothers were the latest fashion; so he hired them – Baroque artists with an awareness of Rococo trends – but then set them to recreate plaster ceilings appropriate to public baths. The stylistic wrangle is evident in the Doric Entrance Hall where the Francini have obediently coffered the ceiling but inserted snippets of Rococo scrolling, shells and swags of flowers in the hollows. It has wooden overdoors that are pure Rococo and charmingly inappropriate in this pompous space, but in almost every room of this reception floor, Leeson has insisted, whatever the decorative treatment, on a regular panel in the ceiling outlined with a bold key fret, his last frontier stand for Roman order.

In the Music Room, domed with public baths coffering, the Francini have made their Rococo point with a centrepiece of two whirling acanthus propellers, while two at least of the four corner pieces are asymmetrical. This was a small rebellion and it was not until they came to the Saloon, discussed in a previous chapter, that a compromise was worked out; neither figurative Baroque nor glacial Palladian, but Irish acanthine and Rococo. It was a splendid invention. Leeson had insisted as usual on his rectangular central compartment, but from shells ranged along it great bursts of acanthus overfly it and soften the rigidity. Whether the pattern of acanthus and rose trails that articulate the cove was evolved first here or at Tyrone House in Dublin is not certain, but it was a close run race. Tyrone House probably has the more fluent composition. In the Russborough Library, originally the Dining Room, the battle of wills between the Francini and Leeson has resulted in a thoroughly bad ceiling, a confused design with a central circle of roses in a rectangle and waving lines of paterae reaching out to the cornices. After that the Swiss-Italians sensibly left Russborough, abandoning the house to their apprentices.

On those apprentice rooms of the south front and the Stair-Hall it is possible to enjoy a true but tardy Irish Baroque with Rococo motifs. McDonnell calls the plasterer, if there was only one, the 'St Peter's stuccodore', on the evidence of some passages of plasterwork in the chancel of St Peter's church in Drogheda, built later in 1752. He also links the eagles at Drogheda with the elegant cranes of 20 Dominick Street, which they in no way resemble.[4] The same team certainly worked first at Russborough, when the Francini brothers had fled, and then at Drogheda, but their glorious excesses are essentially domestic. They were formulated first at Russborough, which was complete by 1751, repeated on a more limited budget at Glasnevin House in the Dublin suburbs a few years later, surfaced again in 56 St Stephen's Green working confusingly alongside other plasterers, and then achieved in the Hall of 12 Merrion Square a last restrained flowering. Regrettably this dramatic native development of the Francinis' country house style never became truly popular in Dublin drawing rooms, perhaps because their work at 56 St Stephen's Green was aesthetically indigestible.

The apprentices' best composition at Russborough, once that first shock has been absorbed, is in the present Dining Room which is the first on the visiting circuit. Leeson has still had his way with a conventional Palladian cornice and Greek key rectangle but the apprentices have overwhelmed this by enormous shells, acanthus twisted into cornucopia, huge rocaille bat wings, eagles and urns. Elegant it is not; but it is most memorable, exuberant and a successful attempt to control space by decorative detail. In the Drawing Room, on the other side of the Entrance Hall, Leeson unwisely allowed the apprentices to devise picture frames for his delicate set of Vernet paintings in the same hefty style and the result can only be described as amusing. Vernet deserved a more sympathetic handling. When they come to the infamous Stair-Hall present-day visitors are confined to an aesthetically sanitary zone at the bottom, where the colossal rocaille forms can only be viewed at an oblique angle (illus. 120). This is a pity as the Stair-Hall is a national shrine. Here Ireland was making an eager leap forward, ignoring England and reaching out, positively if naïvely, towards Europe. Melancholy hounds dangle massive rose wreaths, acanthus turn into cornucopia and these then evolve into flower pots. The scale is all wrong in such a cramped space, but again the impact is tremendous.

To move from Russborough's plasterwork to that of Belvedere in Co. Westmeath is to abandon Brobdignag for a refined Lilliput, but the effete delicacies of Belvedere's three ceilings have been discussed at length in an earlier chapter. It is in its dating that Belvedere is provokingly vague. If, as seems logical, its owner and creator Robert Rochfort, Earl Belvedere, had those ceilings raised as soon as he settled there in the mid-1740s, then he and his anonymous plasterer initiated the true continental Rococo in Ireland. All the other brilliant ceilings from the same hand in Mespil House and Áras an Uachtaráin came later, in the early 1750s. So here a country house was setting the tone and the pace for the capital rather than the other way round. Rochfort's other innovation was to oblige Richard Castle to re-invent the gentleman's house in a new bourgeois form.

Authors can, or should, only describe what they find and we found Belvedere, perhaps because we approached it up that neatly trimmed drive with such high expectations, an ugly and unattractive building. Mark Bence Jones describes it as 'an exquisite villa' of c. 1740.[5] More discerningly, Alistair Rowan and Christine Casey rate it as 'a charming building . . . Sturdy and handsome rather than gracefully elegant, this is nonetheless a sophisticated design which must rank among Castle's best'.[6] What seems to have happened was that Rochfort made Castle, not the greatest of architects and certainly not the most inventive, go back to the drawing board and, in the mid-1740s, design a house which would have been more appropriate to the social needs of a late nineteenth-century bachelor with a moderately good income and no

120 Detail of the wild plasterwork on the Stair-Hall at Russborough, Co. Wicklow (*c.* 1751).

particular feeling for Classicism. That is Belvedere's real importance: it is not in essence a Classical house. Does this mean that here at last is a Rococo exterior design for a Rococo interior?

For a start it completely escapes the confines of the box, with boldly projecting wings on its five-bay entrance front and semi-circular bays at each return elevation. It is astylar but has Venetian windows in each projecting wing and had, originally, a Diocletian window above each of these. The servants were confined in an unpleasant pit, lit meagrely from a cramped trench surrounding three sides of the house. Castle delivered all this with his usual low-browed elevation, achieved this time by undistinguished chamber windows and a plain but heavily moulded cornice. Possibly the nineteenth-century building programme which gave this small house a massive terracing also undertook an unfortunate repointing of the masonry. Belvedere is a house of dull grey stone, matt in finish and depressing in effect (illus. 141); Castle was required to produce a unit for virtually modern living, wide open to a view of lake waters and islands, with all the domestic support structures out of sight. It was a challenge; Belvedere was all that he could manage, and to the authors at least, it was an opportunity missed.

Barmeath Castle is one of the most romantic and paradoxical houses in Ireland: a Rococo mansion enfolded within the semi-ruinous arms of Norman Revival towers and pseudo-Elizabethan ranges. As for Barmeath's commentary upon the Rococo of the capital, it makes two points. The first is negative: the Classical house of about 1750 was so indigestibly plain, as a 1783 painting reveals,[7] that nineteenth-century Bellews, an intensely aristocratic family, were constrained to spend the wealth which they acquired by consistently shrewd marriages on neo-medieval concealments of the house's ugly core. This extends the point made by Belvedere, that the Rococo never achieved in Ireland a satisfying outward dress; the ruthless urban geometry of Dublin's Rococo terraces resulted in a rural indifference to first impressions.

What Barmeath does have is something very rare in Ireland, a room, its Library, where the late Rococo has, with an infinite reserve, absorbed the most refined of Chinoiserie instead of lapsing into the clichés of Robert Adam. The Chinese is less common in Ireland than in England simply because the Rococo was embraced wholeheartedly and satisfied the national need for decorative excess and experimental design. In the Barmeath Library there are only the most sophisticated and underplayed hints of Chinese exoticism. Two of the walls are lined with mahogany break-front bookcases and it is these that suggest the East in their fretwork borders and angular latticing. The frieze of oval interlaced acanthus ropes is sufficiently unusual to sustain the foreign air. On the ceiling wiry rinceaux create a slender race track and the corner pieces have something mandarin and slant-eyed in the way their extended arms sweep outwards and upwards. By the Adam undertones of this last room must date to around 1767 and there is, in one of those late Rococo houses in Upper Merrion Street, now converted along with Lord Mornington's house into a superior hotel, a Stair-Hall with a similar frieze of oval loops. Barmeath's Stair-Hall, however, is earlier than the Library as the fine star on its ceiling has Bérainesque strapwork within its acanthus. All in all Barmeath is very much a castle of the Pale, wide open to Dublin influences but aristocratic enough to make individual variations.

In such a country house chapter it was a relief to be able to strike a sour note over at least one house, Belvedere, if only to break an otherwise monotonous and unconvincing recital of praise. But only praise, even some rapture, is appropriate to Glasnevin where the apprentices had settled when they had done their worst at Russborough. Barmeath was entirely rural, even mountainous in its setting, up north in the rough fields and ragged woodlands of Louth. Glasnevin in contrast, while technically a country house, could never have been much more than a suburban villa, a north Dublin equivalent of that lost, southern Mespil House. Mespil was demolished, Glasnevin has merely disappeared; the nuns have hidden it.

The Convent of the Order of the Holy Faith lies in a religious campus off the Old Finglas Road. In front of the unrevealing brick walls of the Convent a vast smooth lawn sweeps down to the Tolka river and the trees of the Botanic Gardens. There is no sign of the house, nor any indication of whether it was a villa or a mansion, that the ship owner, Sir John Rogerson, built before his death in 1724. It was then extensively redecorated by John Mitchell, MP for Bannow and a neighbour of the Delanys at nearby Delville. After a wait in the stillness of the visitor's parlour the archivist leads the way along corridors of thick brown linoleum. First comes the Stair-Hall then, on the first floor, room after room of Mitchell's Glasnevin, perfectly preserved within the expanding institutional premises. Religious vocations are hard to come by in the late twentieth century and there are no throngs of teaching sisters bustling about the corridors, only a pleasant calm and that extraordinary plasterwork in the great empty rooms.

Because the rooms have no context and little connection with one another Glasnevin is not easy to describe, though unusually easy to photograph as the nuns have favoured dark backgrounds, chocolate and puce, to white raised detail. The hand of the Francini apprentices from Russborough is as plain as if they had signed their work: thick, swirling slices of rocaille loop and bend

121 Glasnevin House,
Co. Dublin: detail from
a first-floor front room
cornice (c. 1760),
a later work by the
plasterer of
Russborough's
Stair-Hall.

in an assertive symmetry of hard, serrated arcs. Sometimes, always in twinned balance, these sprout acanthus leaves to assert an organic life, but here
the rocaille outnumbers the acanthus in a ratio of five to one. That is the
distinguishing mark of the apprentice work. To take the place of the usual
linking acanthus there are flower trails of daisies and roses linking and dangling from the rocaille extremities in florist's shop profusion. As in those south
front Russborough rooms every detail is heavy, delicacy is not a relevant
word at Glasnevin, but the violence, the giganticism of the Russborough
rooms has been modified; here the plasterwork enriches, it does not over-
whelm, it has become heavyweight Rococo (illus. 121), not transitional
Baroque.

One room is coved in the French manner with confident rocaille corner
pieces and cartouche-like cardinal points but the ceiling itself, again in the
French and most un-Hibernian manner, is bare. In the room next door, in
complete stylistic contrast, 21 bold compartments have been hung, divided
in the most assertive way with ribs of paterae and guilloche (illus. 122). A few
of the compartments have flower swags but all the stress of the room is on its
divisions. The cornice has paterae between each modillion and the frieze
below surges with broad acanthus. Whoever designed it, presumably around
1760, deliberately ignored the general Dublin fashion for the reduction of
boundaries and the overflowing of all decorative details. He was designing
against the tide and for that reason perhaps founded no team of plasterers.
Only in the Hall of 12 Merrion Square, that house where the metopes of the
Doric frieze have their own Disneyesque animation, this plasterer was

allowed to work again with open-beaked eagles and abundant swags of flowers. His eagles are not the seagull hybrids of West's team, but upright birds whose feathers are more like a fleece. At 12 Merrion Square he was allowed none of the mad rocaille grossness of Russborough, but at Glasnevin those monstrous stair forms appeared for the last time, far too large for the confined and shadowy Stair-Hall, like giant ears bulging out of smooth surfaces. This was a country house Rococo which Dublin was not ready to accept but whose interior styling would have been perfect for civic buildings.

Dunboyne, remodelled for the gay, hunting widow Sarah Hamilton by a provincial Drogheda architect, George Darley, and Dowth Hall of 1767–9, also by Darley for Viscount Netterville but employing a Robert West team of plasterers, are two houses so closely linked in outward appearances that they will be taken together, slightly out of true sequence. Though both houses have fine plasterwork, they are gently depressing with their reminders of the imminence of Robert Adam and the coming dominance of his Irish apostle, Michael Stapleton, so they would have made a gloomy if honest conclusion to a chapter of great Irish achievements.

Dunboyne Castle and Dowth Hall are both exceptionally ugly houses but, scraped and resurfaced in the nineteenth century with a grey composition stone, Dunboyne is even uglier than Dowth. Darley was no architect in the real sense, just an urban builder accustomed to raising lengths of terrace houses and his Dunboyne is simply that: a seven-bay terrace house dropped down in flat country some eleven miles west of Dublin.[8]

Its front door opens into an elegant dead-end, a low Hall that terminates in a complex apse of concave doors and panels; visitors may go right or left but not straight ahead, so the space works like a moral guessing game. The right-hand door leads to a lofty Stair-Hall. There, at every other broken flight of steps, the climber is conscious of a large plaster boar's head gazing down malignantly from the cove of the ceiling. Emblems of War, the Arts and Crafts are set on the other three walls, but the decapitated boar has an unpleasant life of its own. Apart from this Stair-Hall the house has only two significant rooms, both very large and set one over the other, a Dining Room below, a Saloon above, sure indications of the widow Hamilton's social ambitions.

Darley paid more attention to his able carpenter, Oliver Beahon, than to his plasterers, who were in any case stylistically a mixed and indecisive group. Beahon's doors in both rooms are enormous for the height of the ceilings and gloriously enriched with Corinthian ornaments. The tympanum of the Saloon door has graceful clumps of rush with ribboned trophies of corn and bay: Stapleton rather than Rococo motifs. Bay leaves and husks, the cheap, shallow standbys of Adam work, have infiltrated the flower baskets on the ceiling of this room, and even the urns have been flattened and stylised. Downstairs the Dining Room was plastered perhaps a year earlier and retains as a result some positive Rococo elements of invention. Its ceiling centre of six fruit baskets linked by hoops of flowers supported by doves or ho-ho birds has a lovely flow of predictable forms. Over the chimneypiece at one end of the room a ribboned trophy of hunting horns and pipes responds to a trophy over the doors at the other end of violins and sheet music. The doors themselves, though Beahon masterworks, are badly planned, opening almost into each other in the north-west corner.

Dowth, for all its defiant awkwardness of profile, is a house of urbane, almost Parisian interior sophistication. Far more appealing than Dunboyne, it is set among chestnut trees and farm buildings in that rolling country above the Boyne. There King James's army of Frenchmen and Irish loyalists, strung out incompetently over several miles of battlefield, broke and fled before the determined assault of King William's favourite dragoons. Despite its bucolic setting Dowth captures far better than any actual house in the city the decorative air, furnishings and feeling of a Rococo Dublin town house in the happy days before the Union. It is 86 St Stephen's Green as Robert West would have known it immediately after his team of plasterers had done their work. Dowth is all the more poignant because while its Saloon is pure Rococo (illus. 123), its Dining Room next door is edging over the cusp into the

motifs of Stapleton, Robert West's friend and stylistic Judas. Here the Rococo broke and fled before the assault of Michael Stapleton's modish neo-Classical clichés. As a commentary upon Dublin's Rococo, Dowth testifies to the prevalence of urban manners far out here in the north of the Pale. Viscount Netterville had travelled the Continent and must have valued West's ability, at that late stage in his design career, to offer plaster versions of Parisian boiseries with uninhibited asymmetrical panels.

Kilshannig completely reverses the verdict which Dowth and Dunboyne make on the Rococo. While they suggest an effete but gracious decline, a style played out in wearied sophistication, Kilshannig is the old Rococo, still more than half Baroque, raunchy, rough modelled and vibrantly alive. The more figuratively inclined of the Francini brothers, generally supposed to have been Filippo, appears to have come straight here to Kilshannig after his dismissal at Russborough. This of course is quite impossible as there is a fourteen or more year gap between the Francini work at Russborough and 1765 when Kilshannig was begun, but Kilshannig's four great reception rooms do seem to realize exactly what the Francini would have liked to have created for Joseph Leeson if he had not been fixated upon his Roman public baths.

The house was designed for a Cork banker, Abraham Devonsher, a most untypical and self-indulgent Quaker, by Daviso de Acort, a canal engineer who had recently demonstrated his architectural talents in a custom house at Limerick and a mayoral house for Cork. De Acort is always described as Sardinian, but at that time the Kingdom of Sardinia included a broad strip of Protestant French territory along the south shore of Lake Geneva. If de Acort, or Duckart as the Irish call him, was really French that might explain his choice of details from Tardieu's engraving of Antoine Coypel's ceiling painting *L'Assemblée des Dieux* of 1702, a composition which once covered the ceiling of the gallery of the Palais Royale in Paris, for the ceilings of the Saloon and Library at Kilshannig.[9]

It is, however, vital not to get lost in esoteric scholarly details of provenance. Kilshannig is far more than a compendium of French derivations. The Entrance Hall has the spatial excitement of a Baroque church (illus. 142). When he went on to his second great house, Castletown Cox in Co. Kilkenny (1769–72), Duckart designed another ceremonial entry space but this time, caught up in the Adam wave, he built a rectangular box, ceiled in conventional Rococo garlands but terminated with an Adam-style screen of Corinthian columns and its walls staccatoed with small panels. Kilshannig's Hall is exhilarating in contrast to Castletown Cox's mere grandeur. Light floods into Kilshannig's elliptically vaulted spaces. Ahead there is a three-bayed apse with the door to the Saloon; the Corinthian columns and the half vaults create that sense of purposeful space that a flat roofed rectangle never acquires, however ornately it is embellished. All the flowing, coarsely profiled acanthus work is pure Rococo with ribbons, flower wreaths and fruit baskets, providing a dramatic contrast to the first two reception rooms beyond, even a few seagulls are flying on the frieze. It is a heart warming introduction to a house at least Russborough's equal in its interiors. Castletown Cox is often described as Duckart's finest house, but it has no interior to rival any of Kilshannig's four great rooms or, for that matter, its spiral Stair-Hall.

The enforced alteration of mood and scale from Hall to Saloon at Kilshannig is disturbing. In photographs the Saloon's ceiling appears as a merry little composition of Bacchus revelling in an elegantly disposed symmetry of garlanded circles. The reality is almost frightening and, with a 42 foot by 32 foot ceiling (13 m by 10 m) to cover, grotesquely overscaled. That panther between Bacchus and Pan has teeth like a dinosaur, Pan himself is huge and looks sexually predative, while the cherubs on the linking trapezes are full-sized children. Their modelling is witty and they represent, in the mode of that much earlier ceiling in 9 St Stephen's Green, the Four Elements. But it is all, after that radiant Hall, shadowy, dangerous and dim. Two more astonishing rooms lie left and right. The Library verges upon the French neo-Classical, the Dining Room is an ultimate resounding triumph of the Irish Rococo, underplayed by academically minded visitors because it is original.

The Saloon overwhelms by its crepuscular menace; the Library overwhelms by its crowded order. Each of its four deep coves match each other with their central cameos and flanking French eagles perched on rinceaux (illus. 143). At the central compartment's cardinal points there are big fruit and flower baskets while lively cherubs swing within palmette ovals of the Seasons at the corner points. There are no clear spaces. A first impression of a crowded composition is the enduring one. This plasterer hated vacant spaces; like those south front rooms at Russborough, created almost twenty years earlier, the Library seems a dome of activity but with this difference: the giganticism and violence has gone and as a central focus there is no bland rectangle of Greek key fret but a calm roundel of Apollo and Diana with her hind (illus. 124). In the Saloon the gods were lustful, here they turn away from each other, tranquil and bored.

It is all so hyperactive and similar to that Dining Room ceiling in 9 St Stephen's Green that commentators tend, without being explicit, to credit it to the Francini. There is no solid evidence for that, and before hesitating a guess, the other great room at Kilshannig, the Dining Room, should be considered. This is quite unlike its two neighbours as its plasterwork is wholly Rococo in design and, like the Hall, raises the spirits rather than overwhelms them by any scholarly excess of reference. In a central angular lozenge a bird is flying – phoenix or eagle – surrounded first by flower trails then by symmetrical broad acanthus. Next comes that rarity in Kilshannig, a little clear space, and at each cardinal point is a god's head, full face, with a complexity of oak leaves, bays, acanthus and rocaille, all different, enclosing it. Diana's cartouche has a fox as supporter and trophies of dead birds dangling down on each side (illus. 125): signs that the old figurative vitality of earlier Dublin work has not been lost out here in the provinces. Bunches of flowers in almost three-dimensional relief link these four cartouches of the gods loosely to the central lozenge. The room itself, like the Saloon and the Library, is very high and spacious: 30 feet by 30 feet (9 m x 9 m). The Hall in contrast was modest and welcoming in scale. That frontal mezzanine

floor of the house does not exist at the back, all its space being absorbed by
the reception rooms.

After aesthetic assault upon assault, each one different to the one before, a visitor retreats from these supremely effective interiors to examine
Kilshannig's far from perfect exterior. Naturally it is a pleasure to have
wide Palladian arms with domed side pavilions, now in the process of
restoration, but the contrast of brick and brown stone is less than happy. The
blind oculi over the entrance window fail to lift the rest of that blank, seven-
bay, three-storey façade. Yet again this is an Irish interpretation of Serlio
which lacks Palladio's certainties. It is at least an original front and after such
interiors no one would wish to be too critical. As for the plasterers, the Hall
and the Dining Room could be by the man who worked on the Donabate
pew, while the other two rooms, particularly that central ceiling in the
Library, have to be Francini, but this time when the brothers were working
for Duckart, a French Savoyard with Paris training and strong preferences
of his own. A greater puzzle is the owner, Abraham Devonsher, as he is
supposed to have been a Quaker. What Quaker could entertain under that
eager grasping Pan or dine under such a solemnity of encircling gods and
goddesses? Protestant Ireland was a place of paradox; it was also apparently
a country where styles made quite slow transitions over bad roads. While this
Rococo-Baroque excellence was going up in County Cork, Dublin had
already slipped into thin refinements. Then again a new Dining Room at
Malahide Castle, only five miles on the other side of the city, was being redec-

125 Diana among
trophies of dead birds,
from the Dining Room
ceiling, Kilshannig,
Co. Cork.

126 At Castletown Cox,
Co. Kilkenny, the
Rococo is beginning to
wilt before the
Adamesque in 1769–72.

The Irish Country House as a Commentary on the Urban Rococo   249

orated after a fire with high relief birds and dragons that are the very opposite of those thin refinements. Between the capital and the outer counties there was no uniform stylistic advance.

Two years later in 1769, however, Duckart must have begun to feel the pressure for change from Dublin. The fussy little compartments which irritate the walls of his Hall and Stair-Hall at Castletown Cox are not moves towards Rococo boiseries but towards prim Adam compartments (illus. 126). After the full blooded, if uninventive, Rococo ceiling of the Hall, Duckart's master plasterer, Patrick Osborne of Waterford, tended to graceful vapid designs, unconfined but with nothing to rebel against. There are thin trails of bay leaves, more loops of leaves on wall panels, but never a figurative intrusion or an invention to catch the eye. Osborne was a provincial who had heard what Stapleton was doing in the capital, but was not yet clear on the details. Here once more is an example of ecclesiastical patronage: Castletown Cox was a house for an archbishop. A Quaker banker might get away with that Pan and Bacchus, but an Archbishop of Cashel with £4,000 a year might have been more comfortable under bay leaves. It does appear that Archbishop Michael Cox was not a man of very strong character or decisive tastes. There is an often told, and typically malicious, Irish anecdote about the large vacant space which Cox left on his tombstone. This verse suggests that those commonplace loops of bay and trails of vine could have been his ideal mode of decoration, an outward demonstration of an inner vacancy of mind:

> Vainest of mortals, hadst thou sense or grace,
> Thou ne'er had left this ostentatious space,
> Nor given thine enemies such ample room
> To tell posterity, upon thy tomb,
> A truth, by friends and foes alike confess'd
> That by this blank thy life is best express'd.[10]

CHAPTER XIII

ROCOCO AS THE
ART FORM OF
BOURGEOIS CAPITALISM

Bristol was left behind six chapters ago in the year 1745: a vulnerable, philistine city becoming uneasily aware that architectural fashions were passing it by and that it should be making building gestures commensurate with its wealth. There was even the alarming possibility that William Halfpenny might, for want of a better alternative, become the resident architect. On the credit side an impressive new Corn Exchange was going up, in Bath stone and to immaculate Palladian designs by the Bath architect, John Wood; but this had outraged local feeling and his Bath stone masons were physically threatened when they drank in Bristol ale houses. By way of compensation the open market square at the rear of the new Exchange was being given a riotous Rococo trim by Thomas Paty's team of Bristol stone carvers, flaunting shameless symbols of the city's wealth: negroes' heads, vine trails and the curiosities of three continents. An alien Bath architect might impose Bath's Palladian certainties, but Bristol's provincial craftsmen were directing internal design towards a Rococo in which they could express themselves freely in meaningful, figurative and populist style (illus. 127).

At that point, with the dramatic timing of a villain in a melodrama, Isaac Ware, Lord Burlington's protégé, appeared on the Bristol scene to design Clifton Hill House, a grand suburban villa, for one of the city's rich merchants, Paul Fisher. This was in 1746 and it must have seemed that London's architectural manners were at last being adopted by the country's second city in wealth and population. The site for the villa was close to Clifton parish

127 The continent of
Africa, a Paty overdoor
(1743) in the Corn
Exchange, Bristol.

church, below the level of the road and looking down at the back into an
enclosed east facing combe. But it was more than a hundred feet above the
cloying fumes of the sugar refineries and glass houses, and Ware saw Clifton
Hill as his golden opportunity to make a convincing and fashionable statement. It was thirteen years since he had last had a chance to design a house.

Ware is one of the most equivocal of eighteenth-century architects.
Romantic legend has it that he started his working life as a chimney sweep
who was seen by a benevolent old gentleman, possibly Burlington himself,
drawing Inigo Jones's Whitehall Banqueting House. Such was the latent
talent that the young man was packed off to Italy to study. Whatever the
truth in this Pygmalion episode, he later proved able to translate Italian into
English and Burlington must have considered him a safe convert to ancient
architecture as he secured several administrative posts for him in the
government's architectural establishment. In 1731 Ware published a small
illustrated book, *Designs of Inigo Jones and Others*, the others being Kent and
Burlington. In 1738 he brought out a handsome new translation of Palladio's
Four Books of Architecture, 'all the plates being Engraved in the Author's own
hand'. But then, with all these pure Palladian qualifications, he began working jointly with William Hogarth for two years in the running of the overtly
Rococo St Martin's Lane Academy. Only three years after designing Clifton
Hill House, he would be building Lord Chesterfield's London town house
with half its interiors more committed to Parisian Rococo design than any
other rooms in England. Then to complicate the matter even further the
Complete Body of Architecture, which he published to celebrate his own quite
limited architectural invention, contains the most revealing and quotable
onslaught on Rococo design ever written in the century. Much of this dia-

128 Rococo detail from the Drawing Room ceiling of Clifton Hill House, Bristol (*c.* 1748), Isaac Ware's restrained and compartmented version of the style.

tribe seems to have been inspired by what he had suffered, as a Palladian martyr, in obliging 'the fancy of the Proprietor . . . at the expense of rigid propriety':[1] his recollections of life with Lord Chesterfield and Paul Fisher.

At first sight Clifton Hill House is the perfect 1–3–1-bay pedimented neo-Palladian villa. It is, however, the only house in his *Complete Body of Architecture* that has its window apertures cut directly into the ashlar without any framing architraves. This is refinement taken directly from Palladio himself and suggestive of the coming neo-Classicism – John Wood the Younger's Royal Crescent at Bath for instance – and also more Dublin than London. Indeed the Irish were to build an exact copy of Clifton Hill House at Crosshaven in Co. Cork eight years later, firm evidence of at least a one-way stylistic movement across the Irish Sea. Internally at Clifton Hill, Ware had to cope with Joseph Thomas as his plasterer, and Thomas at his own house in Guinea Street had very recently produced a pure Rococo ceiling, a composition of squirrels, fruits and C-scrolls. From the design of three fine, but by no means brilliant, ceilings in Paul Fisher's Stair-Hall, Dining and Drawing Rooms, Ware and Thomas must have come to a compromise. Thomas confined his invention within heavy compartments (illus. 128), such as Inigo Jones would have approved, but there was some grudging permissiveness. There are no birds, squirrels or grinning mandarins in three-pointed hats, but Thomas was allowed termini. These, Ware claimed to believe, had historical precedent; they were 'those grotesque representations of the human form which we received from the Moors and Arabs'.[2]

This is a revealing passage. Surely, if Ware had really spent time in Italy, he would have known that Raphael, not Moors and Arabs, had perfected grotesque work from the Antique. Could any observant architect who had spent even a short time in Rome have written, as Ware does, 'The antients were of a contrary turn; they admitted ornaments but without luxuriancy. They never indulged fancy at the expense of judgement'?[3] That grotesque work which Bérain had revived at the turn of the century and which, as was well known in 1756, the divine Raphael had derived from fifteenth-century excavations in Nero's Golden House, put Ware into the unavoidable dilemma of the puritan classicist. At one point he wrote of termini with Palladian horror:

> the unnaturalness of the figure is in reality abominable, tho' custom has rendered it familiar. A harlequin letting himself down a funnel is not a more natural object, nor is the representation of the part of a woman's head and neck, terminating in a fish's tail, any more absurd, than the form of a deity ending in a post.[4]

Fifty pages later he had forgotten his disgust and was licking his lips over the same termini as perfect ceiling decorations: 'a very beautiful ornament of figures, boys or virgins to the waist, and from thence terminating in scrolls, wound about with a wild freedom'.[5] He commissioned plate 77 with these termini flourishing in the compartments of a ceiling and acanthine arms spreading out from them. There was not, Ware hastened to write, 'any licence for its spreading out at the edges: it is naturally and necessarily circumscribed'.[6]

Those last four words sum up the whole problem of a Palladian Revival architect coping with the implications of Rococo design: it had to be 'naturally and necessarily circumscribed'. Those were the restraints under which Thomas must have worked at Clifton Hill House. It would be ten years before the Patys could release Bristol plasterers like Thomas from such nervous Puritan reservations. Clifton Hill House is an instance of the delaying action which Burlington's followers were able to stage as late as 1748 and against the wishes of a rich client like Paul Fisher. The Rococo was a popular style; the Palladian was an imposed one.

The very small termini which Thomas introduced into the Drawing Room ceiling were only miniature versions of the motifs which Edward Lovett Pearce had introduced, far more boldly, onto that ceiling in Dublin Castle in 1732–3, fifteen years earlier. We are seeing precisely how far behind Ireland an English Palladian was in 1748, and what agonies he was experiencing in giving way to bourgeois demand for lively ornament in a provincial city. Ware allowed that 'upon the head of a figure may be a basket of fruit or flowers',[7] Kent had featured that motif prominently in the Circular Closet, one of the least Palladian interiors of Burlington's Chiswick villa. From then on the flower basket became as popular a device in Bristol plasterwork as in Dublin and the one on which a plasterer's skill and care can be most easily measured. But Ware drew the line at real French Rococo scroll work: those ceilings 'straggled over with arched lines, and twisted curves, with X and C's and tangled semicircles'.[8] These, Ware insisted, 'may please the light eye of the French who seldom carry their observation farther than a casual glance'.[9] This is such chauvinistic nonsense that one wonders what Ware and Hogarth could have found to agree upon in their two years together at St Martin's Lane; and if he could write vaguely about 'Moors and Arabs', had he never heard of Bérain, Pineau and Oppenord? It is not wise to underestimate the extreme insularity of English, as opposed to Irish, design. Between Dover and Turin there tended to be a cultural void, except where hair styling and women's fashions were concerned.

Clifton Hill House was fitted up and occupied by 1750 and soon Bristol society was ready for another tentative step forward. In 1754 a tontine raised the money for an assembly room and in 1755 the New Musick Room down by the harbour in the old city on Prince Street opened with the ritual performance of *The Messiah*. Outwardly the building was Halfpenny at his very worst, a would-be Palladian entrance front with its pediment plunging forward in Baroque enthusiasm; both windows and door were ridiculously cramped and underscaled. Internally, however, Joseph Thomas had been allowed, on one wall only, a surprisingly free, Rococo hand. Around and above the clock, C scrolls of acanthus curled luxuriantly (illus. 129). A flower basket was centred between rich swags of flowers and on either side a satyr mask topped rich drops with trophies of musical instruments. It was important to focus attention on the clock as the Master of Ceremonies set off the minuets at half-past six, at eight the tempo was stepped up with country dances, and at eleven everyone went home. Subscribers paid two guineas a year, which gave entry to the fortnightly Thursday winter balls for a gentleman and two ladies, provided neither lady wore a hat. Children were not permitted to dance the minuets in frocks, what they were allowed to wear was not stated. Over the entrance was inscribed in letters of lead: 'CURAS CITHARA TOLLIT', or 'Music Dispels Care'; as good an epitaph as any for William Halfpenny, who died in that same year, 1755, still heavily in debt, still writing confidently on the architecture of China, on the strength, perhaps, of his travels in Ireland.

According to a contemporary description, 'Three elegant lustres, that in the middle being very large and beautiful', lit the ballroom, there was an organ with gilded pipes and Chinoiserie-Rococo mirrors on the walls.[10] This puts into perspective the characteristically malicious and inaccurate lines written by Thomas Chatterton, Bristol's own Rococo-Gothick poet, describing a ball there. Chatterton spent most of the seventeen years of his brief (1752–70) life in the city, when almost all its Rococo and Gothick exoticisms were going up. His verse deserves attention as it exemplifies Bristol's own refusal to take itself or polite living very seriously:

> A mean Assembly Room, absurdly built
> Boasted one gorgeous lamp of copper gilt;
> With farthing candles, chandeliers of tin,
> And services of water, rum and gin.
> There in the dull solemnity of whigs,
> The dancing bears of commerce murder jigs;
> There dance the dowdy belles of crooked trunk,
> And often, very often, reel home drunk;
> Here dance the bucks with infinite delight
> And club to pay the fiddlers for the night.
> While Broderip's hum-drum symphony of flats
> Rivals the harmony of midnight cats.[11]

For a 17-year old, striking out in the satiric line of Richard Savage and Dr Johnson, it is precociously clever and captures wonderfully that atmosphere of emulation, mockery and spite engendered by the English class system, even in a city with only two classes: a middle and a lower. In Bristol, as in London and Dublin, the Rococo seems to coincide with and even spring from the great age of the Vauxhalls and the Ranelaghs, public places where the wealthy of any class could mingle for parade and pleasure in gardens and pavilions of extrovert, almost fairground architecture. Quite how Halfpenny's New Musick Room interacted socially with Bristol's Hotwells is not clear, but no city in England or Ireland ever had a spa and a pleasure garden quite as romantic, strange and inconvenient as the Hotwells.

For those not familiar with the city's odd topography, Bristol lies in a widening of the Avon valley between two gorges. The gorge upstream is a mild, wooded affair, though it had been blackened and devastated in the eighteenth century by brass and zinc foundries. These produced, in addition to their metals, a glistening black slag, hard as iron and impervious to decay. Downstream towards the sea on the other side of the city, the land rises much higher, the heights of Clifton close in on the north, Leigh Woods rises precipitately to the south and the tidal river runs between towering red cliffs with only, at that time, tow-paths between the water, the mud and the rock. It was there in this improbably dramatic setting, where Dowry Square and a few brick terraces crowd into the narrowing area of level land, that Bristol had its Hotwells Spa. Perversely, the spring of mildly warm saline water poured out from the banks of the Avon well below high tide level and had, therefore, to be captured in an artificial reservoir built out, like its Pump Room and one of the two Assembly Rooms, right over the river mud. Ships entering Bristol on the tide had to swing around these projecting buildings before they could reach the docks. Everything has gone now except for a pretty little colonnade, originally shops, squashed in under the cliffs. The Portway cuts through the site, carrying a stream of traffic on its way to Avonmouth, Brunel's Suspension Bridge swings high overhead and the warm spring has run dry. What was once the social centre of Bristol is now only a trunk road.

Owen's 1751 *Guide* to Bristol recorded that in a Hotwells Summer Season there were public breakfasts every day followed, on the lively continental pattern, by dancing. Full dress balls were staged twice a week and there was card-playing every night. At the balls a row of seats was reserved for 'Ladies of Precedence and Foreigners of Fashion' who could appear without hats, ordinary visitors had to cover their heads.[12] This was an odd reversal of fashions prevailing at the New Musick Room. Bristolians were only allowed into the Hot Baths on Sundays and, the *Guide* reassured its readers, 'in by a back way and do not disturb the company'.[13] This may appear crudely exclusive, but no one ever writes of Bathonians being particularly welcome in Bath's Pump Room. Spas were for visitors and Bristolians had a bad social reputation in England generally. Thomas Cox in his *Magna Britannia* of 1727 wrote of the city:

> The Trade of many Nations is drawn hither by the Industry and the Opulency of the People. This makes them remarkably insolent to Strangers, as well as ungrateful to Benefactors, both naturally arising from being bred, and become rich by Trade as (to use their own Phrase) to care for no Body, but whom they can gain by.[14]

One visiting Irish gentleman was even more damning, declaring that, 'their souls are engrossed by lucre and they are very expert in affairs of merchandize, but as to politeness it is a thing banished from their republic as a contagious distemper'.[15]

The views of Alexander Pope and Horace Walpole have already been recorded but for both men Bristol was virtually their first experience of a teeming industrial city, and to reach the Hotwells they would have had to pass right through the narrow, stinking streets of the old centre, with no relief from the genteel suburbs up on Kingsdown and Clifton. In fairness, an American visitor, Thomas Hutchinson, thought 'the manners and customs of the people are very like those of the people of New England, and you might pick out a set of Boston Selectmen from any of their churches', which he probably intended as a compliment.[16] Nonconformity was strong, Quakers formed virtually a merchant aristocracy, but the teeming working class population needed to service factories, foundries, collieries and merchant vessels made it a place of riots on any excuse, whether against food prices or bridge tolls, in 1704, 1714, 1727, 1728–9, 1738 and 1749. There were five cockpits in the city and bare knuckle boxing bouts drew big crowds; women boxers were made to hold half-crown pieces in their fists to stop them scratching and tearing each other's hair. One in every ten dwellings in the city was an ale house while serious drinking was organized around clubs and societies: the Loyal, the Union, Colston, Grateful, Dolphin, Anchor, Parent, Gentlemen of Somerset, and the Sons of the Clergy.

It was a rough, tough city, Bath's loathly opposite, yet it was here in Bristol, not in genteel Bath that the delicate, imaginative Rococo style found notable expression in a few grand houses of slave traders and brass founders. The style never became, as in Dublin, a popular decorative mode applied almost as a matter of course in whole rows of superior housing. All the important patrons of Bristol's Rococo were wealthy brethren of the Merchant Venturers. This absurdly self-satisfied and self-perpetuating body acted as an inner government of the city, controlling the forty-two members of the City Corporation, and taking to itself as of right the port dues. It had its own banqueting hall in subdued, panelled Baroque with extraordinary vortices of acanthus carved over its entrance door.[17] Preaching to them at St Stephen's on their Charter Day in 1744, the Revd. A. S. Catcott took as his appropriate text: 'Tyre the Crowning City whose Merchants are Princes, whose Traffickers are the honourable of the Earth', and concluded that:

> the merchant, in exerting his honest and laudable endeavours, may justly hope for the blessing of God, is intitled to the favour and protection of his prince, and deserves the love and esteem of his fellow subjects.[18]

The listening princes and traffickers liked what they heard so much that they had the sermon published. By that time the 'honourable of the Earth' were doing very well on the slave trade. Edward Colston, whose bronze statue, poised on four snub-nosed dolphins, stands in the present city centre, had contrived by clever negotiations to break London and the Royal Africa Company's monopoly on this profitable trade, making himself and his fellow Venturers very wealthy. Still something of a Bristol hero, he founded schools and almshouses and now lies under another statue, marble this time, by Rysbrack, in All Saints church, which shows him suffering a heart attack with urbane insouciance, as if confident of his reward in the hereafter.

Brass, glass, slavery and the Rococo worked together for the Venturers in a chain of commercial consequences. Brass and zinc, or spelter, foundries had proliferated in the city and its surrounding villages – Woolard, Publow, Swinford, Crew's Hole, Kelston and Saltford – ever since the first foundry was set up at Baptist Mills in 1707, while there had been glass works since the mid-seventeenth century. Beads, mirrors, glasses, brass pots and pans were ideal for trading in West Africa in exchange for slaves, and these, of course, were then shipped in the infamous three-cornered trade to the West Indies where sugar and rum were picked up and taken back to Bristol. As a fourth leg in the trade, the refined sugar then went across to Ireland where all the goods which the Irish were not allowed to export directly, could be taken off in Bristol ships.

The relative importance of Bristol's various trading interests can be judged by the 343 ships which left the Avon in 1764. Eighty-five sailed to Europe, 53 to the West Indies, 52 to the American colonies, 32 to Africa, but 107, more than to any other destination, cleared for Ireland. It was safe to trade with Ireland whereas slaving was fraught with dangers. Sometimes entire crews were murdered when their captives escaped from the holds. One slaver captain blew up his whole ship and crew rather than let them fall into the hands of vengeful blacks. Also a considerable capital expenditure in trade goods was needed to launch a successful slaving venture. African princes did not sell their captives or their subjects cheaply and when the slaves had been purchased there were still many risks and potential losses ahead. In one year Onesiphorous Tyndall, a dye and gum merchant in the city, and his partner Isaac Hobhouse, were informed by letters from Jamaica that two-fifths of their slave cargo had died in the middle passage and that many others were almost valueless. But Tyndall had other sources of income and he survived. It was this 'old' money in Bristol which gave the city a head start over Liverpool, its rival in the trade. Liverpool would eventually pull ahead, but only by its superior efficiency. By the end of the century ships from the Mersey could undersell Bristol slaves by 12 per cent a head, while the Merchant Venturers had been milking Bristol harbour dues for 50 years without making any improvements in the grossly inconvenient port facilities. Bristol's Rococo was a brief flowering of those years in the middle century when fortunes were still being made fast and the city's isolation, away in the West, far from the new northern centres of the Industrial Revolution, had not begun to tell against it.

The key to this brief flowering and the inspiration of subsequent Rococo work in and around the city was Thomas Tyndall's Royal Fort, high up on Kingsdown on the site of a Civil War fortification. Visible from most parts of the old city, yet still idyllically retired within its own green landscaped park, this house, built between 1758 and 1762, became a legend in its time and for us the definitive Rococo villa. *Felix Farley's Journal* of 27 June 1767 hailed it with a poem:

> Long in neglect, an ancient Dwelling stood
> With tottering Walls, worn Roofs, and perish'd Wood,
> Till gen'rous Tyndall, fir'd with Sense and Taste,
> Saw here Confusion, – Ruin there – and Waste
> Resolved at once to take the Rubbish down,
> And raise a Palace there to grace the TOWN.[19]

Even allowing for the unctuous writing style of the period, a 'Palace' is not too hyperbolical a description of one of the most poetic and entirely satisfying houses in Britain, though one still very little known or visited. Even now, when it is hemmed in with a range of generally characterless university laboratories, physics, chemistry, medicine and biology, it preserves in its surviving scrap of Repton landscape, an enchanting combination of Classical assurance and the Rococo pastoral.

At this point Thomas Stocking, the supposed 'wild Irish boy' of Bristol plasterwork, has to be introduced, as the Royal Fort's ceilings are always attributed to him, though on stylistic evidence only. The truth is that the Royal Fort, certainly inside, and probably also in its outward elevations, was a team effort of Thomas Paty's firm. Because they were a band of talented craftsmen rather than one dominant designer the Patys were able to put together a brilliant group of carvers in wood and stone with at least two talented plasterers, one an unpredictable poet of the trade, the other a masterly formalist. Thomas Paty himself was the wood carver, more than an equal of Grinling Gibbons, Thomas Stocking, who is listed in the accounts of several later Paty ventures, was almost certainly one of the two principal plasterers. With these working together on a relatively small house for very rich patrons, all that was missing was an architect for the façades and even that seems to have been solved by a team compromise.

Then there were the patrons, Thomas Tyndall and his young wife, Alicia, ten years his junior. Tyndall, third generation wealthy and a grandson of the slaver, Onesiphorous mentioned earlier, was not the usual Bristol philistine but a confident aesthete. If the decoration of the Fort is any guide he enjoyed shooting, fishing, attractive women and music. At a time when the Seven Years War (1756–63) was at its exhilarating peak with new victories reported every other month and France the detested enemy, Tyndall remained wholly committed to the French Rococo, as interpreted, however, by Dublin, with an experimental, figurative freedom.

Instead of entrusting the outer walls of his villa to one architect Tyndall consulted, if a contemporary verse is to be believed, three architects for their ideas:

> For Aid, – he, Jones, – Palladio, – Vanbrough viewed;
> Or Wallis, – Bridges, – Patty's Plans pursued;
> No Matter which, – the Fabric soon uprose,
> And all its various Beauties did disclose.[20]

John Wallis and James Bridges were, like Thomas Paty, Bristol architects, and the verse writer seems to have believed that all three men were involved in the design process. Coincidentally, the Fort has three main elevations of equal importance, not one of which is stylistically related to the other. A particular charm of the house is that it can be walked around and read as a

130 Royal Fort House, Bristol (1758–62): the Palladian and Rococo elevations, with the 'ancient Dwelling' to the right.

chronological essay in eighteenth-century classicism, with sequential chapters on the Baroque, the neo-Palladian and the Rococo, yet all built at the same time. The north or entrance front is sullen with its round-headed windows; Vanbrugh's influence hangs heavily over it, but it sets the correct mood preparation for the Doric severity of the Entrance Hall immediately within. The west front is orthodox Palladian apart from a hint of acanthine curvaceousness in its pediment cartouche. Poised at the top of a steep lawn where students toboggan in Bristol's rare snowfalls, it looks a little lost without supporting quadrant arms (illus. 130). Easily the most sophisticated front looks south, out over the city, or it would do if the University had not blocked the view. This is the Rococo garden front, an elevation as subtle and assured as that of Sir Robert Taylor's exactly contemporary Chute Lodge, Wiltshire. Two matching doors topped with a leafy delicacy of carved scroll work stand, one on each side, of a generously broad, canted bay, laying all this side of the Fort wide open to its garden both for access and for views. Three sensuously modelled female heads, indefinably un-English, are set as keystones to the first-floor windows, and rusticated masonry laps casually over onto the flanking bays. On its fourth side the new villa links up with the pre-existing 'ancient Dwelling' of the quoted poem.

Each of the three elevations has a different style of window architrave, further evidence that there were three designers. Whoever presided over the final scheme pulled the three together by a unifying plat-band and sill-band at the cost of an odd shortening of the Venetian windows on the south front. James Bridges, an American-born architect, constructed the wooden model of the Fort still preserved in the house and so should be regarded as the ultimate architect. A letter from one of the Tyndalls proves that the Paty team 'did all the mason's work for the house' and also handled the interior woodwork and plasterwork.[21] Paty was paid '30 guineas each' for the beautiful ceilings in the Eating and Drawing Rooms, £24 for the brilliant wooden door surround of the Eating Room and £17.10s. for the trophies flanking its chimneypiece.

As the elevations relate a stylistic sequence to anyone walking around them from north to south, so the interiors of the Royal Fort unfold in a stunning chain of linked decorative surprises. The Entrance Hall is a three-part spatial complexity devised to lead visitors out of light, through two areas of shadowy plaster enrichments back into light again and the inspired theatre of a Stair-Hall conceived as a *sala rustica* with direct access to the garden. No stage is meant to be hurried. In the first Hall, lit by two windows, are four ornamental wall pedestals, not with the usual bruised reed motif but with

bruised wheat ears, wilted and drooping gracefully. The busts of Caesars or philosophers which they were meant to support are lost. Then under three arches of Doric pilasters and metopes of military triumph comes a dark space and three more arches, blank this time, with keystones of crowned heads, a Green Man and a plumed girl. An open arch leads out to the left into the third arched space. Here the watchful keystone faces and the acanthus work are hardly noticed, for now light pours in from the right and the garden door as the visitor moves into the Stair-Hall (illus. 131). This has its walls covered in the legendary plasterwork vine.

There is no other Rococo feature like this in England or Ireland. Someone had persuaded the Paty team to realize Chinese wallpaper in plaster and eight separate vines, each rooted in a small area of fantasy, grow up to link their stems together, all entirely asymmetrical and therefore organic in feeling, trailing over all three walls as the stairs mount up. Among its leaves and upon its branches are little worlds of incident: foxes look covetously at birds, birds look thoughtfully at bunches of grapes, one floating island supports browsing goats, another goat stands by a crumbling castle. One vine is rooted by a cottage where a shepherd and his dog guard a flock of sheep. Two monkeys and a lizard have found their perches. The freedom and the invention escapes, just this once, the Classical spirit of disciplined order within which the Rococo usually plays its decorative tricks. On the ceiling above it the central rosette is, in contrast, richly conventional, with roses, ribbons and counterpoised C scrolls. In the centre, like a prophetic celebration of fertility, naked babies romp within a radiant halo.

Inevitably the question rises: who projected this unique work and who realized it? It can only be speculation, but Alicia Tyndall seems the most likely person to have ordered it while Thomas Stocking has been raised up out of nowhere to satisfy the demand for a name of the artist who created it all in an inspired Irish freehand. Sadly Alicia died only four years after her enchanting house was completed, or half completed, for in the finely proportioned rooms of the first floor there are no more substantial flights of plasterwork. Thomas Tyndall as a widower had no heart to decorate a best bedroom in the style of the reception rooms below. It is these with their ceilings which hint at a creative feminine mind working behind the Patys. As the Stair-Hall improvises upon a roll of Chinese wallpaper, so the Drawing Room and Eating Room ceilings improvise upon pages of pattern books like *The Modern Builder's Assistant*, published in 1757 (illus. 132) and Thomas Johnson's *One Hundred and Fifty New Designs*, which came out in 1758, the year the Fort was begun. These are just the books which a young, newly

132 Alternate designs for a ceiling from the *Modern Builder's Assistant* (1757).

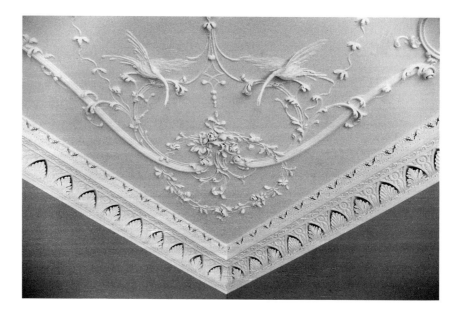

133 Ho-ho birds on the Drawing Room ceiling of the Royal Fort House, Bristol (1758–62).

married wife would have browsed through, looking for the most fashionable effects, as a modern wife in the same house-decorating drive would leaf through the pages of glossy magazines like *House and Garden* and *The World of Interiors*. The result of it all was a sense of light-hearted gaiety that still pervades the main rooms. Neither of the two great ceilings is geometrically confined. Instead, as at Belvedere House, Co. Westmeath, and Mespil House, Dublin, the inner and outer spaces are defined by curvilinear acanthus trails and semi-circles of rocaille work.

The theme of the Drawing Room is pastoral. A shepherdess with a feather in her hat is laughing over the doorway and the chimneypiece of white and ochre Sienese marble has another shepherdess with her swain and a lamb between them. Ho-ho birds are perched in pairs at each angle of the ceiling fronting corner pieces of flower wreaths, airier trails swirl about the centre (illus. 133). Off to one side is an elegant little boudoir – the Alicia sanctum. In the Eating Room the mood is more masculine and the imagery is that of wilder Nature. An eagle has seized its prey in the ceiling centre, but complex flower arrangements circle around it as a humane distraction (illus. 134). Two squirrels scamper along an acanthus trail over the door while another eats a nut over the canted bay. In this room Paty's carving reached a climax of improbable undercarving in soft pine wood with two lean, tall setpieces of angling and shooting impedimenta (illus. 135). Like Thomas Roberts with those plaster trophies in the Octagon of the Nuthall Temple, Paty took everyday objects: nets, rods, guns and angler's pouches, subtly stylizing them into high art, an essentially Rococo celebration of the real world. The door surround is, in contrast, a Classical fantasy. Its Corinthian columns are spiralled with flower trails and their capitals are carved in twisted perspective; the overdoor is a triumphal arch of stalactites, treillage and Rococo complexities with ho-ho birds perched impudently on the top of it all. Both these rooms are decorated so richly and with such invention that they look completely furnished without a stick of actual furnishing, a pure testimonial to Paty's achievement.

As for the wild Irish boy and the Dublin influence, Stocking is not a legend but neither do the known facts about him make up a satisfactory biography. What is reliably documented is that he died, aged 86, in 1808 and was therefore born in 1722, but where is not recorded. He did not become a Free Burgess of Bristol until 1763, a year after the Royal Fort was completed. By then he would have been 41, an indication perhaps that he arrived late in the city, already a skilled plasterer. His wife, Mary, outlived him and they had a son, another Thomas, who became his apprentice in 1765. There are

134 The Eating Room at the Royal Fort House, Bristol (1758–62).

no surviving documents linking him to the work at Arno's Vale or at the Royal Fort, but he was working as part of Thomas Paty's team of builders and decorators at Stoke Park, Bristol (1760–4), Fonmon Castle, Glamorgan (1766–7) and at St Nicholas's church by Bristol Bridge, where he created the entire vast ceiling (1768–9).[22] At Corsham Court, Wiltshire, where he was paid £710 for work between 1763 and 1766, he was in charge of his own team of decorators. Plasterwork at Hagley Hall, Worcestershire (c. 1758), Frenchay House, Bristol (1771) and at Beacon House, Painswick, Gloucestershire (1768–9) has been attributed to him but only on stylistic evidence of varying strength.[23]

The Irish connection is also circumstantial. The number of ships trading across to Dublin and Waterford has already been noted, as has the replication of Clifton Hill House in Co. Cork. Bristol–Dublin links had always been close; the dedication of Dublin's churches deliberately evoked those of Bristol: St Werburgh, St Audoen (St Ewen in Bristol) and all the more usual: Nicholas, Stephen and James. So many Irish came over to Bristol seeking employment that in 1740 the Corporation had to set up a fixed rate of 6s.6d. an adult and 3s.3d. a child to cover their return as vagrants. In the end the connection is supported most convincingly by those Robert West-like flights of birds and by the sheer figurative energy and invention of the Bristol plasterwork, so close to that of contemporary Dublin, so unlike the hesitant,

136 The Black Castle,
Arno's Court, Bristol
(1764), built of slag
from the brass
foundries.

academic or Chinese bias of Rococo plasterwork in England away from the
West Country.

The lives and the residences of Tyndall and Reeve, the two principal
patrons of Bristol Rococo, register like some contrived allegory in a play by
Ben Jonson. Thomas Tyndall lived on the high, healthy top of Kingsdown in
the north of the city; he was rich and he kept his hands, if not his soul, clean
on the proceeds of the slave trade. Down in the valley bottom of Arno's Vale,
south of the Avon, lived an even wealthier patron of the Rococo, the brass
founder, William Reeve. His hands and lungs were far from clean and his
house, Arno's Court, inappropriately renamed Mount Pleasant, bordered a
tract of the Avon valley blackened by the fumes of Reeve's mills and foundry
at Crew's Hole. Where Tyndall was entirely committed to the one style,
Reeve's patronage reflected the indecisions of provincial Bristol, torn between the Rococo and the Gothick. He bestrode the two styles with brash
confidence building first a purely Classical-Rococo villa with two broad
canted bays facing up the main road to Bath, then a few years later clamping
an ogee Gothick trim onto its windows and its porch. Two hundred yards
away across the road he raised in 1764 the Black Castle, probably to the
designs of Halfpenny's son, John. This is a bizarre Gothick complex constructed of the glistening black slag from his brass foundry, the details of its
towers and those 'termany' figures which were a standard Halfpenny ornament executed in contrasting white limestone (illus. 136). The Castle acted
partly as an administration centre for his works and partly as a grotesque
recreational area for rowdy, late night sessions. Returning from his foundry

137 The Dining Room, Riverstown House, Co. Cork (1735–6).

138 The ceiling of the Dining Room at Riverstown House, Co. Cork, based upon Poussin's allegorical painting of 'Time saving Truth from the assault of Envy and Discord'.

139 A show of Rococo
polychromatic
stonework: Newbridge
House, Co. Dublin
(1737).

140 Russborough, Co.
Wicklow (1741–5),
sprawling in a superb,
unmistakably Irish
Palladianism.

141 Belvedere House, Co. Westmeath (1740–6), Richard Castle's uneasy experiment in villa design.

142 The Entrance Hall, Kilshannig, Co. Cork (1765–6): Rococo detail on very late Baroque spaces.

143 The ceiling of the Library in Kilshannig: more French in detail than Irish.

146 The god Pan, with pipes, looks down the stairs at Beacon House, Painswick, Gloucestershire (1767–9), one among several relics of an obsessive eighteenth-century cult.

in the evenings begrimed with soot, Reeve wished to bathe before entering
his house, so between Mount Pleasant and the Black Castle he built a stylistic
compromise: a Bath House with Gothick end turrets, a columned arcade
and a plunge pool roofed over with Rococo plasterwork of dolphins, shells
and water gods.[24]

From the Bath House a tunnel led under the road to Mount Pleasant.
Here a Drawing Room and a Stair-Hall have been preserved in the present
day hotel, with Rococo ceilings which prove how anxious Reeve had been to
imitate his fellow Venturer in north Bristol (illus. 147). A four-armed star of
rose garlands similar to that in Mornington House, Dublin, centres the
Drawing Room ceiling then, enclosed in graceful trails of acanthus and
rocaille work like those at the Royal Fort, a playful sky of birds has been set
flying. Some carry ears of corn, ho-ho birds and swans simply flap their way
along, one eagle is pouncing on a smaller bird as at the Royal Fort, Dowth
Hall and 86 St Stephen's Green. Like all the best Rococo plasterwork it
demands attention and diverts the eye, new details keep emerging. Unlike
Adam-style decoration it can never be taken for granted as mere elegance
laid on by the yard from a set of fixed antique motifs.

Reeve was a Quaker whose entire life seems to have been spent in reversing all the usual expectations of Quaker behaviour except that of hard
work. When he presided as Master of the Merchant Venturers he entertained the Prime Minister, the Duke of Newcastle, to a splendid banquet. On
another occasion he lured the prosecution lawyer who had mocked him at a
trial into a private room, locked the door and challenged him to a duel with

swords, pistols or 'fisty cuffs', only relenting when the frightened man apol-
ogized.[25] In a properly Gothick climax his Bristol career ended in bankruptcy
at which point the Society of Friends expelled him with the pious reproof
that 'it appears the conduct of William Reeve hath been reproachful and
inconsistent with our religious principles'.[26] Bristol nonconformity seemed to
breed internal tensions which found outward and entirely inappropriate
architectural expressions like the Black Castle, which was dismissed, not
unreasonably, by Horace Walpole as 'the devil's cathedral'.[27] Another Quaker
copper smelter, William Champion, with his works a little further to the
north-east of Reeve's Crew's Hole foundry, built himself a perfectly sober
Classical house at Warmley. But then, in a bewildering brain storm, erected
a monstrous twenty-foot idol, the naked 'Warmley Giant' which still stands,
loutishly visible from the house near a demoniacal grotto of black clinkers in
the otherwise formal grounds. The Quaker ladies of Goldney House, next
door to Clifton Hill House, spent thirty years decorating their garden grotto,
but among the usual Rococo shells and glittering minerals they introduced
tableaux of a lion and lioness and a Neptune commanding the flow of waters
at the twist of a hidden tap (illus. 148). Leading away from the grotto there is
a gloomy underground tunnel, sunk beneath a viewing terrace high above

the river and lined with knobbly clinker. This Goldney grotto, Reeve's Black Castle and Champion's naked idol were the dark Gothick response to the chemical fumes, the furnaces and the industrial blight which had made two miles of a pleasant wooded gorge into an environmental disaster. Tyndall's Royal Fort was the sybaritic escape from it all.

In 1752, a mile down the road from the Black Castle, Thomas Chatterton, Bristol's 'marvellous boy', was born; but he appears less marvellous and more of a literary disaster area if his poetry is seen as a written extension to the city's mid-century mixture of Gothick and Rococo, darkness and artificial light. Born the posthumous son of a verger of St Mary Redcliffe church, he was educated to be an office clerk, but by the time he was fifteen he had begun to associate with a group of gullible city antiquaries and was sketching reconstructions of lost Bristol churches and fortifications. His fame rests on the pastiche fifteenth-century poems with which, for a year or two, he fooled the entire English establishment, Horace Walpole included, though not Thomas Gray. Those lines supposedly 'as wroten bie the gode priest, Thomas Rowleie', are the clumsy but engaging parallels to the equally clumsy but charming Black Castle and all the rest of Halfpenny's Gothick. Chatterton's method was to pick out an obscure medieval term here and there from real fifteenth-century sources and scatter them over turgid epics of knightly violence:

> Now, by Saint Mary, if on all the field
> Y-crasèd spears and helmets be besprent,
> If every knight did hold a piercèd shield,
> If all the field with champions' blood be stent,
> Yet to encounter him I am content.[28]

In another, Rococo, mood he could pour out sweetly pastoral verse of deadly mediocrity:

> Seraphic virgins of the tuneful choir,
> Assist me to prepare the sounding lyre!
> Like her I sing – soft, sensible, and fair –
> Let the smooth numbers warble in the air.
> Ye prudes, coquettes, and all the misled throng,
> Can Beauty, Virtue, Sense, demand the song?[29]

His associates, the seedy old bachelors who employed or encouraged him, were all typical Bristol middle-class provincials: the silly bibliophile George Catcott, James Thistlethwaite with his 'literary tastes' and Lambert the attorney who sacked Chatterton when the boy faked a suicide note. They

149 A rare and late
occasion when the
Rococo soared: the
interior of Christ
Church, Bristol
(1786–90).

were the intelligentsia of an industrial city whose historical romance was being lost in soot and squalor. So they responded eagerly to Chatterton's dual registers, his wild medievalism and his polite couplets of compliment. Bristol's Gothick had the same implausible charm of ogee windows in an acceptable Classical order.

In the year when Chatterton was born, Norborne Berkeley, the squire of Stoke Park House on Bristol's northern outskirts, was just beginning to use income from his collieries at Stapleton to add a fake Jacobean castle to his genuine sixteenth-century manor house. Before Chatterton, already ravaged by drugs and venereal disease, took arsenic and died miserably in a London lodging house, Berkeley would have revived in his own favour the faintly absurd, though quite genuine, medieval title of 20th Baron Botetourt. But then he paid Thomas Stocking, working as usual for the Patys, to raise completely inappropriate Rococo ceilings over the reception rooms of his Jacobean-style castle, thoroughly conventional affairs of flower baskets and acanthus trails, further instances of Bristol's dualism.[30] In Chatterton's tragically short lifetime of seventeen years, St Werburgh's and St Nicholas's churches were rebuilt within the old city with dull but almost convincing Gothic outside walls. St Nicholas was given an enormous Rococo ceiling (1768–9), Thomas Stocking's only design disaster, a flat expanse rigidly enclosed in an interminable guilloche ornament with large empty areas and cherubs scrambling up acanthus over the reredos.[31] In the Bristol suburbs Blaise Castle, a Gothick folly on a trefoil plan, was built out at Henbury, Cote House and Stoke Bishop Manor were covered over in Gothick ogees and, as a final stylistic hybrid, Goldney House was given a Gothick gazebo tower enclosed in a Classical colonnade. All these contradictions together with the Rococo work at the Royal Fort and Arno's Vale, made up the confusion to which poor Chatterton's poetry was a natural response. They were a necessary preliminary, like the boy himself, to the coming wave of real Romanticism.

While Rococo-Gothick churches were quite often built in this period of indecision, a committed Classical-Rococo church is rare indeed. Elegant frivolity and the Protestant Church of England did not normally go hand in hand. That is what makes Bristol's Christ Church, built by the Patys but with Thomas's son, William, in charge of the design, so interesting. Many will quarrel with the attribution of a 1786–90 building to the Rococo style, but the point deserves thoughtful consideration. Sir Robert Taylor, who built any number of Rococo villas, was never given the chance to build a Rococo church and William Paty's Christ Church is the Rococo church which Taylor

should have built. Coming so late in time it lacks most, though not all, of the Rococo trim. It is in its spatial qualities, its remarkable airy lightness, that it can claim the style. In 1777, the year when William Paty returned from his training in London, old Thomas Paty had just completed a disastrous botch of a church, St Michael on the Mount Without, a Gothick shell enclosing a nave and sanctuary of sub-Robert Adam columns. To walk from that clumsy interior to enjoy the nave and sanctuary of William Paty's Christ Church is to appreciate the value of a London training and the handicap of mere provincialism.

It may not be possible for a Classical church with round arches to soar, but Christ Church does contrive to stand on tip-toe (illus. 149). Its slim, attenuated Corinthian columns strain up seeming not so much to support the white and gold billow of the shallow saucer domes, as to remind them that they are earth born. Perched on each capital a lean block of entablature is balanced and it is these academic oddities which actually send the ribs up and out to the pendentives over a nave as wide as it is long. The Duke of Beaufort's church at Badminton, designed by Charles Evans in 1785, is usually quoted as the model for this elegant spaciousness, but the Transfer Offices of the Bank of England, designed by Taylor in 1765–8, are much closer, and that would have been a brand new building when William Paty was training in London, one much discussed and admired.[32]

Thomas Tyndall was not only still alive in 1790, he was a prominent parishioner of Christ Church and a sometime Churchwarden. The reredos of the church, brought forward now by an intrusive restoration to serve as a choir screen, has Corinthian columns wreathed round with spiralling flower garlands, and these are exactly like those on the door surround of the Eating Room in the Royal Fort. When the church was first decorated this link between the old man's house and his church would have been even more striking as all the tall columns were painted to resemble Sienese marble and around them, still just faintly visible today, were painted the same spiralling wreaths of flowers. If it could be restored the effect might be more that of a celestial conservatory than of a holy place, but the risk would be one worth taking. It would demonstrate that Christopher Wren's spatial experiments in his City churches had at least one worthy successor here in Bristol, and that the Rococo was not in its last years incapable of the numinous, but actually able to combine it with a sense of worldly optimism.

CHAPTER XIV

ROCOCO IN THE
BRISTOL
HINTERLAND

Four other houses in Bristol's cultural hinterland throw light, not only on
that grey area of the Paty–Stocking relationship, but on the kind of
patron who would still, in the 1759–70 years, opt for uninhibited Rococo
interiors rather than clapped-out Palladian or new wave Adam. Two of
these houses, Fonmon Castle in Glamorgan and Beacon House, Painswick,
Gloucestershire, have one or more brilliant interiors of the first quality and
national importance. One, The Cedars in Wells, Somerset has only mediocre
work and the other, Corsham Court, Wiltshire was, for Stocking, a stylistic
cop-out and a waste of his talents.

It will not have escaped attention in the last chapter that Thomas Stocking
has a tendency to rank as a mythic figure, one to whom any plasterwork of
reasonable quality raised in the West of England between 1755 and 1775 is
liable to be attributed. His surname seems to work in his favour, as Joseph
Thomas's does not. 'Stocking' sounds Dickensian, lively but eccentric, appropriate therefore to plasterwork where squirrels scamper along compartment
mouldings and lurchers dangle dead rabbits from their jaws. Hard documented facts are less supportive to these pretensions of wild genius. The first
squirrel in Bristol plasterwork was in Joseph Thomas's own house in Guinea
Street of about 1743. Stocking's first attested ceilings in Stoke Park, for the
whimsical bachelor Lord Botetourt, are a collection of competent Rococo
clichés, flower basket and scrolls, in no way either inventive or poetic. At
Corsham Court, Stocking was not working for Thomas Paty but was in

charge of his own team of plasterers with Lancelot (Capability) Brown presiding, and the ceilings here are old-fashioned, clumsy or commonplace, hardly Rococo at all in any French or Irish sense of the term. When Stocking had the whole vast canvas of the ceiling of St Nicholas's church by Bristol Bridge to extemporise upon he created delicate conventional scribbles of plaster with wide areas of nothing. Contrary to all this there is the Library at Fonmon Castle where Stocking's activity is chronicled, with payments made in 1766 and 1767, for work which is an unquestionable delight, the very essence of the figurative Insular Rococo.[1] So there is a problem: from which direction did the inspiration come?

The best way to disentangle the two, Thomas Paty and Thomas Stocking, is to work chronologically through the four houses, remembering all the time that at the Royal Fort (1758–62) Paty had been in charge of the entire building operation, carving the woodwork himself and creating an extraordinarily impressive interior with Stocking's name nowhere mentioned either in the accounts or in contemporary comment. Nor, for that matter, is there any proof that Stocking worked at The Cedars in Wells. What The Cedars does prove is how extensive Paty's firm had become, employing large numbers of workmen and craftsmen.

Thomas Paty signed the articles of agreement for The Cedars with Charles Tudway on 23 December 1758, the same year in which he had begun building the Royal Fort for Thomas Tyndall.[2] Both Tudway and Tyndall owed their fortunes, in part at least, to a slave economy but to describe Charles Tudway, who began life as a plain Somerset yeoman, as a slaver might be accurate but a little extreme. He had inherited his slaves and the flourishing sugar plantation of Parham Hill on the island of Antigua in 1748 from a second cousin in another and far more active branch of the Tudway family, merchants and master mariners 'in the Antiguan trade', which could have meant trade in slaves or sugar, but most probably in both. All that Charles Tudway did with his unearned fortune was to enjoy it quietly in the cathedral city of his birth by building The Cedars, a modest house, and setting up a local dynasty which retained possession until well into the twentieth century. It was a perfect instance of the way in which foreign ventures and an expanding British empire could enrich the architecture of a provincial town beyond the resources of that town's own neighbourhood. An instance too of why Britain's eighteenth-century wars with the French were backed with such enthusiasm by the MPs from apparently tranquil rural communities like Wells. Charles Tudway, after serving for several terms as Mayor of Wells, became in 1754 one of the city's two MPs, and his son Clement would follow him in that office. So The Cedars was built as the proper, dignified but not ostentatious seat of a plantation owner and MP, a man who never set foot in the West Indies but controlled his plantation by letters to a series of managers.

Charles Tudway's relationship with slavery was, like Thomas Tyndall's, genteelly distant. His managers saw to it that the slaves were well treated, inoculated against the smallpox long before that treatment was available to Somerset peasants, and fed on a nutritious diet of beans and corn. There were 480 slaves on the Parham Hill plantation and it was commercially vital that they should be happy and contented. A young male, 'an able stout fellow', would sell for £90 to £100 and a 'young able wench' for £80, but only if they were stable and well adjusted to plantation life.[3] If they had a reputation as run-aways their value dropped to £45 and £35 respectively. This emotional interdependence between slave owner and slave is not always stressed, but when Charles Tudway was considering leasing out Parham Hill in 1758, the year when The Cedars was planned, his nephew and manager, Robert Holloway, wrote warning him:

> I am prevailed on even by the poor Negroes of your Estate to desire you not to do it, and who can refrain almost from tears to see such a number of Negroes assembled around me, to know for what reason you would lease it, as they work for you with the greatest pleasure, and rejoice when anything happens for your benefit.[4]

Moved by this 'Uncle Tom' emotionalism, Tudway relented, abandoned the leasing scheme and may well have scaled down his plans for The Cedars as a result.

The house is an unassuming two-storey building with balustraded parapet, a recessed three-bay centre and two-bay wings. There are attic dormers. The only surviving Rococo interiors are the Hall and the Drawing Room; the former is conventionally austere, but with a relief medallion over the chimneypiece of Aeneas rescuing his father Anchises from the blazing wreck of Troy, the latter is richly feminine. As in the Drawing Room at the Royal Fort, Paty's plasterers have avoided any trace of rigid compartments by an agile dance of C scrolls. For corner pieces the ho-ho birds have been abandoned, instead the bust of a woman, rising from a flurry of scroll work, supports with absurd aplomb a large basket of roses and mixed flowers on her head (illus. 150). Flower trails also make up the set pieces at the ceiling's cardinal points and the central, eight-pointed support to the chandelier. Apart from this one outburst of elegant, subdued invention for Charles's wife, Hannah Tudway, The Cedars has none of the Royal Fort's daring or of

150 Stilted Rococo plasterwork from the Paty team in the Drawing Room of The Cedars, Wells, Somerset (1758–60).

its grandeur in miniature. Gainsborough, the ideal Rococo portraitist, painted both Charles and Hannah just before he left Bath for London, and a very dim, solid couple they were.[5] Hannah Tudway is armed with her tatting shuttle and appears impatient to leave off posing and return to proper house-wifely pursuits. Paty's plasterers, whether Stocking or some other, are unlikely to have been pressed into brilliance by the Tudways as they were by the Tyndalls. Indeed the plasterwork for the whole house cost only £19.5.11, Thomas Prowse's commission as architect came to £210, and the bill for the entire project was just over £4,871.[6]

Those flower-pot balancing women in the Drawing Room do have the air of some wilful plasterer going as far as he dared in the face of conventional restraints so Stocking may have worked there. But if he had been artistically restricted at The Cedars he was to find Corsham Court a far more depressing experience. Paul Methuen had bought the Elizabethan house when he was only twenty-one. He was a comparative nonentity who inherited in 1757 a splendid art collection from a distant cousin, the distinguished diplomat and career politician, Sir Paul Methuen KB. To house the paintings and achieve a new suite of state rooms Methuen called in, first Henry Keene, then Lancelot Brown to add a wing to the existing house in a pedestrian Palladian style, old fashioned and outworn by the time the work was begun in 1761.

Lancelot Brown's achievements as a landscape gardener are matters for subjective judgement, but he probably destroyed far more interesting and valuable gardens than he ever created. As an architect he was a straight Palladian who had built Croome Court, Worcestershire, in 1751–2, to a design by Sanderson Miller; so Paul Methuen was not committing himself to a dynamic or forward looking designer. Why Brown should have brought Thomas Stocking in to handle all the new plasterwork if Stocking had a reputation for inventive work in the Franco-Irish style is a puzzle, for Brown designed all the ceilings himself in a sub-Palladian compromise more amateur than truly conservative. It appears that Stocking was now heading a team of plasterers, some 'ornament hands' and some lower paid men who turned out the plaster details from moulds.[7] So his Corsham period (1762–6) may represent a time when he was attempting to break way from Paty and set up as a building contractor in his own right.

The ceilings of the Picture Gallery and the cornice of the Library (now the Breakfast Room) are Stocking's best known efforts at Corsham; neither are remarkable.[8] By 1762 he had completed the cornice of the Library, an almost exact repeat of the cornice in the Drawing Room of the Royal Fort: a Gothic arch enclosing an acanthus leaf, but with the addition of exquisite little heads, comical caricatures acting as drops to each arch. The actual ceiling is a mere maze of Methuen family heraldry, shields strung out on ribbons. For the Picture Gallery in 1764 Stocking had to stick closely to a Brown design with a purely Palladian, coffered central section and a deep cove covered by Brown's concession to the Rococo – a single pre-cast unit of a giant acanthus C scroll repeated and laid side by side all the way round, apart from cherub breaks at the corner and cardinal points. The effect is both heavy and boring, the exact reverse of true Rococo work. For the State Bedroom, Stocking was allowed semi-circles at the cardinal points with a few elegant palm scrolls; for the Cabinet Room Brown imposed heavy compartments of double guilloche which quarter the ceiling diagonally and enclose a central circle.[9] In the quarters are cameo busts of gods and goddesses enclosed in long, symmetrical palm trails. In the Octagon or Ante Room, Stocking was given rather more liberty with octagonal panels of acanthus work around a circular central panel, but it is the compartmentation not the decorative detail which catches the eye.

That Gothic cornice in the Library is a reasonably convincing indication that Stocking had been the plasterer responsible for much of the brilliant work in the Royal Fort even though his name is not recorded in contemporary letters. But the Corsham commission is interesting for several other reasons. It demonstrates clearly that a Rococo plasterer's team could turn its collective hands to any style, though Stocking would not have had to carve many neo-Palladian moulds to satisfy Lancelot Brown's limited design demands. There are also rare human glimpses of Stocking, the foreman plasterer, grumbling at inefficiencies and delays. On 27 December 1763 he wrote to Brown complaining that, though he had completed the cornices of the Cabinet Room and the State Bedroom, Brown had not sent him the designs for their ceilings which would have kept his more skilled workers active doing the freehand details. 'I have been obliged to keep my ornament hands on mouldings for sum time past which is hurtful to me', he explained.[10] They would, of course, have been paid at their usual higher rate for this lesser skilled task. The letter leaves open the question of how much of the actual freehand work Stocking undertook personally if he had 'ornament hands' (plural) for these relatively simple ceilings.

Paul Methuen's daybook records that he paid 'Mr. Stocking the stukoman in full for stuko work and carving done in the library £52.19.0',[11] but in total the plasterwork for that one quite small room cost Methuen 130 guineas while the much larger Picture Gallery, because it was covered for the most part in pre-cast items: rosettes, coffering and cornices, only cost two payments to Stocking of £190 in all.[12] This is why the Adam style of plaster decoration, produced almost entirely from moulds, and very shallow moulds at that, so easily defeated and replaced the Rococo as a general fashion. Anyone who wanted a lively and original Rococo ceiling in deep, shadow-casting relief had to pay over the odds for it. Significantly, at Fonmon Castle where the owner, Robert Jones III, was a virtual Rococo addict, Jones became financially embarrassed half-way through the great Paty-controlled redecorating and rebuilding operation, and had to leave the interiors half-finished and the exteriors an aesthetic disaster.

Fonmon Castle remains, nevertheless, a house of unique character and memorable charm. It lies in a countryside of bizarre contradictions. The Vale of Glamorgan is an un-Welsh, yet equally un-English, part of Wales. Its rolling pastoral landscape, scattered with stumpy church towers and ugly little castles, edges its way down to limestone cliffs and the sea. The runway of a large airport begins within a stone's throw of where Fonmon's gardens end, and an enormous transport hangar towers up over the orchid-rich fields. Then at the end of the drive leading away from the castle, in the strategic position where a Classical temple should end a vista of wind blown, overhanging trees, the gaunt, sand-coloured chimneys of a huge cement works strike aggressively upwards. Like Derbyshire's Renishaw, Glamorgan's Fonmon co-exists with an industrial revolution and gains by the contrast.

In its way the castle fights back effectively against its appalling neighbours. It has a fair claim to be called the ugliest and least stately home in Wales, or even in Britain, yet its charm is almost tangible. A small, late Norman keep with thirteenth-century additions has been crudely classicized with plain rectangular windows, and a seventeenth-century wing has been added to the north. To complete the unprepossessing complex a drab, grey roughcast has been sprayed over the entire fabric in a desperate but vain attempt to fight off the damps which invade its blue lias walls from the salt-laden sea winds. If ever Gormenghast were burnt down Titus Groan from Mervyn Peake's Gothic trilogy would find himself perfectly at home in Fonmon Castle.

Even the history of the place is appropriately bizarre. Deserted by the St Johns, whose home it had been through the medieval period, Fonmon was bought by Colonel Philip Jones, one of Oliver Cromwell's 'Lords in Parliament', a man who earnestly persuaded Cromwell to accept the crown but then settled comfortably with Charles II. The widow of one of his sons married, for comfort in her old age, Judge Jeffreys of the Bloody Assizes. But then came one of those valuable interludes which often precede an eighteenth-century burst of building. Robert Jones II died young, immediately after a Wesleyan conversion, and his widow lived quietly for the years of young Robert Jones III's minority, storing up wealth for her son to splurge gloriously once he came of age.

Robert Jones III's portrait, a three-quarter length by Joshua Reynolds, hangs in the Hall (illus. 151) and tells much that needs to be known about the man. Like so much at Fonmon the painting has had a hard time. It was the result of that period when Reynolds was experimenting with bitumen to enliven his colours. In his fancy dress Hussar's costume, Jones must originally have glistened in cherry reds, carmines, purples and puce. But the inevitable chemical decomposition of the bitumen set in and now Jones's pale, fleshly, self-satisfied face stands out against a murky background, a decayed area of slatey grey frogging and a diseased purple sabre tache. According to family legend he is meant to be dressed as Tancred, the knightly hero of Ariosto's *Orlando Furioso*, but if that is true he can hardly have read the text. He looks exactly like what he was: a Welshman pretending to an English army background in a good regiment.

Jones had inherited Fonmon in 1742 when he was ten. Sensibly enough he reacted against the severe discipline of a Wesleyan boarding school by running back to Fonmon and his mother. Travelling Europe on his Grand Tour he found himself most at ease in Paris. After that French experience he

settled down to enjoy a life of theatre going, gambling and tennis in London and Bath. Aged 30 he married, unexpectedly wisely, a local heiress, Jane Seys of Boverton. That was in 1762 and, as Thomas Tyndall had built the Royal Fort as a home for his young bride, so Robert Jones set about the difficult task of turning Fonmon into an elegant and habitable house for a family with the help of Thomas Paty and Thomas Stocking.

It is difficult to decide what is most admirable about Fonmon's interiors: the ingenuity of Paty's conversion or the exuberance of Stocking's plasterwork. At the Royal Fort Paty had had a clear run, adding a villa of entertainment rooms to existing domestic premises; at Fonmon he had to make an impressive sequence and a spacious modern room, part library, part drawing room, part saloon, out of crabbed medieval spaces with walls three feet thick. His solution was an illogical voyage of spatial discoveries. On entering, via the merest gap in the unwelcoming roughcast, the visitor has to turn sharp right into a long portrait gallery-cum-Stair-Hall. This was created by Paty's demolition of four rooms on two floors, which left the original ceilings of the upper floor still intact and separate. In the first ceiling Stocking placed the cameo bust of a Caesar surrounded by a light garland, in the second, over the stairs, the phantom lost room is recalled by the plasterer's most three-dimensional cornice of vine leaves and fat bunches of grapes. Its quite conventional ceiling, with corner pieces and an eight-pointed central star of abstract C scrolls, comes as a disappointment after such ingenuity. At the very least Stocking could have included a Bacchus.

Next, in a complete about turn, the visitor has to walk back along a side gallery of this long, dysfunctional Hall to enter one of Paty and Stocking's finest rooms. This, the Library, has been forged from the heart of the Norman keep, with all its handicaps turned into spatial advantages, more by engineering than by the normal processes of internal decoration. To make two, or possibly three, quite small rooms into one impressive apartment Paty had to cut through the three-foot wide masonry of the keep. This left him with a handsome and structural depressed arch. To gain symmetry another matching, but non-functional, arch was built on the western side of the new long room. The resulting space is more Baroque than conventionally Classical, with a most satisfying movement and theatricality in its three linked, yet consciously demarcated areas. At the west end is a large Venetian window inset within a recessed arch. To achieve symmetry at the east end, Paty built out a wooden bow with a second Venetian-type window overlooking the deep, wooded dingle which protects the castle on this side. This too is inset within a fourth recessed arch, making up a strong punctuation for one long but quite low room which is already diversified by three non-matching and non-axial doorways.

Those are the bare, Paty bones for Stocking's transformation act. In perhaps no other English, Irish or, it has to be added, Welsh, Rococo space is the figurative element of the plasterwork so vibrant. The ceiling has its full share of invention with an Apollo's head within a glory, very like that in the Dining Room at Dowth Hall. This is surrounded by two rollicking bands of

153 A lurcher and
hare on an arch in the
Library at Fonmon
Castle, Glamorgan
(1766–7).

C scrolls linking four rich corner pieces, where wrynecked ho-ho birds guard
cameo busts of gods and goddesses (illus. 152). Stocking has underplayed the
softer acanthus forms and kept the rhythms of his borders taut by using hard
rocaille forms and giant reversed Cs; the effect is far more masculine than is
usual in a Rococo room. The plasterwork which really catches the eye immediately on entry emphasizes this masculinity. It is not on the ceilings but on
the keystones of the dominant arches and in their spandrels. Each keystone
has a large crowned head or grimacing Green Man with hair of acanthus
leaves; boldly, even grotesquely, modelled they leer across at each other.
Then all four spandrels have dog's heads, three spaniels and one lurcher
(illus. 153), or greyhound, each holding trophies of the chase. The spaniels
suspend grisly groups of pheasant, wild duck and partridge; the fourth, the
most dramatic, that of the lurcher, has a very dead hare dangling from his
jaws.

If all this sounds oppressively grim the reality is the reverse. The Library
is playful and visually a child's delight, with any number of discoveries to be
made by ranging about and looking upwards. Only one of William Burges's
nineteenth-century interiors in the towers of Cardiff Castle could compete
with Fonmon's Library in ingenious surprises and decorative treats, and

there is much more Rococo work in addition to the plaster improvisations. On either side of the Sienese marble chimneypiece is perched a tall, gilt merman taken from Thomas Johnson's designs, their fishy tails twining down saucily (illus. 154); their right and left arms supporting respectively a mantelpiece of richly carved wood which refuses to tolerate a single straight line or to do anything so functional as carry a vase or even a snuff box. Above this virtuoso piece of Paty work a large, four-part Rococo mirror writhes up with birds, branches and swinging candle arms, but this is only an introduction to a positive infestation of Rococo mirrors and girandoles (illus. 155). They are not refined, delicate pieces but obstreperous, assertive chunks of asymmetry, coarsely modelled in gilded wood and gesso. Where Palladian room furnishings assert correct form and Adam ones quiver with their own shallow refinements, the Rococo explores form through unpredictable by-ways and does so with bold mouldings and a challenging directness.

It would be mean spirited not to allow that, in this one committed room, before Robert Jones's money ran out and he fled his creditors to France, he had created, with help from Bristol, a distinctive Welsh Rococo, bucolic and masculine. Here is one great eighteenth-century interior where the word 'elegance' with all its vapid connotations, is not the first that comes to mind. The light laps subtly from eastern and western windows, its flow broken by the coffered acanthus, heavy arches and the army of mirrors. Light coloured fabrics and soft modern furnishings offer easy comfort and everywhere there are faces, Apollo, the fiercely grinning keystones, docile spaniels, little apes in the twisted girandoles, bland deities looking sideways, dead birds drooping, live ho-hos peering. It may have seemed difficult to find another room to rank alongside the Stair-Hall of 20 Dominick Street or the reception rooms of the Royal Fort, but here in this most unlikely setting is their equal.

Stocking, who received 130 guineas for one mediocre room at Corsham Court, was only paid just over £86, in a series of four small sums spread out over 1766 and 1767, for all his work here at Fonmon. The explanation is that at Corsham his team was working on a new wing of the house and would have had to set up the laths on the roof beams and all three layers of the plasterwork. At Fonmon the base work would have been Paty's responsibility and Stocking's £86 was payment only for the decorative detail. It is both satisfying and frustrating to find the forms of this Insular Rococo growing richer and more various as the style approached its cut-off point. Fonmon was late; Beacon House at Painswick was even later, and there the Rococo work in all its maturity of confident composition was shaded to reflect, through all the usual motifs, a spiritual aura of polite devil worship.

154 The riotously decadent Rococo chimneypiece with mermen in the Library, Fonmon Castle, Glamorgan (1766–7).

Painswick today is almost intolerably genteel, a retiree townlet which can run to a delicatessen and antique shops yet still satisfy its ageing residents with a faint whiff of *Cider with Rosie*. In 1769, when John Gardner built Beacon House on a favoured site where the High Street opens out onto the churchyard, Painswick was a prosperous wool manufacturing town set high up above a river that powered a whole chain of woollen mills. Millowners were the local aristocracy, some of them, the Gydes and the Clutterbucks – Timothy Gyde of Stouts Hill and Richard Clutterbuck of Frampton Court – have featured in earlier chapters. The Gardners were another dynasty, almost 'old money' by 1769, but still retaining their urban base and keeping an eye on their mill down in the valley. Within its limited five-bay elevation on the High Street, Beacon House did everything Palladianly possible to assert a gentry status for John Gardner, who had recently served as church-warden.

That church attendance and the proximity of holy ground just across the road in no way excluded Gardner from enthusiastic participation in a local version of that better known Hell Fire Club over which Sir Francis Dashwood presided at West Wycombe in the Chilterns. Painswick's equivalent to Sir Francis was Benjamin Hyett, a Gloucester merchant now settled as the local squire at Painswick House on the town's outskirts. There he had devised that

156 Thomas Robins, *Pan's Lodge in Coldbourn Grove, Near Panswyke in Gloucestershire*, 1750s, gouache and watercolour, with sleazy revels in the foreground.

complex Rococo garden, described earlier, with Van Nost's statue of the Great God Pan standing forbiddingly next to a cold bath (illus. 144). For more private revelries Hyett had built Pan's Lodge, a part-Gothick, part-Classical, three-bay pavilion in woods, the Coldbourn Grove, across the valley from the town. One Thomas Robins painting of the Lodge is bordered in black set round with ill-omened birds of the night and it illustrates an unpleasant scene of sylvan evil with a misshapen Pan figure dancing among his followers (illus. 156).[13] Another Robins is a daylight scene with Pan in the foreground gesturing to distant Painswick as if to claim it: 'Pan's-Wyke', for his own.

Anthropologists are in doubt as to whether this Pan cult was simply something devised to give bored local gentry an excuse for heavy drinking and lewd sessions with girls from the mills or a genuine folk survival from Roman times, when there were wolves on the Cotswolds and shepherds evoked Pan, the god of nature, for protection. Whatever John Gardner may have got up to at night in Pan's Lodge, his official role in the club was more urbane. Beacon House was the venue for the club's dining sessions and accordingly it was given the full Rococo decorative trim appropriate to such meetings. No documentary evidence has survived to link Paty or Stocking with the house but stylistically the evidence is very strong. Thomas Paty's hand is evident in the confident spatial flow of the Entrance and Stair-Hall and in the way in which a design from Thomas Johnson's *Collection of Designs* of 1758 has been manipulated to climb the stair wall and enlivened with some of Stocking's favourite devices.[14]

Such was the brilliance and erotic allure of the plasterwork that in the 1920s an American, possibly Randolph Hearst looking for British treasures to decorate his Californian castle at San Simeon, bought not only the marble chimneypiece in the Entrance Hall with its goat head, but the entire Dining Room, its walls and its ceiling, and carried them away. Their present whereabouts is a mystery, but an old photograph records a room wonderfully crammed with bay wreaths and wild men's heads.[15] Its true prodigy was a life-sized naked statue on its ceiling of the Lycian Apollo, the god who, in later Greek mythology, had taken over the wolf and shepherd roles of the Lycian Pan. One wonders if this overt eighteenth-century sex symbol proved a little too much even for Randolph Hearst, hence its disappearance, but it is a sad loss to the Rococo (illus. 157). These odd psychic explorations, the Pan cult, the Warmley Giant, and the Black Castle, appear to have been natural throw-offs of the mid-century Rococo mood, small rebellions within a Classical framework but also preliminary warnings of the coming Romanticism.

The Dining Room and its Apollo are lost, yet what survives in the Stair-Hall still represents a last epitome of Rococo sophistication and vitality. Thomas Johnson's design articulates a wall by a series of emaciated colonettes, crowned with cherub-topped finials and punctuated by trophies of music and the chase on long drops of flowers. The putative Stocking has pounced upon Johnson's idea, enriched the composition with urns on each lean capital and added linking wreaths of woody nightshade with his favourite reversed C scrolls (illus. 145). Above the colonettes are all the symbolic figures of the Pan cult and Robins's paintings: an owl, a squirrel, oak leaves, lutes, pipes, a fox with a goose slung over his back, and at the turn of the stairs the Great God Pan himself, horned, with his pipes and a wicked sneer on his face (illus. 146). Paty's typical motifs, rose trails and baskets of flowers, find a place and over all this enchanting pageant the ho-ho birds crane their Chinese necks. If it lacks the Baroque theatricality of 20 Dominick Street this Stair-Hall has instead the true lightness and response to the natural world of the Rococo, with a little added touch of spiritual danger besides.

When they took the chimneypiece from the Entrance Hall the raiders from America spared the Rococo overmantel and this, based on another Thomas Johnson design, has a snarling wolf standing precariously on two C scrolls, though it could quite easily be a puppy dog. One obscure Painswick custom, observed into the early years of the twentieth century, was the consumption on one September feast day of puppy dog pie. Apparently in earlier times real dogs (wolf substitutes?) were consumed and the town's culinary tastes were a Cotswold joke with tales of unsuspecting visitors

157 The Dining Room at Beacon House, Painswick, Gloucestershire (1767–9), with the lost ceiling of the Lycian Apollo.

served dog for dinner. By the nineteenth century, gentility had set in and small china dogs were placed inside ordinary fruit pies as a treat for the children. In the Roman Lupercalia, originally a festival of the Wolf God, the Lycian Pan, and held in February not September, goats and dogs were sacrificed and young men raced through the streets lashing women with thongs to confer fertility. Writing in the *Gentleman's Magazine* of 1787 Robert Raikes, the Gloucester founder of the Sunday School movement, described Painswick's September festival as one 'that would have disgraced the most heathen nations. Drunkenness and every species of clamour, riot and disorder formerly filled the town on this occasion'. That was before Raikes instituted a special sermon delivered at the church porch to bring the townsfolk to a more Christian sobriety. Until that time there was apparently a parish race in the spring in which young men and girls ran out of town to the north crying 'High-gates! High-gates!' A scholarly late nineteenth-century parson, who had read his Frazer's *Golden Bough*, interpreted this cry as a debased form of 'aig aitis' or 'goat lover' in Greek.[16] Amazingly he decided to reinstate the custom but this only resulted in further improprieties in the woods. Such then was the Church's suspicion of the whole tradition that a vicar in the 1950s insisted on burying a small stone statue of Pan which had been placed near the church tower. The burial was secret, but a couple of old men still claim to know the site, so a resurrection is not impossible.

No portrait of John Gardner survives except for one curious relic. On the leads of the roof of Beacon House an outline of a gentleman of his period has been carved with his name set underneath. From that position there is a clear view out across the valley to Coldbourn Grove and the site of Pan's Lodge, marked now only by a growth of periwinkle flowers and a former coach house in the fields below it, which Benjamin Hyett built for the convenience of his fellow revellers. The episode of Beacon House, Pan and 'Pan's-Wyke', as Thomas Robins spelt it on his paintings, make a proper ending to this account of Paty and Stocking's work for their art represented exactly that nervous release of the human spirit within surviving Classical confines which Hyett and Gardner seem to have tapped. Is it fair to say that the Rococo could respond to any variety of human moods while the Palladian could only control or ignore them?

CHAPTER XV

THE FALTERING
COURSE OF
ENGLISH ROCOCO

In sharp contrast to its fortunes in Ireland, where it became virtually an aristocratic folk-art, the standard decorative style for any gentry interior, the Rococo in England faltered. There were two reasons for this. The first was that most English plasterers were coarse and unimaginative in their handling of what is, when the mystique of a craft guild is discounted, essentially an easy and responsive medium. The second reason was that, on those rare occasions when the plasterers were both skilled and inventive, what they produced tended to be marvelled at as specimen pieces rather than as integrated parts of a spatial unity. It was only when plasterers and architects worked together that the style succeeded and became popular.

Quite apart from these weaknesses, much of the plasterwork described as 'Rococo' has no Rococo characteristics beyond mere intricacy of workmanship. Notable examples of this are those ingenious framed wall reliefs of scenes from Classical legend or fable. These are no more than equivalents in plaster of old ladies' *petit point* representations of Windsor Castle, St Michael's Mount or Westminster Abbey in laboured stitching. The true Rococo must assert an overall rhythmic perversity of scrolled patterning, but many interiors include just token traces of such work where a few real Rococo elements have been included in generally Palladian compositions. One outstanding and unfortunately influential example of this last category is the Music Room from Norfolk House (illus. 158). This was rescued when the Norfolks' town house was demolished in the vulgarian 1930s and the one room was re-

erected in the Victoria and Albert Museum as that institution's prime and only example of an English Rococo interior when it is in reality an opulent stylistic composite. Many designers had a hand in it. Matthew Brettingham, the second-rate Palladian architect who designed the house for the 9th Duke of Norfolk, was responsible for imposing the heavy ceiling compartments, copied from Inigo Jones's Whitehall Banqueting House as a reverent gesture to a dead master. They inflict the rigidity of a great state apartment of 1619 upon an intimate domestic room of 1756: a delayed instance of that historicist confusion which Lord Burlington's cult of the antique had created in England and which only the full-blooded neo-Classicism of the 1770s would finally resolve.

The compartments of Brettingham's ceiling are only one element in a slick assemblage of several men's craftsmanship and design resulting in an impressive costliness, a cream and gold Grand Hotel style. Hundreds of visitors pass through every day believing the Music Room to be typical of the English Rococo and concluding that the style was neither memorable nor admirable, merely rich. The overall decorative design of the room is attributed to Giovanni Batista Borra, hence the room's cross-Channel indeterminacy, neither English, French nor Italian, but somewhere between the three. So many English aristocrats in the first half of the century patronized Swiss-

Italian plasterers who had been trained in Italy's compromise Rococo, that an English Rococo never really took off except in rare houses where Francophile lords or emigrant Irish plasterers presided.

The only true Rococo details in the Music Room are the exquisitely playful and precisely defined cartouches on the ceiling. On stylistic evidence McDonnell has suggested that these are an early work by Bartholomew Cramillion.[1] But in an explanatory text in the room the Museum attributes them to an Englishman, James Lovel, who had worked with Borra in 1752 at Stowe. In these alone the tantalizing asymmetries of French work of the 1720s have been integrated within Brettingham's rigid rectangles. The remaining plasterwork, the frieze and the guilloche, were by Thomas Clarke, who was Master Plasterer to the Office of Works, but the real impact of the room comes, unusually for an English house, from the boiseries of the Frenchman, Jean Cuenot, who was working to Borra's design.

Very little is known of the personal lives of these talented Swiss-Italians and Borra's own identity is a confusion. One J. B. Borra was a successful Piedmontese architect who is unlikely to have had time in the 1750s to design in England. There was another J. B. Borra, also a Turinese and possibly related, who accompanied Robert Wood as his architectural draughtsman on Wood's tour of Asia Minor and Syria. If it was this second Borra who was working at Norfolk House this would explain the large golden palmettes which are such a pronounced and un-Rococo feature of Cuenot's panelling, but common on the Syrian temple complexes at Baalbeck and Palmyra.

The Music Room is a most interesting composite with some admirable details high up above visitors' heads, but it lacks the lyrical charm and human intimacy of the best Irish and West of England Rococo work. It is easy to criticize the Victoria and Albert curators for deciding to rescue and preserve such a formidable interior, but much less easy to decide what they could have chosen from London's distinctly limited stock of Rococo rooms to offer as a typical example of a style which was nationally so inconsistent.

London, the capital and centre of fashion, exerted a particularly baleful influence on Rococo detail. The city's teams of plasterers had all, by 1750, been trained in 30 years of undemanding Palladian motifs. Hence that coarseness of detail which resulted from the unhappy interaction of Italian plasterers, who had been trained to produce bold Baroque detail, with English craftsmen who had previously got by with a stock of moulds for conventional Palladian details – coffering, rosettes, paterae and fleshy acanthus. These last would still have required some freehand work once the moulded details had been applied, but nothing very demanding. While the very best

Rococo plasterwork is usually bold in its profile and raised sufficiently from its surrounding surfaces to cast clear, defining shadows, it has none of the flat coarseness, that distinctive, dispiriting heaviness, which resulted when English Palladian-trained plasterers were required to work in the Rococo idiom. The best Rococo plasterwork impacts by sharp edges and clearly defined peaks, a constant, nervous animation of line, not by broad planes and wide surfaces.

While Rococo interiors were never common in the capital one ambitious example has survived intact at No. 1 Greek Street in Soho to exemplify this failure by coarseness of detail. The house was built in 1746, but not fitted up until 1754–6, for the rich Jamaican plantation owner and sugar trader Richard Beckford, an uncle of William Beckford of Fonthill.

The links between the Beckfords and the Tyndalls, plantation owners and slave suppliers, would not be impressive if it were not for the fact that Richard Beckford became one of Bristol's two MPs after a fiercely fought election campaign in 1754. That makes the coincidence between his Rococo town house in London and Thomas Tyndall's Rococo villa in Bristol rather more significant. The Greek Street house was fitted up only two years before the Royal Fort was begun, but the disadvantages of employing London as opposed to Bristol, Dublin-influenced decorators, are very marked. With none of the spatial sophistications of the Royal Fort's Entrance Hall, the Beckford house's combined Stair and Entrance Hall is nevertheless impressively cavernous and much taller. In decorative detail it is handsome but uninspired. Two large wall panels are each topped by a face within a scallop shell between flanking rocaille work. The ceiling is compartmented but has graceful flower sprays and more scallop shells, a mould much favoured by its unknown decorator. Over the doors leading off the top landing are lion masks holding flower swags and in an oval frame beside the entrance to the Drawing Room a shepherdess flaunts her bare bosom shamelessly (illus. 159). The Beckfords were a notably lascivious and uninhibited clan. Alderman Beckford, Richard's brother and William's father, claimed 30 bastard children and supported eight of them openly.

Inside the Drawing Room the same blowsy extravagance prevails in a busily sensuous decorative scheme. On the overmantel that head within a scallop shell appears again, flanked by twin baby dragons, from Abraham Swan's 1757 *A Collection of Designs in Architecture* (plate 42); that would make the decoration post-1757. Ribboned acanthus flowers trail over the door, sunflowers alternate with acanthus on the frieze. In the ceiling centrepiece, against a background of notional clouds, four boldly moulded cherubs represent the

159 A blowsy Beckford shepherdess (1754–6) from the staircase landing of 1 Greek Street, London.

Seasons by holding flowers, chasing birds and dangling a torch. The middle compartment of the ceiling has garlands and rough rocaille work and in the outer compartment are jowly medallions of Caesars. It is the kind of room a raw, rich colonial might be expected to commission and which may have helped to give the Rococo a name for overblown, third-hand French amorality. There are two other rooms at the back of the house with the same charming, badly crafted over-kill of detail, the entire interior curiously appropriate to its modern Soho setting as if the district has always been trendy but louche. The building is now the House of St Barnabas, a charitable institution and occasionally open to interested visitors.

What then, since the capital city's plasterers appear never to have become inventively involved in Rococo arabesques or Dublin-style flights of fancy, were the rooms and houses truly representative of an English Rococo?

In his *English Country Houses: Early Georgian*, Christopher Hussey placed Kirtlington, Oxfordshire, and Honington Hall, Warwickshire, in the Palladian section though they both have fine Rococo apartments. The team of eleven which he fielded for the Rococo make an unimpressive showing. Nostell Priory, Yorkshire, Hagley Hall, Worcestershire, and even Hartwell House, Buckinghamshire qualify, though Hartwell has only one fine Rococo room. Buckland, Berkshire, and Edgecote, Northamptonshire, are only Palladian houses with tentative Rococo-Palladian compromises in their decoration. Horace Walpole's Strawberry Hill, Middlesex is Gothick to Gothic Revival without a single real Rococo detail in its rooms. Burton

Constable, Yorkshire has much pseudo-Jacobean work conceived with Rococo frivolity, West Wycombe Park, in Buckinghamshire again, is not Rococo at all but decorated in that antique Roman villa style which Lord Burlington was always straining after and never really achieved. That leaves three houses in Hussey's list: Claydon obviously qualifies, Corsham Court has the half-hearted Stocking plasterwork already discussed and Kyre Park, Worcestershire, is a tame house which once had a possible Stocking domed interior hung with plaster hop vines.

Of the eleven only Claydon, Hartwell, Nostell Priory and Hagley pass the muster, which is not impressive. Hussey rightly excluded Langley Park, Norfolk, whose rooms are more galleries for the exhibition of the naïve skills in plaster reliefs of Charles Stanley (1703–61) than explorations of any precise style, Rococo or Palladian. But Hussey's swift passage over the villas which Sir Robert Taylor built for bankers, businessmen and retired admirals was less than fair. Taylor did, it is true, give Rococo decoration short shrift, passing over it as soon as he sensed that Adam's was the style of the future, but in one of his earliest houses, Harleyford of 1755 on the Thames in Buckinghamshire, he gave the Drawing Room elegant trophy drops (illus. 160). These hardly amount to a committed Rococo interior, but then Taylor was far too aware of Augustan reserve and a gentleman's normal expectations. There is always a feeling in his villas that, for all the domestic convenience of their planning – three rooms around a central stair-hall approached through a domed vestibule – he was designing for men not women, and the best Rococo makes its appeal across the sexes. Bristol's Royal Fort is as conveniently planned as any Taylor house and, by its feminine touches, more radiantly beautiful in its decoration than any Taylor villa. However, Trewithan, Cornwall, of 1763–4, Taylor's last Rococo house, has charmingly understated flower trails and a lean, Ionic arcading in its Dining Room that could have been adopted with advantage in other Rococo interiors: an airy, graceful device, perfect for the essential lightness of the style. The Inner Hall of Honington, probably a house by William Smith of Warwick, has similar arcading but not that defiant gesture of a section of entablature, improbably poised on the capitals, which gives Taylor's arcading its upward reaching qualities. Also, at Honington, Stanley has been allowed a very free hand on the walls of the Hall. Perhaps Stanley's plaster reliefs, or in Ireland the Francini's early efforts, should be seen as insular substitutes for the boiseries of the French; but Stanley never framed his setpieces with any lilting Rococo curvaceousness of line. At Honington his frames are solemn affairs of swan-necked pediments and heavy snail shell curls; at Langley his Grandma Moses-style naïve relief of Diana and Actaeon allows a few acanthus tendrils to overlap its frame, but these only emphasize the difference between the fluent abstract patterning and his crude figurative work.

If any one house in England has perfect interiors where a mature Rococo has been absorbed and allowed to flower with a profuse invention and unapologetic gaiety it is Hagley Hall, built as a completely new house between 1754 and 1760, the vintage Rococo years, for George Lyttelton. Here at least refined plasterwork was applied, not to offer isolated, exotic flourishes of curious craftsmanship, but as essential elements of integrated spatial unities making no apologies for their light-hearted, continental reference. Lyttelton, who had been Secretary for many years to Frederick, Prince of Wales, got the exterior he deserved by asking Sanderson Miller, a well-known Goth, to design it in the Palladian style. The result was an unrewarding, four-square barracks which gives no outward hint of the relaxed grace and decorative profusion of its interiors.

It is apparent, immediately on entering the Hall, that an unusual mind, certainly not Miller's, was in control of the decorative work. There is none of the usual almost obligatory display of the Doric with its frieze of military trophies. Overhead a very light scroll work, chained in with flowery wreaths, occupies the centre. Over the chimneypiece is an ambitious relief of Pan propitiating Diana by sacrificing a sheep (illus. 161). This is the work of the otherwise unknown Italian, E. Vassali, to whom Lyttelton entrusted all the internal decoration. The mantelpiece is supported by two ferocious

Persians making theatrically heavy weather of the urns they have to carry.
There is a sense of individual humour and confidence in the choice of the
pieces, a deliberate avoidance of the predictable.

Approached through the double arch of the Hall, the Saloon is vibrant
with a range of be-ribboned drops representing the Arts and hung from loop
after loop of fruit and flowers (illus. 162). On the window wall opposite are
three huge mirrors of diverting complexity subdivided by tall stems of
bruised reed and floral intricacies, topped by trophies of plenty and serving
as a perch for ho-ho birds. Set between the windows these exuberant artefacts make up a virtual wall of glass, and on the ceiling a bold composition of
C scrolls circuits the room with no frail uncertainties of tentative flower
stems. Here at last the Rococo is being deployed to create a room of stately
consequence, yet alive with movement.

The Drawing Room is equally impressive in another mood. Again the
scrollwork swirls around the ceiling with massive hibiscus-like blooms at
the cardinals of the long sides; and at last painting has been given its natural
place. Cartouche frames, styled confidently in the French manner, branch off
with a hundred agitated curls at the corner points. In these frames 'Athenian'
Stuart had, so Lyttelton wrote, 'engaged to paint me a Flora and four pretty

162 The Saloon (now the Dining Room) at Hagley Hall, Worcestershire.

little Zephyrs'.[2] Flora occupies the central oval, rejoicing with garlands and the Zephyrs blow in the corner frames. Everything else in the room accords with this festive mood (illus. 163). The frieze is gilded acanthine, for over-doors there are portraits redeemed from severity by the spiny C scrolls which leap around them; another hyperactive gilded mirror acts as overmantel and the richest of the portrait frames tops the mirror. Tapestries cover almost every remaining wall space, concealing the absence of boiseries and creating a convincing illusion of France.

Hussey has suggested, but on no direct evidence, that Stocking worked at Hagley but, while it might be satisfying to associate Hagley's Rococo with the Bristol school and so with Dublin, there is absolutely no stylistic link. Lyttelton, who was made a viscount in 1756, was, like Prince Frederick, a Francophile and he knew France and Paris well. He would have made sure that sophisticated French designs, like that for the Drawing Room ceiling, were secured. That Pan sacrificing a sheep in the Hall is no Stanleyesque, ill-drawn composition but one closely based on a Carlo Maratti painting; Rysbrack carved the busts in the Hall and the nude statues in the niches are all quality items.

Like most cultivated aristocrats of the period Lord Lyttelton had active eclectic leanings. Sanderson Miller sketched out a Gothic tower for his park, Athenian Stuart came to Hagley not only to paint Rococo zephyrs but to design the first authentic Greek temple in Britain on a hill in the grounds. Bishop Pococke was reduced to quivering rapture by the Rococo delights and ingenious vistas of Hagley's park. This was an important house for an influential person, someone who might, like Lord Chesterfield, have been in line for the premiership if Prince Frederick had lived to reign, and who, even without Frederick's patronage became Chancellor of the Exchequer. Hagley's Rococo was of the continental mainstream. It might not possess the wild, inventive charms of the Insular Rococo, but it is always committed and consistent, never naïve.

Nostell Priory was another of Christopher Hussey's team of eleven, but it comes as a lame and half-hearted creation after the confidence of Hagley. It was James Paine's first major house, begun in 1737, when he was only twenty. If, as is supposed, the young Paine had studied at the St Martin's Lane Academy, it suggests that the institution was at that time sharply divided between Palladian and Rococo schools of design. For Paine was to become one of those second generation architects who would contrive, by using discreet insertions of washed-out Rococo decoration, to extend the Palladian long past its sell-by date. A second-rate talent who enjoyed first-

163 The Drawing Room at Hagley Hall, Worcestershire, its mirrors fluttering with ho-ho birds.

rate commissions and opportunities, Paine began at Nostell as he intended to go on with an outstandingly dreary Palladian elevation: a lowering pediment hanging over a heavy range of small windows. Its impractical ground plan, never carried through, was based pedantically on Palladio's Villa Mocenigo. There could hardly be a more effective demonstration piece against the entire Palladian revival. In the middle 1740s, decorating some rooms to his own designs with Joseph Rose as the plasterer, Paine evolved a Stanleyesque Rococo compromise with large mythological scenes as the ceiling centre-pieces and token ribbon and flower trails outside their firmly compartmented oval frames. In the cove of the State Bedchamber conventional cartouches and rocaille occupy the cardinal and diagonal points. Nothing is too disturbingly figurative, apart from the plaster reliefs in the centre. Years later Chippendale greatly enriched Nostell and Robert Adam delivered some tense, impressive interiors with every detail closely integrated. There is a world of difference between an Adam interior where Robert Adam in person had kept a tight control over the work and so-called 'Adam' interiors, the Stair-Hall and Saloon at Claydon for instance, where a Joseph Rose team of plasterers went through the Adam motions with clumsy detail and loose compositions.

In his monograph on James Paine, Peter Leach writes of the architect's decorative work at Nostell: 'In these pioneering works of the Rococo style all the major elements of his early manner are immediately present but not surprisingly there are occasional signs of immaturity, the different constituents being at times incompletely integrated.'[3] This is polite. Hussey was more plain spoken on the 'Sitting Room' in the same house describing it as 'flaccid and perfunctory' and as 'tired Palladian tricked out in Rococo'.[4] Nostell Priory is very far from being a great Rococo house, but it demonstrates with chilling clarity how the Palladian limited the style. Nostell, not Hagley, is a truly typical English Rococo house, because it was handicapped from the outset by a blinkered architectural establishment.

Saltram, two miles outside Plymouth, was another house where Robert Adam had to be brought in to rescue a set of interiors from the feeble scale and uncertainties of earlier designers in the Rococo. Lady Catherine Parker, a daughter of Earl Paulett, had married its owner, John Parker, a local landowner and MP, and presided there over the decoration of a particularly lacklustre suite of reception rooms. Instead of pulling down the existing house, the couple wrapped two tall wings around it to conceal its Tudor confusion. The effect can most charitably be described as imposing, which is not an adjective that can be applied to their rooms of state.

Reference has been made to those highly wrought reliefs of Classical plasterwork which are often loosely described as Rococo and the Entrance Hall of Saltram is peculiarly rich in them. Lady Catherine must have been brought up to admire the art of Charles Stanley though, with the new additions to Saltram only begun in the late 1740s, she could not have commissioned the genuine Stanley article as he had been called back to his native Denmark in 1746. What some follower of Stanley provided for this one, surprisingly low, room, where every detail of the plasterwork can be examined closely, were four allegorical representations of the Elements, hung like pictures in relief on the walls with a crowded pastoral scene as the overmantel and a sprawling figure of Mercury in shallow relief as the centrepiece of the ceiling. Though there are the token ho-ho birds, two eagles and some rocaille work on the ceiling, these framed features effectively block out any overall flow of Rococo decoration.

The next two rooms, the Morning Room and the Velvet Drawing Room, are equally low. They have no cove and their complex plasterwork is embarrassingly accessible, with cherubs and large musical instruments in the Morning Room (illus. 164), all the standard Rococo motifs in the Drawing Room. This last room should work well as, unlike the preceding two, its ceiling escapes compartmentation, but the C scrolls are flat, the centrepiece is a weak composition of long stemmed flowers and nothing takes off with any spirit. The stage has been set for a Robert Adam master stroke, a dramatic demonstration of the superiority of the new style in colour and spatial handling.

As a last feeble gesture of the Rococo, the ceiling at the end of the Drawing Room features parrots in the manner of Claude Audran sitting on top of women's heads, then the door opens into the Saloon of 1768–70 and Adam's professionalism takes over. First there is a tremendous spatial release in its height after the Rococo's dwarfish sequence, a generous coving with stately winged sphinxes, husks and garlands that make the parrots of the Drawing Room look amateur and comical. Then there is the colour, a symphony of blues and greys above with reflecting brighter colours in the carpet beneath, and everywhere the assurance of Adam's antique predictables in delicate, undemanding shallow relief. There could be no more convincing demonstration of why one style was dying and another was being launched.

Saltram's Stair-Hall does something to save the honour of the Rococo but even there the walls are thick with lost opportunities. Saltram was closely associated with Sir Joshua Reynolds. The Parkers were his friends and early patrons, he painted them and their children and his competent portraits

feature prominently, but no-one would ever describe Sir Joshua as the ideal Rococo painter. Angelica Kaufmann, on the other hand, with her soft quivering brush strokes, her green and yellow vagueness of background and her scenes of yearning Classical passion could easily qualify for that title and Saltram is rich in Kaufmanns. They litter the walls of the Stair-Hall and if only the Parkers had had the vision to combine her paintings in one long gallery alive with Rococo cherubs and garlands they might have had a masterpiece.

What they have instead is a wide, square Stair-Hall, the broad flights supported improbably on two tall Doric columns, each topped with a section of entablature. On the stair walls is Kaufmann's flattering portrait of Reynolds, a mild, grandfatherly figure, then Kaufmann after Kaufmann: solemn sacrifices in windy places, feathery trysts of fated lovers, all earnestly numinous. A later dome floods the Hall with light revealing unkindly every detail of the ambitious but barely competent plasterwork decorations. At the ceiling's cardinal points flat hen-like eagles (illus. 165) confront creatures more like Tolkein's 'great worms' than conventional dragons. The baskets of fruit and flowers on the friezes have been moulded crudely on the assumption that no one would ever mount the stairs to inspect them closely.

If Saltram was short on skilled craftsmen, Claydon House suffered from a surfeit. At Claydon the second failing of the English Rococo, that of brilliant work inadequately integrated within the whole design of a room, is exemplified with such resounding drama that the failure becomes more memorable and enjoyable than any calm accord between craftsman and architect could

165 Saltram House, Devon: a heavily bucolic detail of an eagle and serpent on the staircase landing.

ever be. Even in its fragmented condition, a great house without a front door, Claydon is one of Britain's architectural experiences to be ranked alongside major cathedrals in importance. With none of Hagley's assured professionalism, its Rococo episodes, by their sheer excess and blundering determination, remain more memorable than the suave sophistication which Vassali delivered for Lord Lyttelton.

Claydon lies deep in hay fever country, in an open, almost featureless landscape, once noble with elms and lost now without its trees. Weed-grown, disused rail tracks and overgrown embankments criss-cross the fields; ungentrified villages sleep in a rural monotony where pubs hold weekend lotteries with £40 as the top prize. Here, in north Buckinghamshire, brick country meets limestone rubble land. It is a curious cultural sink into which successive governments have been able to drop prisons, borstals, army camps and sinister experimental institutions, confident that any organized vocal opposition will be the merest whisper of protest. Its urban metropolis is bucolic Bicester and in the drowsy nondescript heart of it all is Claydon, a house that nearly became Britain's Rococo palace and that remains the Rococo Mecca to which anyone with any feeling for the style must make a pilgrimage at least once in a lifetime. Yet Claydon has no single complete Rococo room, only tremendous Rococo fragments.

The 2nd Lord Verney, who presided over its 1760s additions, was a gloriously unstable character whom none of his contemporaries took very seriously. He was given to wild political ambitions, which got him nowhere except the bankruptcy courts, and to sudden stylistic whims, which resulted in the present west wing of Claydon. Verney probably designed it himself with the help of Webb his steward and Lightfoot, who had been working for Verney earlier on a building speculation in London. The façade bears, however, not the slightest trace of that manic decorative intensity which Lightfoot was soon to imprint on the interiors. The wing was in existence in June 1768, as we have a letter of that date to Verney from Sir Thomas Robinson which mentions that Luke Lightfoot and his team of workers were busy fitting it up.[5] But by that time Robinson, a natural rogue and confidence trickster, had persuaded Verney to make him the architect for a grand and completely inappropriate extension northwards with a Palladian rotunda and a balancing replica of Verney's new west wing to house a ballroom. For the brief twenty years when that enormous 256 foot (78 m) tripartite façade was in existence it must all have looked pleasantly ridiculous. The original and surviving west front is an amateurish elevation, with blind bull's eye windows placed too low, the projection of the central bays too shallow, but the overall composition saved by the fine quality of its ashlar.

It was apparently Lightfoot's drive to impact each and every available wooden surface with rich carving which impressed Lord Verney and made Sir Thomas detest the London carpenter. Apart from being a rogue and, where rich widows were concerned, an old-fashioned bounder,[6] Robinson was a keen Palladian who claimed to have been a friend of Lord Burlington. Riotous Rococo enrichments were anathema to him; but he was an old man by this time and, having outlived most Palladian decorative manners, was prepared to compromise with the Adam style, anything which would upset Lightfoot and interrupt his necessarily slow, labour intensive scheme of decoration. Lightfoot worked in wood not plaster, and if he and his wood carvers had been allowed to undertake the decoration of Robinson's two grandiose new units the work would not have been completed before the end of the century. Armed with this self-evident fact Robinson persuaded Lord Verney to bring in Joseph Rose's team of plasterers and decorators, not only to fit up his rotunda and ballroom, but to actually work alongside Lightfoot's men in the original west wing.

At Saltram there had been a natural chronological progression of styles. The Rococo work had ended in 1768 and then the Adam work had begun. But at Claydon for several years until 1769, when the pernicious Robinson persuaded Verney that Lightfoot was dishonest and had him sacked, Lightfoot's workers and Rose's plasterers were working competitively side by side in the two different styles. This resulted in all manner of remarkable compromises in the three great reception rooms on the west wing's ground floor and explains Claydon's uniquely complex interiors. Here the Rococo did not so much die as suffer psychic torment at the hand of a Palladian fanatic employing, para-doxically, Adam-style plasterers.

At the time of his dismissal Lightfoot had only half-completed the upstairs rooms. To savour his victory to the full the vindictive Robinson pursued Lightfoot back to his builder's yard in Southwark where much of the carved work which Verney had already paid for was still lying around. To ingratiate himself with his employer, Robinson listed it and arranged to have it carted to Claydon where it was put together, more or less as Lightfoot had intend-ed, but in plain, unsuitable settings. The letter which Robinson wrote to Verney describing his sour encounter with Lightfoot in Southwark gives a graphic view of that eccentric genius, who has otherwise been entirely ignored by contemporary diarists:

> He rcd. me in his parlour with his *Hat* on his head an austere look, fierce as an Eastern Monarch, his eyes sparkled fire, his *Countenance* angry and revengeful – did not ask me to sit down, said as he knew what I came about, he had asked a Person to be witness to what passed between us – I asked who he was, he reply'd a gentleman, – on further inquiry I found he was a strong Wilkite.[7]

So the Ruskinian Lightfoot was, as might be expected in someone of his earnest temperament, a left-wing radical, a supporter of the riot-raising MP, Wilkes. Robinson claimed that he persuaded Lightfoot to let him catalogue the carved work and arrange for its transport:

> In the course of our conversation he said he well knew two of a Trade (meaning yr. humble servant.) could never agree. As I went with a resolution not to reply to any impertinence . . . I seem'd not to hear. What to answer properly must have carried me to lengths.[8]

Only two years later the insidious Robinson had also been sacked and the works at Claydon were completed under William Donn, Surveyor to the West-minster Commissioners of Sewers, a worthy successor to Robinson.

Verney himself was a more complex personality than either of these two protagonists. His drive to raise that absurd 256-foot front came from a competitive determination to equal the grandeur of Stowe, a house only a few miles away to the north and the seat of his political rivals the Temple family. The spark which actually set him building himself into bankruptcy was probably the elevation of George Grenville to be Prime Minister in 1763. If a calculating nonentity like Grenville could become First Lord of the Treasury, why not Lord Verney? For a power base a really grand house was needed and subsequent election campaigns for the prestigious county seat of Buckinghamshire cost him as much as £12,000 a time. But he was an extrovert who enjoyed the drama of the hustings and the state required by his rank. One account describes him parading the country in a coach-and-six; perched at the back were 'a brace of tall negroes', the ultimate servant status symbol, 'with silver French horns perpetually making a noise, like Sir Henry Sidney's Trompeters in the days of Elizabeth, blowing very joyfully to behold and see'.[9]

There is something inescapably high camp in this enchanting description and one feature of the interiors which he had created at Claydon is suggestive of an extraordinarily rarefied and poetic sensibility, as refined, self-regarding and perverse as those of nineteenth-century decadents like Huysmans, Wilde and Baudelaire. That feature is the grand staircase, inlaid with holly wood, ivory and mother of pearl, now roped off because it is too exquisite to be trodden on. Lightfoot had suggested five attractive wooden Rococo variants for its balusters. Verney rejected them all and ordered instead the present ironwork balustrade from some unknown smith of genius. At first sight this appears to be still in its original condition, with all its metal garlands, scrolls, flowers and wheat ears, so fragile and so suspended that they can be set whispering together at any normal tread on the inlaid stairs. But as it was first wrought all the wheat stalks were fanned inwards and outwards, not a functional device but one contrived so that anyone ascending or descending would involuntarily become a foretaste of Shelley's 'wild West Wind, thou breath of Autumn's being', and set the wheat ears nodding and rustling as if a breeze was passing over them, while all the other whorls of iron chimed and tinkled against each other. For someone in that mid-century to prepare his stairs to react poetically to his every common passage up or down them was a gesture worthy of the *Yellow Book* and must have produced effects which Ronald Firbank would have relished.

After which the North Hall at Claydon will come as no surprise. Here Lightfoot was given his uninhibited freedom to pursue Rococo excess in that happy time before Sir Thomas Robinson brought in Joseph Rose's men to impose their variant of Robert Adam's style. Before considering the North Hall one reservation has to be made and a subjective judgement offered. While it is all very impressive that Lightfoot should have achieved in wood what lesser men achieved in plaster, there is, even though the wood carving is now all painted white to resemble plaster, a certain almost subliminal hardness to the detail which is marginally less appealing than that which the softer, more responsive, material would have produced. With that minor reservation the North Hall must be acknowledged as the finest room in a house which has at least six other outstanding interiors.

Unfortunately there was never a time when Lord Verney, if he was indeed his own architect, thought out the dimensions of rooms appropriate to the intimacies of Rococo decoration. He simply roughed out three more or less double cubes resulting in spaces too high for the more subtle Rococo effects and then left Lightfoot to make the best of the situation. It is most unlikely that Lightfoot had ever been to Paris or knew anything more about the Rococo than what he could cull from pattern books. Of all the British and Irish Rococo decorators Lightfoot, with his patience and his highly skilled team of carvers, would have been best fitted to reproduce the tall, delicately carved wall panels of French boiseries. Yet, though his dado panels and internal window architraves are carved to a rare perfection, there are no authentic French style boiseries in Claydon. The house has infinite Rococo details but no room with a complete Rococo spatial treatment.

Lord Verney was not committed to the style in an informed way as was Lord Chesterfield. Indeed he was not committed firmly to any style, only to novelties. Lightfoot, lacking the authority and experience of an architect, obediently altered his stylistic direction to satisfy each Verney whim. Provided he was given patterns to copy he could turn out Rococo, Chinese or Gothick work. He even worked effectively alongside Joseph Rose's men creating identical angel brackets to accord with Rose's seraphim ceiling in the Library. Lord Verney had been born at precisely the wrong time, in 1712, only seven years before Horace Walpole, but those seven years were enough to tilt the bias of his stylistic preferences. Walpole would ignore the Rococo, toy briefly with the Chinese and end up a committed Goth. Verney obviously adored the Rococo in a self-indulgent, undiscriminating fashion, was thoroughly addicted to the Chinese but was only a tentative and ill-informed Goth. Then in his flitting, butterfly fashion he would move on easily to the Adam style. Walpole, a scholar and an enthusiast, remained faithful to the Gothick throughout his building life developing it into the more correct forms of the Gothic Revival.

Given by his inconsistent and unpredictable employer a double cube to decorate, Lightfoot relied on brilliant distractions to draw attention away from an awkward 25-foot (7.5 m) high ceiling and the banal motif of guns and cannon within a heavy geometrical frame which he had been obliged to carve for it. The North Hall never quite recovers from that ceiling, which bears no stylistic relation to anything going on beneath it, but Lightfoot fought back resourcefully under its handicap. The room has no less than six doors and two large windows, all framed with wonderful perversity under broken, concave pediments which give a lively impression of how the Classical orders might have been deployed if they had been taken up in Peking (illus. 166). There are in addition four astonishing niches and an overmantel devised in wild Rococo surrealism, but it is these Chinese-Classical doorframes which remain longest in the memory. Theirs is an obvious mockery of true Classicism, yet they are actually superior aesthetically to the forms they mock. Lightfoot may genuinely have gone one better than the Ancients. For good measure his carvers have crammed fruit and flower baskets onto the lintels, clustered grapes and vine leaves down the volutes of the jambs and carved a second wooden garden around the shadow volutes at their sides. All this is repeated eight times in the one room. Lightfoot was an obsessive perfectionist who gave the two windows in each of his state rooms the same full stylistic treatment as the doors, Chinese here, Corinthian in the Saloon, Adam-Neronian in the Library.

· For the design of the niches Lightfoot took the most challenging etchings that Matthew Lock and Thomas Johnson had published for mirrors, girandoles and clocks,[10] he compounded their most eccentric features and then, with his customary manic determination, realized them around the niches. Wyverns fly independently above them, ho-ho birds act as supporters and in between these fantasy creatures every possible contortion of the acanthus has been explored with human faces peering out through the mad foliage.

In the end the visual strain of reacting to and recording the detail of the room begins to tell. Lord Verney, like Duke Orsino at the beginning of *Twelfth Night*, must have demanded:

> Give me excess of it that, surfeiting,
> The appetite may sicken and so die.

but it is a wonderful room, the final affront to Palladian good taste.

Anyone hoping for restful simplicities in the next room will be disappointed. Here in the Saloon, though Lightfoot has not been entirely excluded, Joseph Rose's men have largely taken over. To enter it is a little like walking into an enormous cream trifle (illus. 167). For no obvious reason Rose's team, led by the Italian stuccodore Patroli, reversed the usual concaves of the coffering on the deep cove, turning them into ugly convex bulges. Pastel colours are everywhere and the ceiling has an acceptable imitation of Adam's soothing, shallow reliefs. Robinson described the room as 'not so bad'.[11] That was compared with the North Hall which had shocked his Palladian sensibilities profoundly. The chimneypiece in the Saloon has in the past been attributed to an Italian or to Thomas Carter. Now there is evidence that the Lightfoot team produced it,[12] so Lightfoot may sometimes have designed

166 The North Hall at Claydon House, Buckinghamshire (*c*. 1766). All of Luke Lightfoot's
Rococo detail was carved from wood.

167 The dead-end of Adam-style plasterwork hangs drearily over the Saloon ceiling at Claydon House, Buckinghamshire (*c.* 1768).

with a sense of humour. The piece is a cartoon version of what an imported Italian might have carved for François Premier in the early sixteenth century. In Carrara marble so polished as to seem illuminated, two gangs of fat, naked small boys, half of them upside down, parody the flight of angels to Heaven up and down Jacob's ladder (illus. 168). It may be absurd but it is easily the most memorable feature in a room of insistent, repetitive detail. In the Library, the next room, apart from dutifully Adam-izing the door and window frames, Lightfoot's men were restricted to the unrewarding labour of producing 36 identical angel brackets for the frieze, each angel ensnared in foliage.

In the first-floor rooms, where Lightfoot's workers were interrupted by his 1769 dismissal, there are bursts of cheerful Rococo fantasy, chimneypieces alive with terms and everywhere the patient carving of detail onto barely observed dado panels and architraves. But it is the Chinese and the Gothick rooms which impress the most. Lightfoot must have been given full illustrative directions and models for the Chinese tea scene and the Chinese doors and chimneypieces, but for the Gothick Room he seems to have been given no models. If he had been shown Batty Langley's *Gothic Architecture* he could have devised sharp profiles and inventive niches, gloomy vaults and soaring crockets, but there is virtually nothing of Langley or of any real Gothic detail here. The ceiling has jagged compartments with treillage infilling and three domes inlaid with a children's scribble of ogee aediculae, while neither the doors to the room nor the chimneypiece can rise to an ogival arch. The likeliest explanation, that the room was fitted up after Lightfoot's dismissal, is not tenable as the outraged visitor of 1768, when Lightfoot was still in charge, mentioned 'lesser rooms . . . furnished in all

tastes, as the Chinese Room, the Gothick Room, the French Room, etc., but all bad'.[13]

Claydon's best known interior is the Chinese Room. Its tea party alcove, a room within a room is, like its chimneypiece and its door frames, a virtuoso fusion of Rococo and Chinese forms. The Mandarin's tea party is the essence of quaint charm and delicate carving, and on either side of the tea alcove's central opening the largest sweep of rocaille work in Britain swirls out like the prows of Chinese junks. Yet the room does not work. Its tea party stands like some piece of patient cork-work in a Victorian museum. No one has troubled to relate and link it to the plain walls and ceiling; Lightfoot or Donn, whoever was in charge, has not even bothered to invent a Chinese frieze and cornice. But the door has a lighthearted three-bay pagoda sitting on its lintel, Mandarin terms to its jambs and Chinese patternings on every square inch of its panels. It all looks as though these amazing Chinese carvings had been lying about the house after Lightfoot's dismissal and were then simply applied to the walls of a room which had not been prepared for their reception (illus. 169). So the Chinese Room exemplifies Claydon's failing where individually brilliant set pieces of Rococo craftsmanship have been set out with no overall spatial integration. Pieces so exotic demand not only Chinese Rococo walls but a ceiling billowing up into peaked and fantastic Chinese heavens. Domes were contrived inappropriately for the Gothick Room next door, here, where they were needed, a flat dull ceiling quenches the spirit of the tea alcove and leaves the marvellous stalactitic distortions and inscrutable faces of the chimneypiece as a solo performance. Is it possible that these Chinese setpieces were originally intended for the Gothick Room with its quite un-Gothick domes?

169 The chimneypiece in the Chinese Room at Claydon House, Buckinghamshire (post-1769).

Money was running out. After all the funds he had poured into bribery and banquets Lord Verney lost the election of 1784 by 24 votes. The next, which he won with popular acclaim, cost him a feast for 200 potential supporters in that exotic North Hall. He had won, but it was at a price of almost £15,000, and then came the crash. He is said, and the device sounds typical, to have escaped his creditors at his wife's funeral by hiding in her hearse. Another pathetic tale has a stable boy discovering Verney, a frail and broken old man, wandering the rooms of his closed and shuttered palace, fingering the decorative details and remembering past extravagances. Faithful retainers smuggled him out again and he died in his London house in March 1791. Lightfoot, who had been ruined by the court case with his employer which Sir Thomas Robinson had set in motion, retired to become a grocer in Dulwich where he died in March 1789. The last years of these two wilful and eccentric old men provide a melancholy coda to the fortunes of a continental style on an offshore island arrogantly bent upon an imperial, rather than a European, destiny.

REFERENCES

INTRODUCTION

1   Gervase Jackson-Stops, 'Rococo Architecture and Interiors', in *Rococo: Art and Design in Hogarth's England*, ed. Michael Snodin (London, 1984), p. 190.

2   Quoted by Michael Snodin, 'English Rococo and its Continental Origins', *Rococo: Art and Design*, p. 28.

3   *Ibid.*, p. 27.

4   For illustrations of these houses see James Lees-Milne, *English Country Houses: Baroque 1685–1715* (London, 1970).

5   Jackson-Stops, 'Rococo Architecture and Interiors', p. 192.

6   The *Mercure de France* commented, 'Il paroit une suite d'Estampes en large, dans le goût d'Etienne la Belle'. Quoted by Snodin, *Rococo: Art and Design*, p. 28.

CHAPTER I: THE TROUBLE WITH THE PALLADIAN

1   Howard Colvin, 'A Scottish Origin for English Palladianism?', *Architectural History*, XVII (1974), pp. 5–13.

2   J. H. Plumb, *The First Four Georges* (London, 1956), pp. 39–40.

3   *Ibid.*, p. 41.

4   Lord Chesterfield, *Characters* (Los Angeles, 1990), Appendix, p. 1.

5   *The Complete Correspondence of Lady Mary Wortley Montagu*, ed. Robert Hulsband, 2 vols (London, 1965), I, p. 111.

6   Quoted in Plumb, *The First Four Georges*, p. 39.

7   See Michael McCarthy, 'Baroque Elements in Irish Palladianism', *The Early Eighteenth-Century Great House*, ed. Malcolm Airs (Oxford, 1996), pp. 95–9.

8   Howard Colvin, *A Biographical Dictionary of British Architects 1600–1840*

(New Haven and London, 1995), p. 122.

9   Eileen Harris, *British Architectural Books and Writers 1556–1785* (Cambridge, 1990), pp. 139–44.

10 For a discussion of Leoni's *Palladio* see Rudolf Wittkower, 'English Neoclassicism and the Vicissitudes of Palladio's "Quattro Libri" in *Palladio and English Palladianism* (London, 1974), pp. 73–92.

11 Colen Campbell, *Vitruvius Britannicus*, II vols (London, 1715), I, p. 5.

CHAPTER II: THREE VILLAS TO THE ROCOCO

1   For a scholarly and infinitely allusive account of this period see Katie Scott, *The Rococo Interior: Decoration and Social Spaces in Early Eighteenth-Century Paris* (New Haven and London, 1995).

2   Christopher Hussey, *English Country Houses: Early Georgian 1715–1760* (Woodbridge, 1955), pp. 58–65.

3   *The Yale Edition of Horace Walpole's Correspondence*, ed. W. S. Lewis, 48 vols (New Haven and London, 1937–83), xxxv, p. 143.

4   Michael I. Wilson, *William Kent: Architect, Designer, Painter, Gardener 1685–1748* (London, 1984), p. 36.

5   John Harris, *The Palladian Revival: Lord Burlington, His Villa and Garden at Chiswick* (London, 1994), p. 108.

6   Richard Hewlings, 'Chiswick House and Gardens: Appearance and Meaning', in *Lord Burlington: Architecture, Art and Life*, ed. T. Barnard and J. Clark (London, 1995), pp. 1–149; quote on p. 145.

7   Cinzia Maria Sicca, 'On William Kent's Roman Sources', *Architectural History*, xxix (1986), pp. 134–57.

8   *Country Life*, 28 April 1923.

9   Isaac Ware, *A Complete Body of Architecture* (London, 1756–7), p. 522.

10 *Country Life*, 28 April 1923.

11 Giles Worsley, *Classical Architecture in Britain: The Heroic Age* (New Haven and London, 1995), p. 208.

12 Gervase Jackson-Stops, 'Rococo Architecture and Interiors', p. 190.

CHAPTER III: THE GARDEN AS AN EXPRESSION OF ROCOCO REVOLT

1   Desmond FitzGerald, 'Irish Gardens of the Eighteenth Century', *Apollo* (September 1968), pp. 204–9.

2   *Country Life*, 26 August, 2 and 9 September 1971.

3   Stephen Switzer, *Ichnographia Rustica*, 3 vols (London, 1718), iii, p. v.

4   Michael Symes, *The English Rococo Garden* (Princes Risborough, 1991), p. 45.

5   *Ibid*., p. 30.

6   Sir Henry Wotton, *The Elements of Architecture* (Charlottesville, VA, 1968), p. 109.

7   Sir William Temple, *The Works*, 4 vols (Edinburgh, 1754), ii, p. 24.

8   Lord Shaftesbury, *Characteristics*, 2 vols (London, 1900), ii, p. 125.

9   *Ibid*., ii, p. 98.

10 Robert Castell, *The Villas of the Ancients Illustrated* (1728, repr. London, 1982),

pp. 116–17.

11 For an illustration of these structures see *ibid.*, p. 126.

12 *Ibid.*, p. 117.

13 Langley, *New Principles* (London, 1728), Introduction, p. iii.

14 *Ibid.*, p. v.

15 *Ibid.*, p. viii.

16 These are illustrated in John Dixon Hunt, *William Kent: Landscape Garden Designer* (London, 1987), pls 90–92.

17 William Hogarth, *The Analysis of Beauty* (New Haven and London, 1997), p. 46.

18 Quoted in Bernard Denver, *The Eighteenth Century: Art, Design and Society* (London, 1983), p. 58.

19 Lewis, *Correspondence*, xx, p. 127.

20 Quoted in Denver, *The Eighteenth Century*, p. 58.

CHAPTER IV: A WANDERING BISHOP

1   Richard Pococke, *A Description of the East and some other Countries*, 2 vols (London, 1743/5), ɪɪ, p. 98.

2   The portrait is in the Musée d'art et d'histoire of Geneva and is illustrated in Michael McCarthy, '"The dullest man that ever travelled"? A re-assessment of Richard Pococke and of his portrait by J.-E. Liotard', *Apollo* (May 1996), pp. 25–9.

3   Pococke, *Description*, ɪɪ, p. 162.

4   Richard Pococke, *Pococke's Tour in Ireland in 1752* (Dublin, 1891).

5   J. Cartwright, ed., *The Travels through England of Dr Richard Pococke*, 2 vols, Camden Society (London, 1888–9), ɪɪ, p. 6.

6   *Ibid.*, ɪɪ, p. 138.

7   *Ibid.*, ɪɪ, p. 19.

8   *Ibid.*, ɪɪ, p. 4.

9   *Ibid.*, ɪɪ, p. 76.

10 *Ibid.*, ɪɪ, p. 80.

11 *Ibid.*, ɪɪ, p. 105.

12 *Ibid.*, ɪɪ, pp. 137–8.

13 *Ibid.*, ɪɪ, p. 64.

14 *Ibid.*, ɪɪ, p. 65.

15 These and other paintings by Robins are illustrated in John Harris and Martin Rix, *Gardens of Delight: The Rococo English Landscape of Thomas Robins the Elder*, 2 vols (London, 1978).

16 For the divorce case see Paul Stamper, *Historic Parks and Gardens of Shropshire* (Shrewsbury, 1996), p. 54.

17 Pococke, *Travels*, ɪ, p. 61.

18 *Ibid.*, ɪ, pp. 65–8.

19 Quoted by FitzGerald, 'Irish Gardens of the Eighteenth Century', pp. 204–9.

20 *Pococke's Tour in Ireland*, p. 8.

21 *Ibid.*, p. 4.

22 *Ibid.*, p. 25.

23 *Ibid.*, p. 98.

24 *Ibid.*, p. 162.

25 *Ibid.*, p. 181.

26 *Ibid.*, p. 161.

27 Subsequent quotations which refer to the Duke's improvements at Virginia Water will be found in Pococke, *Travels*, II, pp. 62–4.

28 *Ibid.*, II, p. 43.

29 *Ibid.*, II, p. 260.

30 Batty Langley, *New Principles of Gardening*, p. x.

31 For an account of this garden see Timothy Mowl, 'Air of Irregularity', *Country Life*, 11 January 1990.

32 Pococke, *Travels*, II, p. 261.

33 *Ibid.*, II, p. 66.

34 *Ibid.*, II, pp. 161–2.

35 Subsequent quotations which refer to Hagley Park will be found in Pococke, *Travels*, II, pp. 233–6.

CHAPTER V: GOTHIC AND ROCOCO

1 Lewis, *Correspondence*, IX, p. 71.

2 Worsley, *Classical Architecture*, p. 193.

3 *Ibid.*, p. 188.

4 Terence Davis, *The Gothick Taste* (Newton Abbot, 1974), p. 32.

5 Michael McCarthy, *The Origins of the Gothic Revival* (New Haven and London, 1987), p. 49.

6 Horace Walpole, *Memoirs of the Reign of George II*, 3 vols, ed. John Brooke (New Haven and London, 1985), III, p. 44.

7 *Ibid.*, I, p. 248.

8 *Ibid.*

9 *Ibid.*, I, p. 247.

10 *Ibid.*, II, p. 6.

11 *Ibid.*

12 For this scheme and a Gothick variant of the one that was eventually built, see John Harris, 'Esher Place, Surrey', *Country Life*, 2 April 1987.

13 For Kent's work at Hampton Court see Juliet Allan, 'New Light on William Kent at Hampton Court Palace', *Architectural History*, XXVII (1984), pp. 50–8.

14 *Grub Street Journal*, 6 March 1735.

15 *Ibid.*

16 Batty Langley, *Ancient Masonry both in Theory and Practice* (London, 1736), p. ii.

17 Batty Langley, *Ancient Architecture, Restored and Improved* (London, 1741–2), dedication page.

18 James Lees-Milne, 'Stout's Hill, Uley, Gloucestershire', *Country Life*, 5 July 1973.

19 For a sketch of Woodside see Harris and Rix, *Gardens of Delight*, I, pl. 62.

20 Moore Abbey is illustrated in Mark Bence Jones, *Burke's Guide to Country*

Houses, I, *Ireland* (London, 1978), p. 210.

21 Merlin's Cave is illustrated in John Dixon Hunt, *William Kent: Landscape Gardener*, pl. 32.

22 *Ibid*., pl. 29.

23 The Westminster screen is illustrated in Michael I. Wilson, *William Kent: Architect, Designer, Painter, Gardener, 1685–1748* (London, 1984), pl. 62. The pulpit is illustrated in McCarthy, *Gothic Revival*, pl. 194.

24 *Ibid*., plate 191.

25 The most plausible analysis of the complicated architectural history of Shobdon church is given in McCarthy, *Gothic Revival*, pp. 151–4.

26 Pococke describes Old Windsor in his *Travels*, II, pp. 64–5; Thomas Robins's illustrations of Bateman's house and garden are in Harris and Rix, *Gardens of Delight*, I, plates 8–17.

27 Keene's Hartwell church is illustrated in McCarthy, *Gothic Revival*, pls 199 and 204.

28 The cloister design is illustrated in McCarthy, *Gothic Revival*, pl. 142.

CHAPTER VI: BRISTOL – THE UNSOPHISTICATED CITY

1 For this design see Timothy Mowl, *To Build the Second City: Architects and Craftsmen of Georgian Bristol* (Bristol, 1991), p. 49.

2 *The Correspondence of Alexander Pope*, ed. George Sherburn, 5 vols (Oxford, 1956), IV, p. 204.

3 Lewis, *Correspondence*, X, p. 232.

4 Patrick McGrath, *Bristol in the Eighteenth Century* (Newton Abbot, 1972), p. 129.

5 These designs are in the British Architectural Library RIBA; one is illustrated in Mowl, *Second City*, p. 52.

6 Both houses are illustrated in Mowl, *Second City*, pp. 50–01.

7 J. Charlton and D. M. Milton, *Redland 791 to 1800* (Bristol, 1951), Appendix II, p. 67.

8 Now in the Public Library, Deanery Road.

9 The Goldney interior is illustrated in Andor Gomme, Michael Jenner and Bryan Little, *Bristol: An Architectural History* (London, 1979), pl. 93.

10 Plates 141–6.

11 The Meissonier soup tureen was sold at Sotheby's and previewed with an illustration in *The Daily Telegraph*, 20 April 1998, p. 18.

12 Kenneth Morgan, *Bristol and the Atlantic Trade in the Eighteenth Century* (Cambridge, 1993), pp. 19–22.

13 Walter Ison, *The Georgian Buildings of Bristol* (Bath, 1978), title page.

14 Isaac Ware, *The Complete Body of Architecture* (London, 1756–7), p. 251.

CHAPTER VII: DUBLIN – THE PROTESTANT CITY

1 These were reproduced in papier mâché during an Edwardian restoration of 1902.

2 Woodfall diary of travels, 16 August 1785; quoted in Samuel Fitzpatrick,

Dublin, a Historical and Topographical Account (Cork, 1907), p. 37.

3   Lady Llanover, ed., *The Autobiography and Correspondence of Mary Granville, Mrs Delany*, 1st Series, 3 vols (London, 1861), I, p. 343.

4   *Journal of the Royal Society of Antiquaries of Ireland*, cxv (1985), pp. 13–25. See also Nicholas Sheaff, 'Jarratt and Rococo', *Irish Arts Review*, I (Autumn 1984), pp. 50–51.

5   *Country Life*, 6 August 1970.

6   Joseph McDonnell, *Irish Eighteenth-Century Stuccowork and its European Sources* (Dublin, 1991).

7   *Ibid.*, pls 5–6.

8   *Ibid.*, pls 17–26.

9   *Ibid.*, pls 4 and 6.

10   For Mitelli see Peter Ward-Jackson, *English Furniture Designs of the Eighteenth Century* (London, 1958), fig. 34.

11   McDonnell, *Irish Eighteenth-Century Stuccowork*, p. 8.

12   See John Turpin, *A School of Art in Dublin since the Eighteenth Century* (Dublin, 1995).

13   Quoted in Anne Crookshank and the Knight of Glin, *Painters of Ireland c. 1660–1920* (London, 1978), pp. 70–71.

14   *Ibid.*, p. 71.

CHAPTER VIII: THE PLAYGIRL OF THE WESTERN WORLD

1   Simon Dewes, *Mrs Delany* (London, 1930), p. xi.

2   *Ibid.*, p. 206.

3   This and subsequent quotations from Mrs Pendarves are taken from Llanover, *Mrs Delany*, I, p. 288.

4   *Ibid.*, I, p. 289.

5   *Ibid.*, I, p. 288.

6   *Ibid.*, I, p. 291.

7   *Ibid.*, I, p. 292.

8   A ceiling, now destroyed, at Delville House in the north Dublin suburbs had similar pairs of birds sitting on twigs. C. P. Curran tentatively dated this to *c.* 1729: *Journal of the Royal Society of Antiquaries of Ireland*, lxx (1940), p. 10.

9   This and subsequent quotations concerning the Clayton house are from Llanover, *Mrs Delany*, I, p. 305.

10   *Ibid.*, I, p. 288.

11   *Ibid.*, I, p. 290.

12   *Ibid.*

13   *Ibid.*

14   Dr Matthew Maty, *Memoirs of Lord Chesterfield*, 2 vols (London, 1777), I, p. 163.

15   Llanover, *Mrs Delany*, I, p. 294.

16   *Ibid.*, I, p. 295.

17   *Ibid.*, I, p. 301

18   *Ibid.*

19   *Ibid.*, I, p. 309.

20 John Cornforth, 'Dublin Castle – II', *Country Life*, 6 August 1970.

21 Llanover, *Mrs Delany*, I, p. 317.

22 *Ibid.*, I, p. 318.

23 *Ibid.*

24 *Ibid.*, I, p. 338.

25 *Ibid.*, I, pp. 345–6.

26 *Ibid.*, I, p. 346.

27 *Ibid.*, I, p. 353.

28 *Ibid.*, I, p. 355.

29 *Ibid.*, I, p. 365.

30 *Ibid.*

31 *Ibid.*, I, p. 373.

32 *Ibid.*

33 *Ibid.*, I, pp. 370–90.

34 *Ibid.*, I, p. 409.

CHAPTER IX: LORD CHESTERFIELD AND DUBLIN

1 Llanover, *Mrs Delany*, II, p. 336.

2 *Ibid.*, II, p. 362.

3 *Ibid.*, II, pp. 314–17.

4 John Turpin, *A School of Art*, p. 6.

5 *Ibid.*, p. 7.

6 *Reflections and Resolutions proper for the Gentlemen of Ireland as to their Conduct for the Service of their Country* (Dublin, 1738).

7 Turpin, *A School of Art*, p. 10.

8 *Ibid.*, p. 11.

9 *Ibid.*

10 *Ibid.*, p. 32.

11 *Ibid.*

12 *Ibid.*, p. 16.

13 *Letters of the 4th Earl of Chesterfield*, ed. Bonamy Dobrée, 6 vols (London, 1932), III, p. 656.

14 *Ibid.*, III, p. 659.

15 Maty, *Memoirs of Lord Chesterfield*, p. 151.

16 *Ibid.*, IV, p. 766.

17 *Ibid.*, IV, p. 832.

18 Turpin, *A School of Art*, p. 13.

19 Robert Dodsley, 'Of drawing', *The Preceptor* (Dublin, 1748), pp. 361–78. For a full account of its instructions see Turpin, *School of Art*, pp. 39–42.

20 *The Walpole Society*, XXII (1933–4), Vertue III, p. 127.

21 *Ibid.*

22 For a discussion of Paine's possible membership of the Academy see Peter Leach, *James Paine* (London, 1988), p. 23.

23 Mark Girouard, 'Coffee at Slaughter's: English Art and the Rococo', *Country Life*, 13 and 27 January, 5 February 1966.

24 *William Hogarth, The Analysis of Beauty*, ed. Ronald Paulson (London, 1997), p. 30.

25 *Ibid.*, p. 23.

26 *Ibid.*, p. 33.

27 *Ibid.*

28 *Ibid.*, p. 34.

29 *Ibid.*, p. 36.

30 *Ibid.*, p. 48.

31 Illustrations of these paintings and engravings are most readily accessible in David Bindman, *Hogarth* (London, 1981).

32 Llanover, *Mrs Delany*, II, p. 400.

33 FitzGerald, 'Irish Gardens of the Eighteenth Century', p. 207.

34 Llanover, *Mrs Delany*, II, p. 408.

35 For illustrations of these Rococo interiors, see *Country Life*, 25 February and 4 March 1922.

36 David Coombs, 'The Garden at Carlton House of Frederick Prince of Wales and Augusta Princess and Dowager of Wales', *Garden History*, xxv/2 (Winter, 1997), pp. 153–77.

37 For Egmont's castle see Timothy Mowl, '"Against the time in which the use of gunpowder shall be forgotten": Enmore Castle, its origins and its architect', *Architectural History*, xxxiii (1990), pp. 102–19.

38 Three copies of *The Music Party* were made by Mercier; for illustrations of two see exhibition catalogue, ed. Stephen Jones, *Frederick, Prince of Wales and his Circle* (Gainsborough's House, Sudbury, 1981), catalogue nos 2 and 3.

39 *Daily Telegraph*, 12 August 1998.

40 The barge is illustrated in Wilson, *William Kent*, pp. 130–31.

CHAPTER X: RENAISSANCE ON THE NORTH BANK

1 McDonnell, *Irish Eighteenth-Century Stuccowork*, pls 69–70.

2 *Ibid.*, Appendix 1a and Appendix 1b (pp. 125–6).

3 Curran, *Dublin Decorative Plasterwork*, pp. 53–5.

4 C. P. Curran, 'Dublin Plasterwork', *Royal Society of Antiquaries of Ireland*, LXX (1940), pp. 31–6.

5 Catalogue no. 77/6.

6 No. 77/6. 9/10.

7 West was paid £125.16.10. according to Ensor's general accounts. See Curran, *Dublin Decorative Plasterwork*, pp. 59–60.

8 McDonnell, *Irish Eighteenth-Century Stuccowork*, pls 74–6.

CHAPTER XI: WIDE STREETS AND AN EMBARRASSMENT OF RICHES

1 McDonnell, *Irish Eighteenth-Century Stuccowork*, pl. 73.

2 Turpin, *A School of Art*, pp. 13–14.

3 *Georgian Society Records*, 5 vols (Dublin, 1909–13), IV, p. 125.

4 See Henry-Russell Hitchcock, *Rococo Architecture in Southern Germany* (London, 1968), pl. 133.

5 Quoted from the Earl of Egmont's diary by Mark Girouard, 'Belvedere House, Co Westmeath, Eire', *Country Life*, 22 June 1961, p. 1480.

6 Curran, *Dublin Decorative Plasterwork*, pp. 54–5.

7 *Country Life*, 22 June 1961, p. 1483.

8 *Country Life*, 29 June 1961, p. 1538.

9 Llanover, *Mrs Delany*, II, p. 474.

10 *Ibid.*, II, p. 562.

11 McDonnell, *Irish Eighteenth-Century Stuccowork*, pls 81–4.

12 Curran, *Dublin Decorative Plasterwork*, p. 62.

13 See Martha Blythe Gerson, 'A Glossary of Robert Adam's neo-Classical Ornament', *Architectural History*, XXIV (1981), pp. 59–82.

CHAPTER XII: THE IRISH COUNTRY HOUSE AS A COMMENTARY ON THE URBAN ROCOCO

1 Semple's authorship was discovered by David Griffin of the Irish Architectural Archive in part 22 of the Architectural Publication Society's *Dictionary* of 1887; cited by Gervase Jackson-Stops, 'Newbridge Restored', *Country Life*, 18 February 1988.

2 The accounts are quoted by Jackson-Stops, *Country Life*, 18 February 1988.

3 A key to the church can be obtained from the bungalow across the road. A railway station is only a step away and the Donabate pew should become a regular pilgrimage for Rococo addicts. Newbridge House itself is the property of the County Council and opened to the public with a relaxed charm which could be a model for all such properties in Ireland and Britain.

4 McDonnell, *Irish Eighteenth-Century Stuccowork*, pp. 11–12.

5 Mark Bence Jones, *Burke's Guide*, p. 39.

6 *The Buildings of Ireland: North Leinster*, 1993, p. 168.

7 The painting is preserved in the house.

8 When the authors visited Dunboyne the house had been empty for some years but it was in good condition. Expanding industrial estates in the neighbourhood should soon give it a secure future as a social venue.

9 McDonnell, *Irish Eighteenth-Century Stuccowork*, pls 59-63.

10 Quoted in *Country Life*, 14 September 1918. After which Swiftian summary it would be churlish not to mention that the Archbishop's house has been perfectly restored for its present owner by Quinlan Terry, and to make it clear that Dunboyne, Dowth, Barmeath, Glasnevin and Kilshannig are private houses only opened to the present writers by the good nature of their owners. They are not generally open to the public, neither is Castletown Cox.

CHAPTER XIII: ROCOCO AS THE ART FORM OF BOURGEOIS CAPITALISM

1 Ware, *Complete Body*, p. 522.

2 *Ibid.*, p. 498.

3 *Ibid.*, p. 470.

4 *Ibid.*, p. 451.

5 *Ibid.*, p. 500.

6   *Ibid.*, p. 516.

7   *Ibid.*, p. 249.

8   *Ibid.*, p. 522

9   *Ibid.*

10 C. F. W. Denning, *The Eighteenth-Century Architecture of Bristol* (London, 1923), p. 107.

11 From 'Kew Gardens', lines 137–48.

12 Quoted in *Bristol and its Adjoining Counties*, eds C. M. MacInnes and W. F. Whittard (Bristol, 1955), p. 235.

13 *Ibid.*

14 Thomas Cox, *Magna Britannia* (London, 1727), pp. 744–5.

15 Quoted in McGrath, *Bristol in the Eighteenth Century*, p. 30.

16 *Ibid.*, p. 26.

17 The banqueting house was lost in the air raids, but the interior is illustrated in Denning, *Eighteenth-Century Architecture*, pl. 67.

18 Quoted in Patrick McGrath, *The Merchant Venturers of Bristol* (Bristol, 1975), p. 96.

19 Quoted in Ison, *Georgian Buildings of Bristol*, p. 190.

20 Written pseudononymously by J. W. Shirehampton (possibly John Wallis) and quoted in Ison, *Georgian Buildings of Bristol*, p. 153.

21 From T. O. Tyndall to Onesiphorous Tyndall Bruce (S.R.O. GD 152/53/6/9/7). Cited and quoted with the approval of the Keeper of the Records of Scotland.

22 For Stocking at Stoke Park: Gloucester Record Office, Badminton Muniments, D2700; Corsham Court: Frederick J. Ladd, *Architects at Corsham Court* (Bradford-on-Avon, 1978), appendix D; Fonmon Castle: Glamorgan Record Office, Fonmon Archives, 11/50/5 (We owe this information to Sir Brooke Boothby); St Nicholas Church: Ison, *Georgian Buildings of Bristol*, pp. 65–70.

23 Attributions to Stocking at Hagley: Christopher Hussey, *English Country Houses: Early Georgian*, p. 198 and pl. 355; Frenchay House: Department of the Environment List of Buildings of Special Architectural or Historic Interest; Beacon House: David Verey, *The Buildings of England: Gloucestershire*, I, *The Cotswolds* (1970), p. 363 (giving William Stocking).

24 The Bath House colonnade was rescued by Clough Williams-Ellis after 1958 and re-erected at Portmeirion.

25 John Latimer, *The Annals of Bristol in the Eighteenth Century* (Bristol, 1970), p. 285.

26 Sheena Stoddard, *Mr Braikenridge's Brislington* (Bristol, 1981), p. 42.

27 Lewis, *Correspondence*, x, p. 232.

28 From 'The Tournament'.

29 From 'Acrostic on Miss Clarke'.

30 See Timothy Mowl, 'The Castle of Boncoeur and the Wizard of Durham', *Georgian Group Journal* (1992), pp. 32–9.

31 The St Nicholas ceiling is illustrated in Andor Gomme, Michael Jenner and Bryan Little, *Bristol*, pl. 139.

32 For the Transfer Offices see Marcus Binney, *Sir Robert Taylor: From Rococo to Neo-Classicism* (London, 1984), pl. 11.

CHAPTER XIV: ROCOCO IN THE BRISTOL HINTERLAND

1 Glamorgan Record Office, Fonmon Archives, 11/50/5. The authors are most grateful to Sir Brooke Boothby and Patricia Moore for this information.

2 The agreement is quoted in full in David Tudway Quilter, *Wells Cathedral School*, II, *The Cedars and the Tudways* (Wells, 1985), pp. 67–8.

3 *Ibid.*, p. 62.

4 *Ibid.*, p. 67.

5 *Ibid.*, plates on pp. 70, 71.

6 *Ibid.*, p. 68.

7 Frederick J. Ladd, *Architects at Corsham Court* (Bradford-on-Avon, 1978), p. 65.

8 *Ibid.*, plates 49 and 42.

9 *Ibid.*, plates 51 and 53.

10 *Ibid.*, p. 65.

11 *Ibid.*, p. 65, note 67.

12 *Ibid.*, p. 65.

13 For this and other Painswick illustrations by Robins see Timothy Mowl, 'In the Realm of the Great God Pan', *Country Life*, 17 October 1996. See also Roger White and Timothy Mowl, 'Thomas Robins at Painswick', *Journal of Garden History*, IV/2 (April–June, 1984), pp. 163–78.

14 Thomas Johnson, *One Hundred and Fifty New Designs* (London, 1758), plate 25.

15 *Country Life*, 21 August 1915.

16 The Revd. W. H. Seddon, *Painswick Feast: Its Origin and Meaning* (Painswick, 1916), p. 4.

CHAPTER XV: THE FALTERING COURSE OF ENGLISH ROCOCO

1 McDonnell, *Irish Eighteenth-Century Stuccowork*, p. 13.

2 *Ibid.*, p. 199.

3 Leach, *James Paine*, p. 147.

4 Hussey, *English Country Houses: Early Georgian*, p. 190.

5 Christopher Hussey, 'Claydon House, Buckinghamshire', *Country Life*, 31 October 1952, p. 1399.

6 Robinson had married in Barbados the widow of a rich Jewish ironmonger and then left her on the island.

7 Hussey, *Country Life*, 7 November 1952, p. 1483.

8 *Ibid.*, p. 1483.

9 Gervase Jackson-Stops, *Claydon House* (London, 1984), p. 27.

10 A design by Lock and Copland for 'Two Mirrors', published 13 November 1752 offers several of the features used in the niches. For an illustration see Peter Ward-Jackson, *English Furniture Designs* (London, 1958), pl. 32.

11 *Country Life*, 31 October 1952, p. 1401.

12 Tim Knox's recent researches have suggested this; his revised National Trust guidebook to the house will be published in 1999.

13 Jackson-Stops, *Claydon House*, p. 29.

ACCESSIBILITY
AND THE ROCOCO:
A GAZETTEER

The following is a list, by no means exhaustive, of buildings which have some Rococo details of interest, interior or exterior. One reason why the style is not widely appreciated in Britain is that many of the best examples are either inaccessible to the public or accessible only for one or two days a year. Even National Trust properties with Rococo rooms are usually closed for several winter months. In every case the opening times, if advertised, vary from year to year, so we have made no attempt to list these. Easily the best course is to buy, early in any particular year, a publication such as *Historic Houses, Castles Gardens* and then work through the complex index. Many properties are only open by pre-arrangement with an owner. Church keys can be hard to locate. Some churches, like Christ Church, Bristol, may be open at certain lunch-times and for Sunday services; the Rotunda Chapel in Dublin is part of a busy maternity hospital.

Ireland has not yet become as conscious as England of the commercial charm of country-house visiting and, in any case, most of the best Irish Rococo plasterwork is in one-time Dublin town houses, now converted into offices. Busy Irish solicitors and architects have invariably been most generous in allowing the authors access to their premises, but they are hardly likely to remain hospitable if they become part of a regular tourist trail. This is a problem which the Irish Tourist Board has yet to solve. 20 Lower Dominick Street is as important aesthetically to Dublin as the Parthenon to Athens, and access will have to be regularized sooner rather than later. It will remain, however, isolated in a street of unattractive council flats.

ENGLAND & WALES

Bristol
· 15 Orchard Street (private commercial premises)
· Arno's Court, Brislington (now Parkside Hotel)
· Christ Church, Broad Street
· Clifton Hill House, Lower Clifton Hill (Bristol University Hall of Residence)
· Goldney Hall & Grotto, Goldney Avenue (Bristol University Hall of Residence)
· Redland Chapel, Redland Green
· Royal Fort House, Tyndalls Park (Bristol University)

Buckinghamshire
· Claydon House (National Trust)
· Hartwell House, Stone (now hotel)

Devon
· Saltram House, Plymouth (National Trust)

Glamorgan
· Fonmon Castle, Barry

Gloucestershire
· Beacon House, Painswick (privately owned)
· The Orangery, Frampton Court, Frampton-on-Severn (Mrs P. M. F. Clifford)
· Painswick Rococo Garden, Painswick
· Stouts Hill, Uley (now Stouts Hill Club)

Herefordshire
· Croft Castle, Leominster (National Trust)
· Shobdon Church

London
· 1 Greek Street, Soho (privately owned)
· Chiswick House and Gardens (English Heritage)
· Kew Gardens
· Victoria & Albert Museum (Norfolk House Music Room)

Norfolk
· Felbrigg Hall, Felbrigg (National Trust)

Northamptonshire
· The Menagerie, Horton (privately owned)

Oxfordshire
· Rousham House & Garden, Steeple Aston

Shropshire
· Palmer's Guildhall, Ludlow
· Shipton Hall, Much Wenlock

Staffordshire
· Speedwell Castle, Brewood (privately owned)

Warwickshire
· Alscot Park, Stratford-on-Avon (privately owned)
· Honington Hall, Shipston-on-Stour

Wiltshire
· Corsham Court, Corsham

Worcestershire
· Hagley Hall, Stourbridge
· Hartlebury Castle, Kidderminster (The Church Commissioners)

Yorkshire
· Castle Howard, York
· Fairfax House, Castlegate, York
· Nostell Priory, Wakefield (National Trust)

IRELAND

Co. Cork
· Riverstown House, Cork

Co. Dublin
· Donabate Church
· Malahide Castle
· Newbridge House, Donabate

Dublin
· 20 Lower Dominick Street (youth centre/office)
· Áras an Uachtaráin, Phoenix Park
· Dublin Castle
· Newman House, St Stephen's Green
· Rotunda Hospital Chapel

Co. Fermanagh
· Florence Court (National Trust)

Co. Westmeath
· Belvedere House, Mullingar

Co. Wicklow
· Russborough House

SELECT BIBLIOGRAPHY

PRIMARY PRINTED SOURCES

Cartwright, J., ed., *The Travels through England of Dr Richard Pococke, 1750–1757*, 2 vols, Camden Society (London, 1888–9)

Castell, Robert, *The Villas of the Ancients*, reprint of 1728 edn (London, 1982)

Chambers, William, *Designs of Chinese Buildings, Furniture, Dresses, Machinery and Utensils*, reprint of 1757 edn (New York, 1968)

Crunden, John, *Convenient and Ornamental Architecture* (London, 1767)

Dobrée, Bonamy, ed., *The Letters of Philip Dormer Stanhope, 4th Earl of Chesterfield*, 6 vols (London, 1932)

Dodsley, Robert, *The Preceptor* (London, 1748)

Halfpenny, William, *Chinese and Gothic Architecture Properly Ornamented*, reprint of 1752 edn (New York, 1968)

Halfpenny, William and Halfpenny, John, *The Country Gentleman's Pocket Companion and Builder's Assistant* (London, 1756)

Harris, Eileen, ed., *ARBOURS and GROTTOS. A facsimile of the two parts of Universal Architecture (1755 and 1758), with a catalogue of Wright's works in architecture and garden design* (London, 1979)

Herbert, J. D., *Irish Varieties for the Last Fifty Years* (London, 1836)

Hogarth, William, *The Analysis of Beauty*, reprint of 1753 edn (Oxford, 1955) [compare III n.17]

Johnson, Thomas, *One Hundred and Fifty New Designs* (London, 1758)

Langley, Batty, *New Principles of Gardening or The laying out and planting Parterres, Groves, Wildernesses, Labyrinths, Avenues, Polls & etc After a more Grand and Rural Manner than has been done before* (London, 1728)

——, *Ancient Masonry both in Theory and Practice* (London, 1736)

——, *Ancient Architecture, Restored and Improved by a Great Variety of Grand and Useful Designs, entirely new in the Gothick Mode for the ornamenting of Buildings and Gardens* (London, 1741–2); re-issued as *Gothic Architecture, Improved by Rules and Proportions* (London, 1747)

——, *The City and Country Builder's and Workman's Treasury of Designs* (London, 1750)

Latimer, John, *The Annals of Bristol in the Eighteenth Century* (Bristol, 1970)

Lady Llanover, ed., *The Autobiography and Correspondence of Mary Granville, Mrs Delany*, 3 vols (London, 1862)

Lewis, Wilmarth Sheldon, *The Yale Edition of Horace Walpole's Correspondence*, 48 vols (New Haven and London, 1937–83)

Pococke, Richard, *A Description of the East and some other Countries*, 2 vols (London, 1743/5)

——, *Pococke's Tour in Ireland* (Dublin, 1891)

Swan, Abraham *A Collection of Designs in Architecture* (London, 1757)

——, *The British Architect or The Builder's Treasury of Staircases* (London, 1758 edn)

Switzer, Stephen, *Ichnographia Rustica* (London, 1718)

Ware, Isaac, *A Complete Body of Architecture* (London, 1756–7)

SECONDARY PRINTED SOURCES: BOOKS

Arnold, Dana, ed., *Belov'd by Ev'ry Muse: Richard Boyle, 3rd Earl of Burlington and 4th Earl of Cork (1694–1753)* (London, 1994)

——, ed., *The Georgian Villa* (Stroud, 1996)

Ballard, Martin, *Bristol: Sea-Port City* (Bristol, 1966)

Barnard, Toby and Clark, Jane, eds, *Lord Burlington: Architecture, Art and Life* (London, 1995)

Beard, Geoffrey, *Decorative Plasterwork in Great Britain* (London, 1975)

——, *The Work of Robert Adam* (London, 1978)

——, *Craftsmen and Interior Decoration in England 1660–1820* (Edinburgh, 1981)

——, *The National Trust Book of The English House Interior* (London, 1990)

Beckett, J. C., *The Making of Modern Ireland* (London, 1981)

Bence-Jones, Mark, *Burke's Guide To Country Houses*, I: *Ireland* (London, 1978)

Bindman, David, *Hogarth* (London, 1981)

Binney, Marcus, *Sir Robert Taylor: From Rococo to Neo-Classicism* (London, 1984)

Bowron, Edgar Peters, *Pompeo Batoni and his British Patrons* (London, 1982)

Breffny, Brian de, ed., *The Irish World: The History and Cultural Achievements of the Irish People* (London, 1977)

Burnell, Agnes, ed., *Decantations: Tributes to Maurice Craig* (Dublin, 1992)

Casey, Christine and Rowan, Alistair, *The Buildings of Ireland: North Leinster* (London, 1993)

Chase, Isabel Wakeling Urban, *Horace Walpole, Gardenist* (Princeton, 1943)

Coffin, David, *The English Garden: Meditation and Memorial* (Princeton, 1994)

Colvin, Howard, *A Biographical Dictionary of British Architects 1600–1840* (New Haven and London, 1995)

Conner, Patrick, *Oriental Architecture in the West* (London, 1979)

Craig, Maurice, *Dublin 1660–1860* (Dublin, 1952)

——, *Classic Irish Houses of the Middle Size* (London, 1976)

Crookshank, Anne and the Knight of Glin, *Painters of Ireland c. 1660–1920* (London, 1978)

Cruickshank, Dan and Burton, Neil, *Life in the Georgian City* (London, 1990)

Curran, C. P. *Dublin Decorative Plasterwork: Seventeenth and Eighteenth Centuries* (Dublin, 1967)

Davis, Terence, *The Gothick Taste* (Newton Abbot, 1974)

Denning, C. F. W., *The Eighteenth-Century Architecture of Bristol* (Bristol, 1923)

Denver, Bernard, *The Eighteenth Century: Art, Design and Society* (London, 1983)

Dewes, Simon, *Mrs Delany* (London, 1930)

Fitzpatrick, Samuel, *Dublin, a Historical and Topographical Account* (Cork, 1907)

Fowler, John and Cornforth, John, *English Decoration in the 18th Century* (London, 1974)

Girouard, Mark, *Cities and People: A Social and Architectural History* (London, 1985)

Gomme, Andor, Jenner, Michael and Little, Bryan, *Bristol: An Architectural History* (London, 1979)

Gorce, Jerome de la, *Bérain Dessinateur du Roi Soleil* (Paris, 1986)

Guinness, Desmond and Ryan, William, *Irish Houses and Castles* (London, 1971)

Harris, John, *Sir William Chambers, Knight of the Polar Star* (London, 1970)

——, *The Artist and the Country House: A History of Country House and Garden View Painting in Britain 1540–1870* (London, 1979)

——, *The Palladian Revival: Lord Burlington, His Villa and Garden at Chiswick* (New Haven and London, 1994)

Harris, John and Rix, Martin, *Gardens of Delight: The Rococo English Landscape of Thomas Robins the Elder*, 2 vols (London, 1978)

Hayward, Helena, *Thomas Johnson and the English Rococo* (London, 1964)

Hibbert, Christopher, *The Grand Tour* (London, 1987)

Hind, Charles, ed., *The Rococo in England: A Symposium* (London, 1986)

——, ed., *New Light on English Palladianism* (London, 1988)

Hitchcock, Henry-Russell, *Rococo Architecture in Southern Germany* (London, 1968)

——, *German Rococo: The Zimmermann Brothers* (London, 1968)

Howley, James, *The Follies and Garden Buildings of Ireland* (New Haven and London, 1993)

Hunt, John Dixon, *William Kent: Landscape Garden Designer* (London, 1987)

Hunt, John Dixon and Willis, Peter, eds., *The Genius of the Place: The English Landscape Garden 1620–1820* (London, 1975)

Hussey, Christopher, *English Country Houses: Early Georgian, 1715–1760* (Woodbridge, 1955)

Ison, Walter, *The Georgian Buildings of Bristol* (Bath, 1978)

——, *The Georgian Buildings of Bath* (Bath, 1980)

Jackson-Stops, Gervase, *An English Arcadia, 1600–1900* (London, 1992)

Jacques, David, *Georgian Gardens: The Reign of Nature* (London, 1983)

James, Francis Godwin, *Ireland in the Empire 1688–1770* (Cambridge, MA, 1973)

Johnson, R. Brimley, *Mrs Delany at Court and among the Wits* (London, 1925)

Johnston, Edith Mary, *Ireland in the Eighteenth Century* (Dublin, 1974)

Jones, Barbara, *Follies and Grottoes* (London, 1974)

Jourdain, Margaret, *English Interior Decoration 1500 to 1830* (London, 1950)

Kearns, Kevin Corrigan, *Georgian Dublin: Ireland's Imperilled Architectural Heritage* (London, 1983)

Kimball, Fiske, *The Creation of the Rococo Style* (Philadelphia, 1943)

Levey, Michael, *Rococo to Revolution: Major Trends in Eighteenth-Century Painting* (London, 1966)

MacInnes, C. M. and Whittard, W. F., eds, *Bristol and its Adjoining Counties* (Bristol, 1955)

Maxwell, Constantia, *Dublin Under the Georges, 1714–1830* (London, 1946)

McCarthy, Michael, *The Origins of the Gothic Revival* (New Haven and London, 1987)

McGrath, Patrick, *Bristol in the Eighteenth Century* (Newton Abbot, 1972)

——, *The Merchant Venturers of Bristol* (Bristol, 1975)

McDonnell, Joseph, *Irish Eighteenth-Century Stuccowork and its European Sources* (Dublin, 1991)

McDowell, R. B., *Ireland in the Age of Imperialism and Revolution 1760–1801* (Oxford, 1979)

Morgan, Kenneth, *Bristol and the Atlantic Trade in the Eighteenth Century* (Cambridge, 1993)

Mowl, Timothy, *To Build the Second City: Architects and Craftsmen of Georgian Bristol* (Bristol, 1991)

——, *Palladian Bridges* (Bath, 1993)

——, *Horace Walpole: The Great Outsider* (London, 1996)

O'Brien, Jacqueline and Guinness, Desmond, *Dublin: A Grand Tour* (London, 1994)

O'Donnell, E. E., *The Annals of Dublin: Fair City* (Dublin, 1987)

O'Dwyer, Frederick, *Lost Dublin* (Dublin, 1981)

Paulson, Ronald, ed., *William Hogarth, The Analysis of Beauty* (New Haven and London, 1997)

Pons, Bruno, *Grands Décors Français 1650–1800* (Paris, 1995)

Scott, Katie, *The Rococo Interior: Decoration and Social Spaces in Early Eighteenth-Century Paris* (New Haven and London, 1995)

Shellabarger, Samuel, *Lord Chesterfield and his World* (Boston, MA, 1951)

Snodin, Michael, ed., *Rococo: Art and Design in Hogarth's England* (London, 1984)

Somerville-Large, Peter, *Irish Eccentrics* (Dublin, 1975)

Stutchbury, Howard, *The Architecture of Colen Campbell* (Manchester, 1967)

Summerson, John, *Architecture in Britain 1530–1830* (Harmondsworth, 1977)

Symes, Michael, *The English Rococo Garden* (Princes Risborough, 1991)

Thornton, Peter, *Authentic Decor: The Domestic Interior 1620–1920* (London, 1984)

Turpin, John, *A School of Art in Dublin since the Eighteenth Century* (Dublin, 1995)

Uglow, Jenny, *Hogarth* (London, 1997)

Ward-Jackson, Peter, *English Furniture Designs of the Eighteenth Century* (London, 1958)

White, Roger, *Georgian Arcadia: Architecture for the Park and Garden* (London, 1987)

Whitehead, John, *The French Interior in the Eighteenth Century* (London, 1992)

Williamson, Tom, *Polite Landscapes: Gardens and Society in Eighteenth-Century England* (Stroud, 1995)

Worsley, Giles, *Classical Architecture in Britain: The Heroic Age* (New Haven and London, 1995)

Wilson, Michael I., *William Kent: Architect, Designer, Painter, Gardener 1685–1748* (London, 1984)

Wilton, Andrew and Bignamini, Ilaria, eds., *Grand Tour: The Lure of Italy in the Eighteenth Century* (London, 1996)

SECONDARY PRINTED SOURCES: ARTICLES

Allan, Juliet, 'New Light on William Kent at Hampton Court Palace', *Architectural History*, XXVII (1984), pp. 54–8

Beard, Geoffrey 'Italian Stuccoists in England', *Apollo* (July 1964), pp. 48–56

——, 'Italian Masters of Stucco', *Country Life* (24 November 1960)

——, 'A Family's 50 Year Supremacy' (Rose family), *Country Life* (8 December 1960)

Robert, Bell, 'Archaeology and the Rococo Garden: The Restoration at Painswick House, Gloucestershire', *Garden History* (Summer 1993), pp. 29–45

Cocke, Thomas, 'Gothic at Gloucester', *Country Life* (31 December 1981)

Colvin, Howard, 'A Scottish Origin for English Palladianism?', *Architectural History*, XVII (1974), pp. 5–13

Conner, Patrick, 'China and the Landscape Garden: Reports, Engravings and Misconceptions', *Art History*, II (1979), pp. 429–40

——, 'Britain's First Chinese Pavilion?', *Country Life* (25 January 1979)

Downes, Kerry, 'The Publication of Shaftesbury's "Letter Concerning Design"', *Architectural History*, XXVII (1984), pp. 519–23

FitzGerald, Desmond, 'Irish Gardens of the Eighteenth Century', *Apollo* (September 1968), pp. 204–9

Gerson, Martha Blythe, 'A Glossary of Robert Adam's Neo-Classical Ornament', *Architectural History*, XXIV (1981), pp. 59–82

Girouard, Mark, 'Coffee at Slaughter's: English Art and the Rococo', *Country Life* (13 and 27 January, 5 February 1966)

Harris, Eileen, 'The Wizard of Durham: The Architecture of Thomas Wright', *Country Life* (26 August and 2, 9 September 1971)

Harris, John, 'Painter of Rococo Gardens: Thomas Robins the Elder', *Country Life* (7 September 1972)

——, 'Esher Place, Surrey', *Country Life* (2 April 1987)

——, 'A Pioneer in Gardening: Dickie Bateman Re-assessed', *Apollo* (October 1993), pp. 227–33

Hayes, John, 'English Painting and the Rococo', *Apollo* (August 1969), pp. 114–25

Hellyer, Arthur, 'Only One Of Its Kind: Painswick', *Country Life* (15 June 1989)

Jackson-Stops, Gervase, 'Sharawadgi Rediscovered: The Chinese House at Stowe', *Apollo* (March 1993), pp. 217–22

Jacques, David, 'On the Supposed Chineseness of the English Landscape Garden', *Garden History*, XVIII/2 (Autumn, 1990), pp. 180–91

McCarthy, Michael, 'Thomas Wright's "Designs for Temples"and Related Drawing for Garden Structures', *Journal of Garden History*, I, 1 (1981), pp. 55–65

——, '"The dullest man that ever travelled"? A Re-assessment of Richard Pococke and of his Portrait by J.-E. Liotard', *Apollo* (May 1996), pp. 25–9

——, 'Baroque Elements in Irish Palladianism', *The Early Eighteenth Century Great House*, ed. Malcolm Airs (Oxford, 1996), pp. 95–9.

Mowl, Timothy, 'In the Realm of the Great God Pan', *Country Life* (17 October 1996)

——, 'The Castle of Boncoeur and the Wizard of Durham', *Georgian Group Journal* (1992), pp. 32–9

Pevsner, Nikolaus, 'The Genius of the Picturesque', *Architectural Review* (June 1944), pp. 139–45

Rowan, Alistair, 'Batty Langley's Gothic', *Studies in Memory of David Talbot Rice*, eds. Giles Robertson and George Henderson (Edinburgh, 1975), pp. 197–21

——, 'The Irishness of Irish Architecture', *Architectural History*, XL (1997), pp. 1–23

Sicca, Cinzia Maria, 'On William Kent's Roman Sources', *Architectural History*, XXIX (1986), pp. 134–57

Sutton, Denys, '*Le Bon Ton* and *The Roast Beef of Old England*' (editorial), *Apollo* (August 1969), pp. 129–33

White, Roger and Mowl, Timothy, 'Thomas Robins at Painswick', *Journal of Garden History*, IV/2 (1994), pp. 163–78

Worsley, Giles, 'Nicholas Hawksmoor: A Pioneer Neo-Palladian?', *Architectural History*, XXXIII (1990), pp. 60–74

PHOTOGRAPHIC
ACKNOWLEDGEMENTS

The authors and publishers wish to express their thanks to the following sources of illustrative material and/or permission to reproduce it and/or permission to take photographs and reproduce them:

Bodleian Library, Oxford: 12, 42, 132; Sir Brooke Boothby Bt.: 151, 152, 153, 154, 155; Bord Failte Photo: 111; Bristol City Library: 20, 33, 35, 36, 37, 156; Bristol University Special Collections: 6, 7, 8, 9, 29, 30, 31, 32, 38, 40, 41, 48, 49, 75, 77, 78, 80, 81, 82, 129; Mrs P. M. F. Clifford: 58; Country Life Picture Library 18, 83, 157; Courtauld Institute of Art (Photographic Survey of Private Collections): 76; Musée d'Art et d'Histoire, Geneva: 34; The Irish Architectural Archive, Dublin: 69, 70, 72, 73, 74, 85, 86, 87, 89, 90, 91, 92, 93, 94, 107, 108, 109, 110, 112, 113, 114, 116, 117, 120, 123, 126; Gordon Kelsey: 3, 50, 51, 52, 53, 54, 64, 128, 130, 131, 134, 136, 147, 148 , 149, 151, 152, 153, 154, 155; A. F. Kersting: 1, 13, 14, 15, 17, 161, 162, 163; Lord Faringdon: 22; National Library of Ireland, Dublin: 79; National Trust: 10, 164, 165; Lady Nutting: 11; Palace of Westminster: 39; Royal Commission on Historical Monuments of England: 2, 16, 19, 46, 47, 160; RCHM England (by courtesy of the National Trust): 166, 167, 168, 169; L. G. Stopford Sackville: 76; V&A Picture Library (Photo © The Board of Trustees of the Victoria & Albert Museum): 158; Mrs J. West: 60, 61; Peter Stephenson Wright: 144; and the authors: 4, 5, 10, 11, 21, 22, 23, 24, 25, 26, 27, 28, 43, 44, 45, 55, 56, 57, 58, 59, 60, 61, 62, 63, 65, 66, 67, 68, 71, 84, 88, 95, 96, 97, 98, 99, 100, 101, 102, 103, 104, 105, 106, 115, 118 , 119, 121, 122, 124, 125, 127, 133, 135, 137, 138, 139, 140, 141, 142, 143, 145, 146, 150, 159, 164, 165.

INDEX

Individual properties are indexed by name (e.g., Alscot Park); numbered houses in streets will be found listed under those streets under their town or city. Properties outside cities are also given a general entry under their county. Illustration numbers appear in *italics*.